MILITARY LIFE

MILITARY LIFE

The Psychology of Serving in Peace and Combat

Volume 2: Operational Stress

Edited by Amy B. Adler, Carl Andrew Castro, and Thomas W. Britt

PRAEGER SECURITY INTERNATIONAL

Westport, Connecticut · London

Library of Congress Cataloging-in-Publication Data

Military life: the psychology of serving in peace and combat / edited
by Thomas W. Britt, Amy B. Adler, and Carl Andrew Castro.
  p. cm.
Includes bibliographical references and index.
ISBN 0-275-98300-5 ((set) : alk. paper)—ISBN 0-275-98301-3 ((v. 1) :
  alk. paper)—ISBN 0-275-98302-1 ((v. 2) : alk. paper)—ISBN
  0-275-98303-X ((v. 3) : alk. paper)—ISBN 0-275-98304-8 ((v. 4) :
  alk. paper)
1. Psychology, Military. 2. War—Psychological aspects. 3. Combat—
  Psychological aspects. 4. Peace—Psychological aspects. 5. United
  States—Army—Military life. 6. Combat disorders. 7. Post-traumatic
  stress disorder. I. Britt, Thomas W., 1966– II. Adler, Amy B., 1963–
  III. Castro, Carl Andrew.
  U22.3.M485 2006
  355.1'0973—dc22   2005017484

British Library Cataloguing in Publication Data is available.

Library of Congress Catalog Card Number: 2005017484
ISBN: 0–275–98300–5 (set)
  0–275–98301–3 (vol. 1)
  0–275–98302–1 (vol. 2)
  0–275–98303–X (vol. 3)
  0–275–98304–8 (vol. 4)

First published in 2006

Praeger Security International, 88 Post Road West, Westport, CT 06881
An imprint of Greenwood Publishing Group, Inc.
www.praeger.com

Printed in the United States of America

The paper used in this book complies with the
Permanent Paper Standard issued by the National
Information Standards Organization (Z39.48–1984).

10 9 8 7 6 5 4 3 2 1

To Kit Adler—ABA

To Christopher and Bea—CAC

To my brother and friend, Richard Britt—TWB

CONTENTS

PREFACE

The psychological health and well-being of military personnel is important to the effectiveness of a nation's military, the adjustment of military families, and the integration of military personnel into the larger civilian community. A careful examination of the psychological issues confronting military personnel must necessarily be broad in scope and include a range of disciplines within psychology and the social sciences to provide a comprehensive assessment of the factors that affect the performance, health, and well-being of military personnel and their families. Such a multidisciplinary approach ensures researchers, military leaders, policy makers, and health care providers with a framework for understanding key factors relevant to modern military operations.

This four-volume set, *Military Life: The Psychology of Serving in Peace and Combat*, is organized around four defining fields of applied military psychology: military performance, operational stress, the military family, and military culture. Each volume begins with a riveting account of an individual's experience. These first-person accounts leave no doubt that the topics covered in this set are real, relevant, and deeply felt. The accounts are from the front line: the war and home front, as told by a veteran of Vietnam, the Gulf War, and Iraq; the precarious mental health of military personnel in a combat zone, as told by a military psychiatrist who served alongside Marines in combat; the anxiety and hope of military families on the front line of family separation, as told by an Army wife and mother of two service members turned military sociologist; and a psychologist with a front-row seat to observing the U.S. military's cultural shifts from Vietnam to the global war on terror. The stories told in these first-person accounts are stories of the authors' personal struggles with the challenges wrought by military conflict, incorporating the perspective that comes from their expertise, compassion, and humor. Three parts follow each of these first-person accounts. The chapters in each section are written by authorities selected for their knowledge in the field of military psychology, sociology, and other social sciences and shed light on the reality of life in the armed forces.

This set integrates the diverse influences on the well-being and performance of military personnel by developing separate volumes that address different facets of military psychology. By focusing on *Military Performance*, the first volume addresses the need to understand the determinants of how military personnel think, react, and behave on military operations. Several of the chapters in Volume 1 also have implications for the well-being of military personnel—such as the consequences of killing, how stress affects decision making, and how sleep loss affects operational effectiveness. Newly emerging issues in the armed forces are also discussed, including the role of terrorism, psychological operations, and advances in optimizing cognition on the battlefield. The impact of morale, the small military unit, and individual personality also provide insight into what influences the well-being and performance of military personnel.

The second volume in the set, *Operational Stress*, examines issues related to preparing military personnel to meet operational demands, details the psychological consequences of potentially traumatic events experienced on deployment, and reviews possible interventions that can support military personnel as they face such events. This volume includes descriptions of the experience of combat stress control teams on deployment, prisoners of war and the challenge of repatriation, the secular and spiritual role of military chaplains, the impact of military leaders, and the enduring role of small unit climate.

The third volume in the set takes an in-depth look at *The Military Family*. This comprehensive volume tackles the major stressors facing military families head on: family separation, family relocation, and dealing with the death of a service member. The particular issues confronting single parents, military children, and dual-military couples are also addressed. Another chapter addresses the balance between military work and family life. The problem of military family violence is the topic of the next chapter. A final chapter focuses on strategies for reducing military family conflict.

The fourth volume in the set, *Military Culture*, addresses the wider context of values, group diversity, and perceptions of the military, each of which has potential implications for the well-being and performance of military personnel. The role of values is explored in three chapters that address crosscultural values, the link between military values and performance, and the concept of courage. The next section explores specific groups within the military and the larger cultural trends that affect these groups: military reservists, women in the military, and the issue of gays serving in the armed forces. The final section of the volume examines how the military is perceived: the attitudes of service members about quality of life in the military, the role of the media in covering military operations, and the development of public attitudes toward the military and how these attitudes influence recruiting.

Producing this set required the effort and support of numerous people. In addition to thanking the authors for their outstanding chapters, we would like to thank Judy Pham, Hayley Brooks, Whitney Bryan, and Sarah Brink for their technical assistance in formatting the chapters. We would also like to thank Debbie Carvalko and the team at Praeger for providing valuable support and encouragement throughout the project. Finally, we appreciate the support provided by the Military Operational Medicine Directorate of the U.S. Army Medical Research and Materiel Command, Fort Detrick, Maryland. Note that the views expressed in this set are those of the authors and do not reflect the official policy or position of the Department of the Army, Department of Defense, or the U.S. Government.

We express our gratitude to the military personnel who have served their country in times of war and the families who have supported them. We hope this set in some small way can improve the lives of the next generation of service members and their families.

PART I

FIRST PERSON

CHAPTER 1

KILROY WAS HERE: REFLECTIONS OF A PSYCHIATRIST IN COMBAT

Robert L. Koffman

Inscribed on a war-torn pillar of sun-weathered cement, fortifying a guard post in war-weary Fallujah, is scrawled: "It takes the taste of the bitter to truly know the sweet." This saying is attributed to an old Jewish proverb, and I can only imagine that an ever-so-vigilant sentry inscribed the graffiti while standing guard for long hours of boredom punctuated with heightened alert provoked by each approaching vehicle. I muse how such a Semitic reference could be found on the very entrance to the formerly premier Iraqi military installation. If indeed, the pen is mightier than the sword, would-be authors, pundits, and urban graffiti artists stride confident from battle only to pass large periods of quiescence chronicling their victories in much the same way the ancients did through their use of petroglyphs.

Throughout my multiple tours of duty in Iraq, I have come to appreciate how connected we, the combatants of the new millennium, are with our brethren soldiers of other great wars. Consider for a moment the now-forgotten World War II and Korean War caricature of Kilroy, the funny little man with a long nose and two big round eyes peering over what appeared to be a wall. Comically, Kilroy appeared everywhere there was a service member. In fact, the game quickly became to put the likeness of Kilroy and his slogan, "Kilroy was here," in the most unlikely places.

Gazing at the ordinance-pocked pillar, I am intrigued and reassured by the literary bent of this particular graffiti and wonder for another moment about the bitterness tasted by that 19-year-old lance corporal. As I have been so many times before, I am singularly impressed by the elite membership of his peer group, a uniform-clad

The views expressed in this chapter are those of the author and do not reflect the official policy or position of the U.S. Department of Defense or the U.S. Government.

cohort this nation gratefully praises . . . a peer group that, unfortunately, now knows the taste of bitterness. Bitter is an apt depiction. Indeed, each time I return to this perilous but strangely beckoning nation, life seems to grow increasingly acerbic. How long will our warriors continue to taste bitterness? I also wonder, when will the sweetness begin again for the common Iraqi?

Healthy Coping in Combat

How does that 19-year-old soldier or Marine do it? How does he—or increasingly now, she—moderate colossal stress levels, much less, negotiate adolescence tumult at its peak? How does the combatant cope with combat, a war that is mostly feared for its random application of death through the instrument of indirect fire: clandestine roadside bombs, incoming mortar rounds, hastily launched but lethal rocket attacks?

As a military psychiatrist, I understand the value of adaptive coping, furthermore I appreciate that not all coping mechanisms, or defense mechanisms in therapist's parlance, are healthy and adaptive. Imagine if alcohol was not against Central Command regulations and "liquid courage" was liberally served and consumed; perhaps it is just as well that alcohol is not one of the coping strategies available to U.S. military personnel on deployment. While other maladaptive coping strategies remain available to deployed personnel, some adaptive coping strategies are not only available but frequently engaged. One of the healthiest and most effective ways to mitigate the stress of combat is to burnish an organization's sense of eliteness and esprit de corps. Cohesion is the fundamental principle behind a healthy organization. Furthermore, sharing laughter is a wonderful way to cohere. The late Bob Hope knew this best; for nearly six decades he brought laughter to the troops. Long a cliché, laughter truly is good medicine. In fact, so prognostic is the ability to maintain a sense of humor that I consider laughter to be the fifth vital sign, a psychological flak jacket.

Curiously associated with humor as another high-order defense is altruism. Evidenced in Medal of Honor and Bronze and Silver Star recipients, altruism facilitates the courageous acts understood as selfless sacrifice. It is a gross misunderstanding to believe that the reason a soldier throws himself on a grenade is in service to his country or his country's freedom. Rather, just as he owes his life and safety to his buddy, he gives his life for his buddy.

Nevertheless, I am still intrigued by the sentry's posting. It was neither humorous nor spoke of benevolence. Sometimes the demonstrated goal is simply to leave one's indelible mark. In marking territory, we take our cue from nature. Absent the gift of sophisticated scent and only able to beat our chests like our simian cousins for so long, we make up for our limited olfaction with an adjunctive tool, the Magic Marker®. Humph.

I wonder if marking, or tagging, as it is known sociologically, is predominately committed by the male of the species. Had Kilroy's creator been female, would she have been as prolific leaving her calling card throughout Europe and Asia? These may not seem to be important questions in a time of war, but to the psychiatrist or psychologist, all behavior is meaningful. Moreover, the opportunity to observe behavior particularly in response to inordinate pressure, gripping fear, and overwhelming demands cannot, should not, be dismissed lightly. Similarly, in the confined environment of urban combat, all markings are meaningful…

My musings continue: How many other mental health providers recognize the green PVC walls of the ubiquitous Porta-John® as the warrior's tabula rasa, or blank screen. Prurient in our clandestine ability to study typically scatological or anatomically explicit artwork, we are afforded good indicators of a unit's morale, their faith in their leadership, their level of discipline. Free expression is even more difficult to suppress. When the commanding general of the camp issued an order that no service member would deface any Porta-John® in any fashion, he made the grievous error of referring to such stealthy vandals as "ninjas." Thereafter, as artwork and political commentary skyrocketed following his decree, each exposé and statement was signed, "The Ninja." Rich content, indeed.

However, the richest psychiatric content came early in the war during the first rotation in Operation Iraqi Freedom (OIF I). Before the commanding general issued an edict to the contrary, virtually every service member used the desert-colored fabric —designed solely to cover the generically green Kevlar helmet—as their personal canvas. Whereas only the service member's name and, ominously, blood type were required, in true adolescent fashion and as if not to be outdone, a nonspoken race was on to wear the most candid Kevlar statement. Enter "helmet art," the grunts' version of World War II nose art seen adorning the nose sections on airplanes. Gone— at least from most—was the sexual innuendo depicted in leggy Betty Grable, straddling the nose cone section of the plane. Replacing the cultural icon for its time was the theme of what can only be termed "getting back at the bastards." What is thoroughly amazing, particularly for those who know how well the U.S. military services pride themselves on being uniformly uniform, was the bawdiness, the rawness, the outspokenness of an otherwise blank screen. Hours of down time, coupled with the ubiquity of a Magic Marker® and inspired by sheer adolescent lunacy and unflappable warrior spirit, led to creations that could only be described as the analytic Holy Grail. From epithets to epitaphs, service members etched what they could not recite. One helmet had a pair of aces drawn with the caption, "Not Today"; another helmet solemnly illustrated dog tags of his fallen comrades. Verses from Corinthians were popular, so was the defiant bull's eye, taunting the enemy to "come and get me."

My amazement and delight in the unflappable spirit of America's best continued. A tall combatant, at least one full helmet's height above his comrades, caught my eye. I spied his canvas with the black marker pastiche "Cry HAVOC! Unleash the Dogs of War." Catching up to him, my amazement turned to awe. I was struck that this gangly twenty-something knew enough of the classics to quote none other than William Shakespeare, who penned this line four centuries ago. But the pangs of couth and class I savored were short-lived. I asked the young man if he was characterizing the inhumanity of betrayal uttered by Mark Antony, who anguished over a murdered Julius Caesar (from William Shakespeare, *Julius Caesar*, act 3), and the naïve E-4 looked back at me and reported, "No sir, I heard it in *Full Metal Jacket*. Pretty cool, huh?"

If humor is an essential defensive operation for binding anxiety, within the Sunni Triangle there is much anxiety to bind. One warrior who was attached to the unit I visited sought my assistance to help him understand how it was that the mere chance of seat selection in his Humvee—front vs. back—meant the difference between seeing his buddy die a grizzly death or dying himself from a roadside improvised explosive device (IED) attack. Whereas chance alone (some may add, fate or faith) saved his life, chance alone could not assuage his survivor guilt.

In another instance, yet another service member shared with me how he struggled with the increasing likelihood of being taken out by a mortar or rocket at this particularly dangerous location. He determined that he had about a one in a hundred chance of meeting a similar fate. He did not like these odds, noting that if this were a game of Texas Poker, I believe the game to be that wildly popular Hold-Em, he would fold. (Note the effective use of humor.) My intervention was to help the service member better develop his use of rationalization—a defensive operation not quite as mature as altruism and humor. Since this individual used numbers to help him understand or explain the chaos of combat, we talked about probabilities and how his odds could be improved just by incorporating better situational awareness—in this case by listening for the all-too-familiar whistle of rocket and judiciously wearing his "battle rattle." We figured he could improve his odds by at least a factor of 10, maybe even 20. Indeed, none of the recent fatalities in camp had been wearing their flak and Kevlar at the time of the attack. Though the member still felt like he was a "sitting duck," he was at least a sitting duck with a sense of control over his fate. Mastery is crucial in an environment wherein one feels he or she is held captive, hostage within his or her own compound. Rationalization is a powerful sedative.

But rationalization only works when the grieving service member can emotionally venture beyond guilt. Not uncommonly, of the truculent I attended, those steeped in the most intense recrimination were the medics, the corpsmen, who experienced immense remorse for not being able to save the lives of their buddies. It is one of the great injustices of war that those who are trained to render assistance are those who are personally closest to the dying. Helplessness is little consolation when you can only provide solace and comfort. With total disregard for their own safety, the role of lifesaver not only defines the role that the medic or corpsmen plays, but it also reinforces the justification for the sacrifices they must make. Indeed, no ache is greater than that experienced by a 19-year-old, who previously believed himself and the rest of his fire team invincible, to cradle the dying all the while being powerless to stave off massive hemorrhage. Such was the situation of one such healer who sought—albeit reluctantly—the services of this healer after his officer was hit in the neck by fragments from an errant RPG round. Being a squad or fire team's corpsmen or medic means being reposed with entirely unrealistic levels of faith, confidence, and trust. And this special conviction reinforces the role of the healer, which both sustained him and destroyed him. If the willingness to die for your buddy could only be parlayed into medical craft, nearly no losses would occur on the battlefield. But on this sweltering summer day, it did, and the anguish of loss seared hotter and deeper than any piece of fragment. In trying to console this youthful, tormented soul, a man left only with haunting memory of cradled death, I was at once stuck by his tattooed forearm prophetically touting, "Death is certain, life is not."

New Challenges, New Warfare

Though military compounds are likely to be targeted regularly, these encampments are the farthest things (except for the presence of desert camouflage) from starkly sanitized worlds. Festooning every wall (bulkhead) and door (hatch) are the thank-you notes, the banners, and the grade school works of art personalizing a campaign of support indicative of a grateful nation. Through ongoing efforts to bring America closer to the war fighter, as well as to show the solidarity of a unified country, countless schools, churches, civic groups, and grateful citizens alike took the time to thank those who serve.

Like an infinite number of stars twinkling in a moonlit sky, flickers of Americana are everywhere imaginable. Exemplified best by Abigail Van Buren's "Operation Dear Abbey" letter-writing program for service members deployed abroad, the intention was always to connect the service member with a home town—a photograph; a name—and, in doing so, to personalize the appreciation. However, the unseen and underappreciated reality of this war is the psychological inability to grapple with, much less work through or reconcile, combat with an enemy who knows no sense of fairness. This reality to which I refer (and one that needs to be broached in schools of infantry) is represented in the following letter actually sent to a service member and the service member's response. (Note: for anonymity, names and identifying details have been changed.)

Dear SPC Todd,
My name is Bobby Smith. I live in Texas. I am nine years old. I am in the 3rd Grade. I like to play fastball. What does SPC mean? The name of my school is Washington Elementary School. I like to eat meatloaf. Do people really do all those push-ups?
Love, Your Friend,
Bobby Smith

Smitty,
My name is Specialist Todd, your friend. I am 28 years old. I live in Texas, too. Sucks to be us. I was in the 3rd grade a couple of times. I have not done fractions in 15 years, but I did shoot a 10 round burst into one Iraqi man's gut, that equals half of a man, is that right? I have a 240 G that I shoot people with. So you are nine years old, I shot a nine year old who had an AK 47. I like to eat MREs. It hurts when I (expletive).
Love, Your friend,
SPC Todd

Whereas staff noncommissioned officers or commanders may bristle to learn that a service member sent such an alarming note, the mental health care provider tries to understand even what cannot, should not, be condoned. Sick humor need not always be the musings of a sick mind, just a broken one. In the case of "SPC Todd," the psychological state remaining after witnessing unfathomable carnage is a sick, grievously wounded spirit.

To better understand the morose nature of "SPC Todd," consider that only days earlier this service member lost a sizable percentage of his unit in an all-too-common ambush, an attack wherein the enemy defied long-established protocols of war by using children as shields—and as combatants! Another member of SPC Todd's unit shared with me that he and several members of his fire team were pinned down by an enemy mortar. After the insurgent's mortar tube was silenced by the business end of a 7.62 mm round, what troubled SPC Todd was that a young boy who "couldn't have been older than eight or nine years old," subsequently appeared to "man" the tube, dropping rounds in it. But what really tore that combat-hardened OIF vet apart was watching this youngster know enough about how to aim a fairly complicated weapon system and to walk rounds right into the vicinity of Todd and his team. The boy was soon to share a similar fate with the man, who the fire team later learned was the boy's father.

Being a mental health provider during Operation Iraqi Freedom defines job security. Even those not embarked on regular patrols must take stock of their psychological health. With indirect fire lobbed intermittently "inside the wire" and the unpredictable detonation of an IED "outside the wire," the randomness at which a comrade is killed or injured is most unsettling. However, there is perhaps an even greater challenge to healthy coping. Adding to the random nature of being attacked, the soldier or Marine must also reconcile significant ambiguity associated with his or her combat role. In Iraq the insurgents and Jihadists we fight resist identification and trade their loyalty and allegiance for RPGs and mortars. The same citizens soldiers risk their lives defending take up arms against us. The ability of the insurgents to reappear and challenge Coalition Forces at will parodies the childhood game of "Whack-A-Mole." We are fighting an enemy who lays siege to religious sanctuaries, uses women, children, and innocent civilians as shields, and then feigns piety. How confusing must this be for the 19-year-old? This fundamental contradiction of combat duty in Iraq adds to the ambiguity of ever-changing warrior roles and is further complicated by yet another dynamic.

Unlike the "great wars" wherein allies primarily waged conventional war replete with a forward edge of battle area and a relatively secure rear encampment, we now encounter an asynchronous battlefield, euphemistic for an enemy who is all around you. What this means is that the battlefield is no longer subdivided into the near, close, and deep. Where once the rear area provided sanctuary, there is no true rear area in Iraq. Another useful synonym for the urban combat environment in Iraq: the "360° battle space." Eloquently stated, Lieutenant General James Helmly, chief of Army Reserves, characterizes this "nonpermissive" environment best: "Driving that truck is one of the most hazardous damned occupations we have in Iraq." He added, "Truck drivers and frankly, MPs [Military Police] are front-line troops these days" (Kennedy, 2004, p. 2).

Emblematic of this unorthodoxy, General Charles Krulak, the commandant of the Marine Corps from 1995 to 1999 posited the challenge of the "three-block war." In this three-block war, troops would at once be engaged in peacekeeping operations, unrelenting combat (so called "kinetics ops"), and humanitarian operations, all conceivably within the same three-block urban environment. Central to operations was General Krulak's construct of the "strategic corporal." To succeed in this new battle, General Krulak remarked that the strategic corporal requires "unwavering maturity, judgment and strength of character" (Krulak, 1999, p. 29). To this I would add, healthy, adaptive coping mechanisms.

To be sure, the moxie and mettle displayed by our troops is worthy of all the praise and superlatives afforded these tireless heroes. Whether apparent in their narratives, depicted in their graffiti, worn on their Kevlar, or humbly understated by their pride of purpose and duty, combat veterans from Operation Iraqi Freedom and Enduring Freedom set a new standard for healthy coping.

First evident in Kosovo, then East Timor, and now Iraq, the three-block war, the urban war, is the face of combat today. Moreover, with redefined warrior ethos and changing warrior roles, mental health care providers in the combat setting are redefining combat stress. As mental health providers, our task has become to understand the unique challenges associated with providing proximate, immediate, and expectant care in an asynchronous, 360° battle space in which our troops live, fight, and work. Although not visibly or specifically inscribed, Kilroy was here, too.

References

Kennedy, H. (2004, December). Army reserve seeks to toughen up training for part-time soldiers. *National Defense*. Retrieved September 29, 2005, from http://www.nationaldefensemagazine.org/issues/2004/Dec/ArmyReserveSeeks.htm

Krulak, C. C. (1999, January). The strategic corporal: Leadership in the three block war. *Marines Magazine*, 29–34.

PART II

PSYCHOLOGICAL PREPARATION FOR WARFARE

CHAPTER 2

JOINING THE RANKS: THE ROLE OF INDOCTRINATION IN TRANSFORMING CIVILIANS TO SERVICE MEMBERS

Dennis McGurk, Dave I. Cotting, Thomas W. Britt, and Amy B. Adler

"Four brave men who do not know each other will not dare to attack a lion. Four less brave men who know each other well, sure of their reliability and consequently of mutual aid, will attack resolutely" (Ardant du Picq, 1870, p. 48). Taking "less brave" men and women and training them to know and trust each other in order to attack the enemy is what military indoctrination is all about.

Military indoctrination is a process by which civilians are transformed into military service members. To indoctrinate is to instruct in a doctrine, principle, or ideology; to imbue with a specific partisan or biased belief or point of view (Nichols, 2001). Military indoctrination in U.S. forces goes far beyond this; it is the process of turning civilian men and women into service members—soldiers, sailors, airmen, and Marines. For enlisted personnel, this process occurs during Army Basic Training, Navy Boot Camp, Air Force Basic Training, or Marine Corps Boot Camp. Indoctrination for military officers takes place during Reserve Officer Training Corps (ROTC) training, at one of the service academies (U.S. Military Academy [West Point], the Naval Academy [Annapolis], or the Air Force Academy [Colorado Springs]), or in officer candidate school (OCS). Enlisted training varies in length from 6 to 12 weeks, depending on the branch of service, while officer training is generally conducted during the four years cadets are in ROTC and the service academies or 13 weeks for OCS.

However, all indoctrination has the same overarching goal, to train recruits/cadets physically and mentally and instill in them an understanding of, and willingness to

The views expressed in this chapter are those of the authors and do not reflect the official policy or position of the U.S. Department of Defense or the U.S. Government.

live by, the values held by each service (TRADOC Regulation 350-6). Said differently, indoctrination changes civilian individuals into part of something larger, a collective group that shares a unique identity. Indoctrination has three specific goals: (1) to remove characteristics that are detrimental to military life (that is, to subordinate self-interest to follow orders), (2) to train individuals to kill when necessary, and (3) to enable recruits to view themselves in collective terms. In this chapter, we describe general theoretical models of indoctrination and apply these models to the indoctrination of service members into the U.S. Armed Forces. In doing this, we note how military indoctrination deviates from more traditional "cult" forms of indoctrination and make the argument that indoctrination can be used in the service of laudable goals.

The Nature of Indoctrination

Military indoctrination can be viewed under the broader framework of "intense indoctrination." Baron (2000) provides a model for understanding the underlying processes and mechanisms that facilitate indoctrination and provides examples of indoctrination in the religious, philosophical, and political arenas. Lay views of "indoctrination" are undoubtedly influenced by such highly publicized news stories as the Branch Davidians led by David Koresh, the Heaven's Gate sect group suicide in California, and the case study of Patty Hearst being indoctrinated into the Symbionese Liberation Army. One unfortunate consequence of these dramatic examples is the perception that only troubled individuals are subject to the process of indoctrination and that indoctrination can only be used in the service of malevolent or dysfunctional goals. Even Baron's (2000) analytical approach toward indoctrination implicitly suggests an inherent immoral process. Before describing how military indoctrination both conforms to and deviates from general models of intense indoctrination, it is first necessary to ask the question of *why* there is a need for indoctrination in the armed services and how military indoctrination may differ from "cult" indoctrination.

The Need for Military Indoctrination

Intense indoctrination is necessary when the behaviors required of members of a group or organization entail a radical departure from the individual's prior experience, and it is only through engaging in the techniques involved in indoctrination that individuals will perform these new behaviors. In most organizations, such processes of socialization are not necessary; less intense or "softer" techniques, such as group bonding, are sufficient to persuade workers and group members to adopt the goals and values of the organization. Grojean and Thomas (this set, Volume 4) discuss the processes by which organization members (including service members) are socialized to take on the values and goals of the groups to which they belong. In a military context, softer socialization processes will be most effective in instilling values that service members already believe are reasonable, moral, and desirable (e.g., integrity, honesty, commitment).

However, intense indoctrination will be necessary to enable service members to engage in behaviors that represent a more radical departure from their prior experiences and worldview. What types of behaviors require more intense persuasion? Two classes of behaviors in a military context represent (1) killing someone else in the service of a mission to protect one's country, and (2) the willingness to subordinate self-interests, including survival, in the service of group goals. The leaders of traditional religious, political, and terrorist "cults" employ the process of indoctrination for similar reasons. The more extreme of these groups may require group members to kill other people in the service of their organization's goals, and the group members need to be willing to sacrifice (even by giving up their own life or the life of their child) for the group.

Military Versus Cult Indoctrination

How does military indoctrination differ from indoctrination into a cult-like organization? Unlike cult-like indoctrination, the process of military indoctrination simultaneously prepares individuals to kill and/or potentially sacrifice one's life while developing more traditionally accepted standards of conduct and socially acceptable values. These latter values, such as integrity and honor, along with adherence to standards, such as killing only enemy combatants, are designed to prevent the service member from becoming an automaton that simply follows any order regardless of its moral consequences.

Service members are not trained for the sole purpose of killing and sacrificing their lives when necessary. Although these behaviors represent a critical aspect of their training and may be necessary during military operations, service members must also be prepared to invoke more complex decision-making strategies to ensure mission success. Current and future operational environments will require service members to operate relatively independently, take on multiple responsibilities, and demonstrate a diversity of skills. For example, in the same operation, a soldier may be required to attack an enemy combatant, negotiate with civilians in the war zone, and help rebuild and provide security for a school devoted to the education of local children. To accomplish these diverse tasks, service members will need to demonstrate success at complex decision making that takes place within the context of a detailed professional and ethical framework.

Despite the increased reliance on technology to accomplish military missions, individual service members are still the ones ultimately responsible for mission execution. Thus, the focus on developing individual military values remains a necessary priority (Walsh, 2000). Recruits must learn the values of their organizations, and a good deal of their time is spent being inculcated into a culture with specific values (e.g., Army values of loyalty, duty, respect, selfless service, honor, integrity, and personal courage). These kinds of values guide the military's actions (*Field Manual 7-21.13 The Soldier's Guide*) and are the cornerstone of each of the armed services.

The values are intended to guide individual decision making well beyond basic training. It is this emphasis on values that serves as a key mechanism by which civilians entering military service are indoctrinated into military culture.

The Process of Indoctrination

Baron (2000) provides an excellent review of the dynamics and stages of intense indoctrination. His description helps to illustrate the ways in which military indoctrination both conforms to and deviates from his global indoctrination model. Ultimately, successful indoctrination results in a dramatic change in the individual's self-concept, which is both maintained and reinforced by the individual's social environment. The change in self-concept, which involves internalization of the group's values, ultimately leads the individual to seek the fulfillment of not only personal goals but also group goals. The goal of military indoctrination is to produce service members who have internalized the values of the armed services so as to drive individuals to behaviors in defense of the nation that may involve killing or sacrificing oneself, while thinking and problem solving in the presence of complex contingencies.

Stages of Indoctrination

Various authors have described different stages that make up the indoctrination process (Baron, 2000; Lifton, 1961; Schein, Schneier, & Barker, 1961; Stahelski, 2004). Despite some diversity in how these stages are conceptualized, these authors construe indoctrination as following roughly the same sequence of stages. Because of its focus on the process of indoctrination across a variety of situations, we use Baron's (2000) stage model as a basis to illustrate military indoctrination, although we integrate other approaches as well. The fundamental stages of intense indoctrination consists of the "softening-up stage, compliance stage, internalization stage, and consolidation stage" (Baron, 2000, p. 240). A brief summary of each stage and its military application is provided in Table 2.1.

Softening-up Stage

Baron argues that the first stage involves laying the groundwork for the individual to adopt the new values and behaviors of the group by separating the individual from prior contacts and by exposing the individual to a variety of stressors. This initial stage also involves an attempt to decrease an emphasis on the unique aspects of an individual's identity and, instead, to expose and reinforce the key tenets of the group. It is generally believed that an initial period of stress and some disorientation ultimately provide more fertile ground for engaging in social psychological processes that will cause an individual to de-emphasize his or her personal identity and embrace the identity of the group. Stahelski (2004) (see Figure 2.1) refers to this stage of indoctrination as "depluralization," which consists of removing all other group identities from the individual's self-concept. When individuals encounter stressors such as lack of sleep and intense physical activity on a continuous basis, their

Table 2.1
Baron's Stage Model of Intense Indoctrination Applied to the Military

Stage of Indoctrination	Critical Features	Military Application
Stage 1: Softening-up	–isolation from family/friends –exposure to stress (physical, psychological) –instigation of fear	–service member (SM) isolated from outside world –SM trains for long, intense hours –some emphasis on fear of drill instructor
Stage 2: Compliance	–recruit tries out new behaviors –done for extrinsic reasons –social pressure may be primary motivator	–SM quickly "falls into line" and performs expected behaviors, even if for fear of reprisal
Stage 3: Internalization	–identity of recruits incorporates new values –behaviors performed out of intrinsic desire to please group members	–SM incorporates military values into value system –role of SM takes on central importance
Stage 4: Consolidation	–recruit allegiance to group solidified –recruit totally accepts new values/beliefs	–SM completely committed to values of service –SM willing to kill and be killed in service of unit and country

Source: Baron, 2000.

attention resources are depleted, making them less resistant to persuasion attempts (Baron, 2000; Easterbrook, 1959; Wine, 1971).

In the context of indoctrination into the U.S. Army, recruits are told they have left their family, friends, and all else behind them and are now part of the military family. Recruits work continuously from early in the morning until bedtime, with little time for reflection about how their experiences are consistent or inconsistent with their prior life. In most Army indoctrination settings, new members are allowed minimal or no contact with outsiders, including their immediate families. In addition, military training is very often conducted in isolated environments, away from outside influence. Recruits are generally restricted to the post during the initial phases of indoctrination. Cadences, the songs that are sung when marching or running in formation, are rich with references to things that are "back on the block," referring to the civilian world as if it is another world. In addition, no tattoos or other group markings are allowed to be seen when in uniform. Taken together, this facilitates what Ward (1999) referred to as the social incubator and enables the indoctrination process to occur.

The softening-up stage also includes Stahelski's (2004) stage of self-deindividuation, where personal identity is de-emphasized and group identity is emphasized in

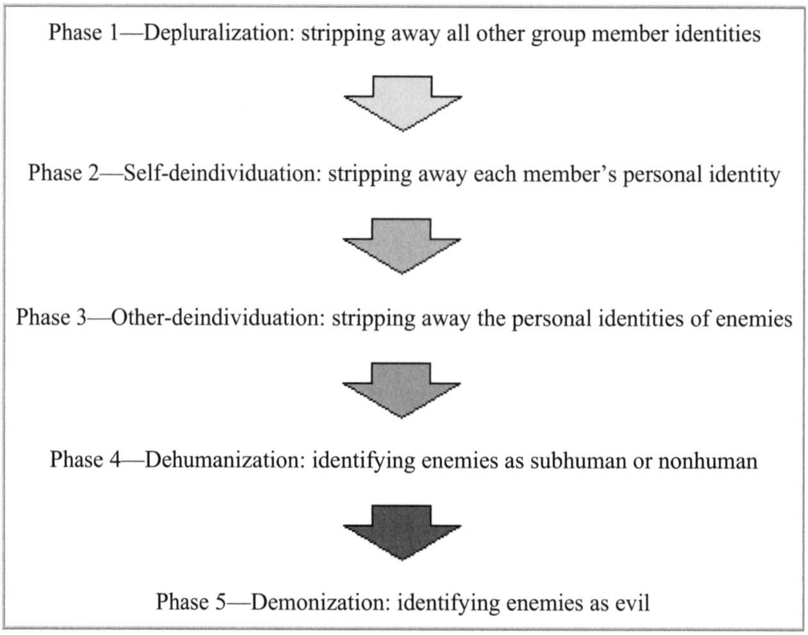

Phase 1—Depluralization: stripping away all other group member identities

Phase 2—Self-deindividuation: stripping away each member's personal identity

Phase 3—Other-deindividuation: stripping away the personal identities of enemies

Phase 4—Dehumanization: identifying enemies as subhuman or nonhuman

Phase 5—Demonization: identifying enemies as evil

Figure 2.1
Stahelski's Five Phases of Social Psychological Conditioning

Source: Stahelski, 2004.

its place. This is what is commonly referred to in the military as "breaking down" recruits before they are rebuilt in the military organization's image. One striking example of this is when new recruits are no longer referred to by their first name. New enlisted soldiers are called Private Smith or Private Jones, while officer recruits are referred to as Cadet Smith or Cadet Jones. The extreme case of deindividuation is the Marine Corps requiring recruits to refer to themselves in the third person. When recruits want to talk to the drill instructor, they must state "the private requests to speak." To further stress the formation of a group identity, all recruits wear identical uniforms and have identical haircuts so that everyone looks as similar as possible. Prior research suggests that these types of activities promote a sense of anonymity and loss of self-awareness, leading to a greater likelihood of immersion in the social role or group (Diener, 1975). This stage sets the groundwork for what Goffman (cited in Bourne, 1967) termed the "mortification process," during which the recruit is stripped of his or her previous self. Previous achievement, family, and individuality are ignored, and the institution's own indicators of achievements, reference group, and status are demanded in their place. For example, high school sports jackets with uniform numbers on the sleeve are replaced by battle dress uniforms (BDUs), with name tapes that spell out "U.S. Army" sewn over the heart and an Army unit patch sewn on the sleeve.

The process of military indoctrination certainly contains essential features of the "softening-up" stage of general intense indoctrination, but it is also worth considering the ways in which military indoctrination is unique. Although the initial training of service members provides a heavy dose of workload and stressors to ultimately enhance resiliency under the severe conditions of combat, even at an early stage recruits are also trained to recognize morally suspect actions and to take personal responsibility for actions that may have life-and-death consequences for others. A more complex code of values guiding the behavior of service members is introduced during basic training and then is expanded throughout the rest of a service member's military training. (See Grojean & Thomas, this set, Volume 4.) In this way, the softening up, or deindividuation, plays a role in ensuring the adoption of the behaviors necessary to excel and thrive in combat situations, but service members are also trained to be decision makers who are aware of the values guiding their behaviors.

Compliance Stage

According to Baron (2000), the second stage of intense indoctrination involves the individual beginning to experiment with newly learned behaviors: "The recruit tentatively 'tries out' some of the behaviors requested by the group, more or less going through the motions or paying lip service to many of the demands made by the group" (p. 241). At this stage, individuals are basically modeling what they believe is expected of them to avoid punishment and reprimands, not conforming because of an intrinsic interest in supporting the group.

It is almost certainly the case that military recruits go through this compliance phase or period of engagement in the early stages of training (Bourne, 1967). Behaviors such as singing cadences and group exercises may at first be done out of an extrinsic desire to avoid disapproval or punishment. Even learning and advocating the values espoused by a service member's branch of the military may at first be done with a relatively superficial commitment. However, research has shown that behaviors initially performed for extrinsic reasons have a higher likelihood of being internalized by the individual when repeatedly performed and reinforced (Cialdini, 1993). Desired behaviors, such as using proper military courtesies when addressing the drill instructor, are required numerous times each day, and compliance is strongly supported by the group. In addition, group reinforcement of positive actions is encouraged by drill instructors.

Internalization Phase

The third phase of indoctrination represents a more active incorporation of the group's actions, values, and standards into the individual's worldview, which is facilitated through constant social confirmation and continued emphasis on group norms and activities (Baron, 2000). At this stage, the individual has come to privately believe the central tenets of the group and begins to seek inclusion within the group. The private acceptance of group norms and influence represents a critical step in the indoctrination process, as the individual comes to personally adopt the group's belief system. It is during this stage that the individual starts to change his or her self-conception to one in which membership of the group takes on central importance (Schein et al., 1961).

From the perspective of military indoctrination, internalization will likely take place at different times for different service members, with some service members failing to reach this stage. Service members who are motivated to join the military for relatively extrinsic reasons (e.g., financial rewards, parental approval) may fail to progress from compliance to internalization, and instead may continue to "go through the motions" throughout training. However, service members who internalize the central values of the armed services will be changed as individuals and will be more internally motivated to behave in ways consistent with those values (Ryan & Deci, 2000).

Consolidation Stage

The final stage of intense indoctrination involves individuals solidifying their identity as a group member and expressing an unwaivering commitment to the group's goals and activities (Baron, 2000). To simplify their lives, individuals in this consolidation stage, like many individuals, generally categorize people as those similar to them (in-group) versus those different from them (out-groups). In examples of intense indoctrination, the individual may unquestioningly respond to group requests and may even distort reality in the service of maintaining a positive perception of the group.

In discussing this stage as part of terrorist indoctrination processes, Stahelski (2004) notes how this final phase contains a number of processes relevant to how so-called out-groups are treated by terrorist organizations. Terrorist groups de-emphasize the prospective enemy as unique individuals, a process referred to as other-deindividuation. Beyond other-deindividuation is the process of dehumaniza-tion, in which the enemy is portrayed as not merely lacking in individuality but as nonhuman. The enemy is perceived to have negative characteristics such as low intel-ligence, lack of compassion, and/or a corrupt nature. Often the enemy is likened to a rat or other vermin (Stahelski, 2004).

One final aspect of views of the enemy within indoctrination is demonization, when the enemy is identified as evil or of the devil. Differences in religion are often evoked, and enemy soldiers are described as godless. This creates a view of the enemy as less than human and, like dehumanization, makes it much easier to kill them. The former Soviet Union was labeled "the evil empire" by President Ronald Reagan. In some foreign countries, the United States is referred to as the "Great Satan," and Americans are called infidels. Similarly, some cultures instruct their soldiers that kill-ing the enemy will earn them eternity in Valhalla, 72 virgins in heaven with Mohammed, or other "heavenly" rewards. While these kinds of rewards are not promised during United States military indoctrination, being part of the righteous side of a conflict is emphasized, and "dying with your boots on" is considered an honorable way to die.

Consistent with this emphasis on killing, indoctrination is used to train individu-als in the attitudes and behaviors required to kill. It is typically assumed that civilians enter the military with an inherent reluctance to kill, and so the task of indoctrina-tion is to shape attitudes toward killing and to train individuals in the behaviors nec-essary to kill. The processes used to shape attitudes toward killing include depluraliza-tion, other-deindividuation, and dehumanization; the process of desensitization to discharging weapons is used to shape behavior. Whether or not service members remain reluctant to fire their weapons despite this indoctrination has been the subject of some debate (see Grossman, 1996; Marshall, 1947; Spiller, 1988), but this partic-ular goal of military indoctrination has remained consistent. Interestingly, Stahelski (2004) posits that democratic militaries use these methods but are careful to apply these techniques only to enemy soldiers, not noncombatants or civilians. Democratic militaries regard this distinction as critical and pride themselves on limiting collateral damage, injuries, or deaths of innocent civilians.

Overall, whether developing an identity that incorporates the organization's values or developing attitudes that meet the organization's needs, indoctrination involves a series of systematic stages. These stages of indoctrination lay out the pattern that individuals entering the organization follow. The mechanisms underlying these indoctrination stages encompass active methods of persuasion as well as the influence of the group and changes in individual identity.

Mechanisms of Indoctrination

The indoctrination process follows a number of steps. Individuals are removed from their former selves, a new self is formed, and group goals and values are inter-nalized. The mechanisms of such a process involve techniques that have been fre-quently studied in social psychological research. Many of these techniques, despite their deceivingly mild nature, have powerful effects. While many social psychological theories can be used to understand the indoctrination process, three key theories are described here: persuasion, group dynamics, and identity development.

Persuasion-related Processes

In a sense, indoctrination represents an extreme form of persuasion, in which the goal is to persuade an individual to perform some behaviors that before the indoctrination experience would have been considered ludicrous. Baron (2000) describes in detail the social psychological research on persuasion critical to understanding how an individual progresses through the various stages of indoctrination. The persuasion principle most relevant to the process of indoctrination is related to the diversity of negative emotional states capable of undermining the cognitive elaboration of a persuasive message. The individual is left relying on persuasive cues such as the degree of expertise and/or the authority of the source (Baron, 1986; Gleicher & Petty, 1992; Sanbonmatsu & Kardes, 1988).

The intense workload and sleep restriction experienced by military recruits leaves them little attention capacity for processing the messages they receive about new norms and guidelines that should govern their conduct (Easterbrook, 1959; Kahneman, 1973). Therefore, recruits should be less likely to devote their remaining cognitive effort to judging the quality of persuasive messages and will be more likely to be persuaded by the messages because the messages come from a military authority or expert. Some controversy currently exists about the extent of attitude and identity change that results from such peripheral route processing (see Petty & Wegener, 1998). However, it is possible that changed beliefs and attitudes as a result of superficial processing may later be consolidated through more thoughtful analysis in later military training programs that do not tax the resources of trainees. (See Grojean & Thomas, this set, Volume 4.)

Group Dynamics and Conformity

Intense indoctrination always occurs in a powerful social context for the recruit (Baron, 2000; Lifton, 1961; Schein et al., 1961). New recruits face immense social pressure to conform to the values of the group or risk psychological (e.g., group exclusion) and possibly physical consequences. Individuals have a basic need to belong to meaningful groups (Baumeister & Leary, 1995), and the feeling that one has been excluded from important and meaningful reference groups can lead to anxiety and a loss of self-esteem (Leary, Tambor, Terdal, & Downs, 1995).

One obvious way to avoid the negative consequences of being excluded by a group is to conform to that group (Cialdini, 1993). Furthermore, researchers have found that individuals are more likely to conform to existing group norms when experiencing such stressors as time pressure, loud noise, or threat of physical pain from shock (Darley, 1966; Kruglanski & Webster, 1991). As already discussed, intense indoctrination settings are inherently stressful, and therefore the pressures to conform to group and authority norms for proper conduct will be great. Within a military context, conformity during indoctrination occurs on multiple levels: conformity to the actions of fellow unit members, conformity to the demands of authorities (e.g., drill sergeants), and conformity to the more abstract values emphasized by the particular branch of the armed service. In addition, conformity is more likely because all aspects of training are conducted with accompanying stressors (e.g., time limits, while drill instructors are yelling, and/or the threat of physical pain from performing push ups or other physical exercises).

Identity Processes

According to Tajfel, social identity is "that part of the individual's self-concept which derives from his knowledge of his membership of a social group (or groups) together with the value and emotional significance attached to that membership" (1981, p. 255). In addition, social identity distinguishes itself by calling attention to the competition, real or imagined, between the group with which one identifies (i.e., the in-group) and another group (i.e., the out-group). Social identity, in fact, suggests that identification both stems from and is being fed by a need for positive distinctiveness between the in-group and the out-group. This need is satisfied by intergroup downward comparisons that often heighten group differences (Oaker & Brown, 1986). The group in this approach is based on both perceived similarities between in-group members and differences between in-group and out-group members. We note, however, that although the distinction between the "we" and the "they" is fundamental, the "they" may not have any independent existence, and its members may not have anything in common other than not being a "we" from the definer's perspective (Deaux, 1996). Social identification theory may capture an intrinsic element of military indoctrination: its emphasis on bettering the self. The process of military indoctrination presumably betters the self by making the individual part of a distinguished group (e.g., "the few, the proud, the Marines"). To both motivate for and maintain this "transformation," a degree of downward comparison is required. Airborne school instructors, for example, emphasize that paratroopers are better than "regulars" (who are often referred to as "dirty, nasty legs," implying that regular troops go to war on foot, while paratroopers jump from aircraft).

Each individual has a general orientation by which he/she views the self and others who can be captured by the concept of collectivism. Collectivism represents the general disposition to (a) define the self as part of groups, (b) subordinate personal goals to group goals, and (c) show strong emotional ties to the group. In contrast, individualism (most often construed as the opposite tendency on a single continuum with collectivism) represents an orientation toward self-reliance, independence, personal goals, and achievements. As a general dispositional variable, this concept has mostly been studied at a cultural level of analysis.

Although it is beyond the scope of this chapter to investigate cultural factors in military identification processes, we note that the work of Markus and Kitayama (1991, 1994) in Japan and the United States indicates that Asian cultures emphasize the interdependence of the self with others, using the self-in-relation-to-other as the basic unit of self-definition. In contrast, Western cultures emphasize the differences between the self and others and a self-as-distinct-from-others approach to self-definition. Whether collectivism results in quicker military indoctrination or whether collectivist cultures (or individuals) require different indoctrination strategies than do individualist cultures (or individuals) are questions that have not as yet been studied empirically. However, we cannot but wonder about the importance of this general orientation in an individual selecting a branch for service in the United States Armed Forces ("the few, the proud, the Marines" versus "the Army of one" may attract recruits from different cultural orientations). Indeed, if such self-selection is based on collectivism, we can speculate that molding specific military indoctrination strategies for individuals with collectivist and individualist orientation may result in more effective military indoctrination.

The Experience and Success/Failure of Indoctrination

While the processes of indoctrination may be operating on the recruits, the recruits themselves experience the process from their unique perspective. To study the phenomenology of indoctrination, we turned to where the majority of concentrated indoctrination occurs: initial training courses. We identified two studies that specifically examined the experiences of incoming military recruits.

In Gold's (2000) study of West Point cadets undergoing their first exposure to the military during the six-week cadet basic training session known as "beast," interviews revealed three major stressors identified by the recruits. First, the novelty of the experience is profound. Being thrown into a completely new environment, with a new identity, and a new set of rules and expectations that are not yet clear create the basis from which the old identity can be shed and the new identity can be developed. This period of transition from civilian to cadet is a type of culture shock. The culture itself, the group of reference, has shifted to such a dramatic degree that the cadets are left dazed and confused, but motivated. The importance of the new peer group is critical for transitioning into this new military identity. As one cadet notes, it feels like "a thousand of you who are nothings together" (Gold, 2000, p. 149). This camaraderie provides support for surviving this harsh but exhilarating transition.

Interestingly, in a study conducted 30 years earlier with enlisted soldiers drafted into the military, Bourne (1967) reported similar findings. The soldiers experienced what he termed environmental shock, similar to Gold's concept of culture shock. The worst of this stress is experienced during the phase before the actual training begins, because the individual has lost his identity but has not yet been provided with a new one and also has not yet been able to test himself on the much-anticipated challenges of the training course itself. Self-doubt and lack of confidence place the individual in a stressful no-man's-land.

The second stressor identified by the West Point cadets was the stress of not being able to anticipate what will happen next. The shifting expectations and demands are a component of stressors (Lazarus & Folkman, 1984). Again, Bourne also notes that this inability to anticipate demands is a major source of stress for the basic trainees. By focusing on the unknown, individuals are left in an unstable condition that prepares them for accepting a new certainty, the certainty of the group and the group's goals.

The third and final stressor reported by the West Point cadets was the stress of sheer workload in the form of time management pressures. Bourne's study did not reveal the same stressor but did mention that the draftees worked 20 hours a day, so much that there was little time to contemplate the changes that were occurring (consistent with the softening-up phase described by Baron, 2000).

Despite the externally applied pressure of indoctrination, individuals being indoctrinated, at least in the case of the military, are quite aware that they are being subjected to an active change process. This self-awareness may not be typical of other kinds of indoctrination. In the studies cited here, both the cadets and the basic trainees were conscious that they were in the midst of a life-changing experience. They were quite aware that they were going to be subjected to stressful events designed to turn them into members of the organization. They were motivated participants in that transition. They also contemplated the process itself. In the case of the cadets, Gold reported that even incidental training-related demands were perceived by the cadets as part of the overall training process, as part of some overall plan to prepare them as military leaders. In the case of the basic trainees, Bourne reported that upon reflection, many wished that the training had been harder. They were hoping to see themselves transformed into men by the experience.

Other components of military indoctrination that play an important role in the life of the trainee and that are not typically described in theories of indoctrination are the physical demands of the training. One physical demand is sleep restriction or deprivation. A consequence of sleep restriction may well be reduced resistance, which may reduce the ability of recruits to critically analyze cognitive information regarding attempts at persuasion. Another physical demand is intense physical training. Despite the exhaustion that such a demand places on individuals, a paradoxical effect may, in fact, be to increase an individual's resistance to stress. Research has shown that physically fit soldiers are better able to cope with stressful experiences (e.g., Brown, 1991; King, Taylor, Haskell, & DeBusk, 1989). Physical training may keep the trainees busy and tired, but it is also a kind of coping strategy that can aid the trainees in dealing with other training stressors. Additional coping techniques Gold identified included relying on social support and the emerging cohesiveness of the cadets. The very dynamic that supports the indoctrination process is perceived by the cadets as a useful tool for handling the stress of "beast." Other coping strategies identified by Gold included using humor, rationalization, and distraction. While these coping strategies assisted the self-selected and motivated cadets, each cadet also had his or her own unique experience and response.

While the emphasis in the Gold and Bourne papers was on those who completed the training process, not all trainees succeed. Those who are unable to complete the challenge of indoctrination (the military's perspective) or basic training (the recruit's perspective) may have encountered a level of expectation and challenge beyond their resources. One of the most difficult aspects of the indoctrination process is that following the period of environmental shock, the self is redefined. The redefinition

may be voluntary (in a time of an all-volunteer force), but the process is still externally applied—individual trainees must respect the authority of those in command,
they must subordinate their own needs and desires, and they must be able to tolerate
the "mortification process" of the loss of identity and the anger that such a loss
engenders (Bourne, 1967) and to meet these challenges consistently. It may be that
those without strong internal defenses do not succeed in making this kind of psychological transition.

Indeed, the research suggests that those who are unable to complete the basic
training process are likely to have had a difficult early home life when such defenses
and a fundamentally stable self could be developed (e.g., Carbone, Cigrang, Todd, &
Fiedler, 1999; Shulman, Levy-Shiff, & Sharf, 2000). Specifically, one of the most
common reasons for failing basic training is psychiatric. Those who fail have had less
support at home, as demonstrated in a study of Israeli recruits (Shulman, et al.,
2000). These recruits have also experienced more abuse as children. In their study
of Air Force basic trainees, Carbone and colleagues (1999) found those more likely
to be referred for a psychiatric exam were more likely to have a history of physical abuse. They also are more likely to have a history of psychological problems
(Williams, 2004). In fact, stable temperament is also associated with completing
the basic training course, suggesting the need for a stable response to the demands
on identity and the self (Elsass, Fiedler, Skip, & Hill, 2001; Lubin, Fiedler, &
Van Whitlock, 1996). Good coping strategies are also helpful for those entering basic
training. Such strategies include optimism (Carbone et al., 1999) and physical fitness
(Pope, Herbert, Kirwan, & Graham, 1999).

Given the high rate of attrition among those entering basic training (a finding reported across many of the services; Carbone et al., 1999; Hoge et al., 2002;
Hoge et al., 2005; Talcott, Haddock, Klesges, Lando, & Fiedler, 1999; Williams,
2004), early intervention programs designed to shore up the coping strategies of
these recruits should be able to help them confront the psychological challenge
of basic training indoctrination. In a study with Air Force recruits, two-session
stress-management training did not make a difference in the attrition of at-risk
trainees (Cigrang, Todd, & Carbone, 2000). However, in a study of Navy recruits, Williams (2004) describes an intervention designed to reduce emotional
reactivity and improve cognitive-behavioral coping strategies in at-risk recruits.
Those completing weekly cognitive behavioral skills training were more likely to
complete basic training than were at-risk recruits who did not receive such training. This result suggests that recruits provided with ongoing support and new
evidence-based skills can cope better with the tough demands of basic training.
This kind of proactive support is another way in which basic training differs from
cult-like indoctrination. Those who are psychologically strong and stable to start
with actually make better candidates for the military's indoctrination program,
which is quite a contrast to the profile of cult recruits (see Lifton, 1961; Schein
et al., 1961).

Thus, from the perspective of the recruit who successfully adapts to the beginning
phases of military training, the demands of military indoctrination are exhilarating,

seen in a context of achievement and life transition. The recruits are well aware that the process is something powerful, and they are eager to embrace it, despite its demands. The indoctrination, while attempting to be a redefining of self, may in fact be, from the perspective of the recruit, a reshaping of their already-strong sense of self. Such an interpretation of the indoctrination process is based not only on the accounts of recruits, but also on the fact that those who do not start with a fundamentally sound self are less likely to succeed in reshaping it. If there was a completely new self, then the lack of a stable preindoctrination self would not be a particular disadvantage. The fact that it is suggests that the reshaping is a dual process in which the basic trainee plays an active role.

Future Directions

Indoctrination is believed to be a vital part of successfully incorporating individuals into strongly defined organizations to promote that organization's agenda and values. The process of indoctrination involves many interrelated steps and procedures that guide the individual's journey from outsider status to status as a member of the organization who not only understands the organization but also identifies with it. While there are many similarities in indoctrination across a range of organizations, from cults to the military, we have outlined the fundamental ways in which these processes differ.

Much of the research on indoctrination up to this point has focused primarily on case studies and broad questions of social psychological processes that are believed to underlie the indoctrination process. Little systematic research has examined the extent to which thorough indoctrination is indeed necessary for an organization like the military. For example, how can the success of indoctrination be measured? Do individuals perform better if they are more indoctrinated? Does the group function more effectively? Does the individual, once integrated into an existing unit, have less conflict than one who isn't indoctrinated? Does indoctrination affect intention to remain in the organization? These outcomes are the assumed results of indoctrination but have not yet been studied. Similarly, what aspects of indoctrination would be measured to determine the degree of indoctrination? A valid measure of indoctrination needs to be identified, whether it be duration, intensity, or some other characteristic of indoctrination.

Another area that requires investigation is the most effective way to indoctrinate individuals within the military context. In many countries with strong democratic traditions, the military must balance between having its individuals adapt to a specific worldview that includes following orders and killing when necessary with the need to question unlawful orders and consider the ethics of particular situations.

Facilitating the development of the individual within the military structure as a service member capable of simultaneously following orders, thinking independently, and evaluating the legality of the order is a difficult task. Whether the objective of developing individuals who follow orders and question them is internally inconsistent, or whether the two parts of the objective can be reconciled is unclear. How these goals can be optimally reflected in the indoctrination process is also an area of indoctrination that has not yet been systematically examined. For example, can the recruit learn simultaneously to follow orders while questioning them, or should this be a two-step process? Research into this question could lead to recommendations regarding how best to develop basic training strategies so that individuals are ready to both follow and question orders simultaneously.

As mentioned previously, different methods of indoctrination may be more effective for collectivist and individualistic groups and/or individuals. This may be especially important within the United States because of the diversity of Americans' ethnic background ranging from strongly collectivist (e.g., Japanese-Americans) to strongly individualistic (e.g., Western European-Americans). An evaluation of whether collectivism results in quicker military indoctrination or whether collectivist cultures (or individuals) require different indoctrination strategies than do individualist cultures (or individuals) could prove beneficial to the military.

While we have discussed indoctrination, assuming it is a prerequisite for successful functioning and survival of the organization, it is not clear to what extent indoctrination is a requirement for organizational sustainment. For example, there is great diversity in the degree of commitment to the organization on the part of service members. Some decide to leave the service after their initial obligation, while others remain until retirement. Yet, each has undergone similar types of indoctrination experiences. Clearly, early indoctrination is not the cause of deep organizational commitment, which leads to the question of whether additional indoctrination continues to influence members of the military beyond that found in basic training. Another possibility is that there are personality differences that affect how the indoctrination process influences individuals or that individuals arrive at basic training in different stages of indoctrination readiness. Some may be highly skeptical and some may be quite ready to assume the values of the organization (see Grojean and Thomas for a discussion of the importance of the individual x experience interaction, volume 4), or perhaps indoctrination is not the driving force behind organizational commitment.

Indoctrination into the military is epitomized by the experience of basic training. Reflected in film and novels, the world of basic training is portrayed as a harsh, intense, and unforgiving experience in which individuals are turned into killing machines. This portrayal contrasts sharply with the reports of basic training from the recruits themselves. While psychological processes evidently are at work that influence individual identity, individuals are not passive participants in the process. Recruits make a conscious decision to join the ranks of the military. The trainees are as much a guide in their developmental journey as is the external process itself. The future of research examining the dynamics, components, and effectiveness of indoctrination would do well to remember that turning civilians into service members is a multidetermined, iterative, and interactional process.

References

Baron, R. S. (1986). Distraction conflict theory: Progress and problems. In L. Berkowitz (Ed.), *Advances in experimental social psychology* (Vol. 19, pp. 1–40). New York: Academic.

Baron, R. S. (2000). Arousal, capacity, and intense indoctrination. *Personality and Social Psychology Review, 4*, 238–254.

Baumeister, R. F., & Leary, M. R. (1995). The need to belong: Desire for interpersonal attachments as a fundamental human motivation. *Psychological Bulletin, 117*, 497–529.

Brown, J. D. (1991). Staying fit and staying well: Physical fitness as a moderator of life stress. *Journal of Personality and Social Psychology, 60*, 555–561.

Bourne, P. G. (1967). Some observations on the psychosocial phenomena seen in basic military training. *Journal of Psychiatry, 20*, 187–196.

Carbone, E. G., Cigrang, J. A., Todd, S. L., & Fiedler, E. R. (1999). Predicting outcome of military basic training for individuals referred for psychological evaluation. *Journal of Personality Assessment, 72*, 256–265.

Cialdini, R. B. (1993). *Influence: Science and practice* (3rd ed.). New York: HarperCollins College Publishers.

Cigrang, J. A., Todd, S. L., & Carbone, E. G. (2000). Stress management training for military trainees returned to duty after a mental health evaluation: Effects on graduation rates. *Journal of Occupational Health Psychology, 5*, 48–55.

Darley, J. M. (1966). Fear and social comparison as determinants of conformity behavior. *Journal of Personality and Social Psychology, 4*, 73–78.

Deaux, K (1996). Social identification. In E. T. Higgins & A. W. Kruglanski (Eds.), *Social psychology handbook of basic principles* (pp. 777–798). New York: Guilford Press.

Department of the Army, *Field Manual 7-21.13. The Soldier's Guide.* Retrieved August 18, 2004, from http://www.globalsecurity.org/military/library/policy/army/fm/7-21-13/

Department of the Army, Training and Doctrine Command. (2003). *TRADOC Regulation 350-6. Enlisted initial entry training (IET) policies and administration.* Retrieved August 18, 2004, from http://www-tradoc.army.mil/tpubs/regs/r350-6/r350-6.htm

Diener, E. (1975). Effects of altered responsibility, cognitive set, and modeling on physical aggression and deindividuation. *Journal of Personality and Social Psychology, 31*, 328–337.

du Picq, A. (1870). *Battle studies ancient and modern battle.* Translated from the eighth edition in French by Colonel John N. Greely, U.S. Army and Major Robert C. Cotton, U.S. Army. Harrisburg, PA: Military Service Publishing Co., 1947.

Easterbrook, J. (1959). The effect of emotion on cue utilization and the organization of behavior. *Psychological Review, 66*, 183–201.

Elsass, W. P., Fiedler, E., Skop, B., & Hill, H. (2001). Susceptibility to maladaptive responses to stress in basic military training based on variants of temperament and character. *Military Medicine, 166*, 884–888.

Gleicher, F., & Petty, R. E. (1992). Expectations of reassurance influence the nature of fear-stimulated attitude change. *Journal of Experimental Social Psychology, 28*, 86–100.

Gold, M. A. (2000). Cadet basic training: An ethnographic study of stress and coping. *Military Medicine, 165*, 147–152.

Grossman, D. A. (1996). *On killing.* Boston: Little, Brown and Company.

Hoge, C. W., Lesikar, S. E., Guevera, R., Lange, J., Brundage, J. F., Engel, C. C., et al. (2002). Mental disorders among U.S. military personnel in the 1990s: Association with high levels of health care utilization and early military attrition. *American Journal of Psychiatry 159*, 1576–1583.

Hoge, C. W., Toboni, H. E. Messer, S. C., Bell, N., Amoroso, P., & Orman, D. T. (2005). The occupational burden of mental disorders in the U.S. military: Psychiatric hospitalizations, involuntary separations, and disability. *American Journal of Psychiatry, 162*, 585–591.

Kahneman, D. (1973). *Attention and effort.* Englewood Cliffs, NJ: Prentice Hall.

King, A. C., Taylor, C. B., Haskell, W. L., & DeBusk, R. F. (1989). Influence of regular aerobic exercise on psychological health: A randomized, controlled trial of healthy middle-aged adults. *Health Psychology, 8*(3), 305–324.

Kruglanski, A. W., & Webster, D. M. (1991). Group members' reactions to opinion deviates and conformists at varying degrees of proximity to decision deadline and environmental noise. *Journal of Personality and Social Psychology, 61*, 212–225.

Lazarus, R. S., & Folkman, S. (1984). *Stress, appraisal and coping.* New York: Springer.

Leary, M. R., Tambor, E. S., Terdal, S. K., & Downs, D. L. (1995). Self-esteem as an interpersonal monitor: The sociometer hypothesis. *Journal of Personality and Social Psychology, 68*, 518–530.

Lifton, R. J. (1961). *Thought reform and the psychology of totalism: A study of brainwashing in China.* New York: Holt.

Lubin, B., Fiedler, E. R., & Van Whitlock, R. (1996). Mood as a predictor of discharge from Air Force basic training. *Journal of Clinical Psychology, 52*, 145–151.

Markus, H. R., & Kitayama, S. (1991). Culture and the self: Implications for cognition, emotion, and motivation. *Psychological Review, 98*, 224–253.

Markus, H. R., & Kitayama, S. (1994). A collective fear of the collective: Implications for selves and theories of selves. *Personality and Social Psychological Bulletin, 20*, 568–579.

Marshall, S. L. (1947). *Men against fire.* Norman: University of Oklahoma Press.

Nichols, W. R. (Ed.). (2001). *Random House Webster's Unabridged Dictionary* (2nd ed.). New York: Random House.

Oaker, G., & Brown, R. (1986). Intergroup relations in a hospital setting: A further test of social identity theory. *Human Relations, 39*, 767–778.

Petty, R. E., & Wegener, D. T. (1998). Attitude change: Multiple roles for persuasion variables. In D. T. Gilbert, S. T. Fiske, & G. Lindsey (Eds.), *Handbook of social psychology* (Vol. 1, pp. 323–390). New York: McGraw-Hill.

Pope, R. P., Herbert, R., Kirwan, J. D., & Graham, B. J. (1999). Predicting attrition in basic military training. *Military Medicine, 164*, 710–714.

Ryan, R. M., & Deci, E. L. (2000). Self-determination theory and the facilitation of intrinsic motivation, social development, and well-being. *American Psychologist, 55*, 68–78.

Sanbonmatsu, D. M., & Kardes, F. R. (1988). The effects of physiological arousal on information processing and persuasion. *Journal of Consumer Research, 15*, 379–385.

Schein, E. H., Schneier, I., & Barker, C. H. (1961). *Coercive persuasion: A socio-psychological analysis of the "brainwashing" of American civilian prisoners by the Chinese communists.* New York: Norton.

Schulman, S., Levy-Shiff, R., & Scharf, M. (2000). Family relationships, leaving home, and adjustment to military service. *Journal of Psychology, 134*, 392–400.

Spiller, R. J. (1988). S.L.A. Marshall and the ratio of fire. *The Rusi Journal, Winter*, 63–71.

Stahelski, A. (2004). Terrorists are made, not born: Creating terrorists using social psychological conditioning. *Journal of Homeland Security.* Retrieved March 22, 2004, from http://www.homelandsecurity.org/journal/Articles/stahelski.html

Tajfel, H. (1981). *Human groups and social categories: Studies in social psychology.* Cambridge, UK: Cambridge University Press.

Talcott, G. W., Haddock, C. K., Klesges, R. C., Lando, H., & Fiedler, E. (1999). Prevalence and predictors of discharge in United States Air Force Basic Military Training. *Military Medicine, 164*, 269–274.

Walsh, J. S. (2000). *Moral factors: The 10th principle of war.* Newport, RI: Naval War College.

Ward, M. (1999). *An analysis of socialization incubators in selected military commissioning institutions.* Unpublished doctoral dissertation, Southern Illinois University at Carbondale.

Williams, A. (2004). Psychosocial effects of the Boot Strap intervention in Navy recruits. *Military Medicine.* Retrieved October 10, 2005, fromhttp://www.findarticles.com/p/articles/mi_qa3912/is_200410/ai_n9464194

Wine, J. (1971). Test anxiety and direction of attention. *Psychological Bulletin, 76*, 92–104.

CHAPTER 3

SCENARIO-BASED TRAINING: IMPROVING MILITARY MISSION PERFORMANCE AND ADAPTABILITY

Eduardo Salas, Heather A. Priest, Katherine A. Wilson and C. Shawn Burke

Current military soldiers are constantly required to operate in complex, stressful, and ambiguous environments. In fact, it has been said that "Gone are the days of a predictable enemy who will allow U.S. intelligence to distribute a common template of threat doctrine. The Army now faces an incredible variety of potential threats" (Brown, 2003, p. 1). This statement is not only true of the U.S. Army, but also of all military services. The modern military must deal with an unpredictable, deceptive enemy in war and peace. Furthermore, the use of coalition forces to combat this new enemy adds additional complexities (e.g., communication difficulties, culture clashes) to these teams. Future forces will find that "military successes will result from rapid and accurate decision-making" (Machamer, 1995, third section, para. 3), when facing uncertain situations in dynamic environments.

In the past, it has been safe to assume that anytime our U.S. military was not at war, the forces were training for war. However, more recently the nature of the U.S. military's tasks (as well as those of allied troops) has broadened beyond that of war fighting to peacekeeping and even counterterrorism. These new missions require that our soldiers be properly trained to adapt to any number of situations. Consider the U.S. military's most recent war efforts—Operation Iraqi Freedom. Although an end to war was declared on April 9, 2003, U.S. and coalition troops continue to fight guerrilla warfare, assist the Iraqi population in peacekeeping missions, and continuously seek out terrorist cells operating in the Middle East. The tasks being conducted may change each day—and sometimes within the same day—requiring that troops be ready for any situation. As such, U.S. and coalition troops need to be adaptive, make complex decisions, and problem solve in war fighting and peacekeeping. To acquire these skills, practice-based, structured training is required that can target the complex competencies that will make this new brand of military operations successful.

The U.S. military is one of the largest investors in training, spending an estimated $17 billion each year to train soldiers (House Committee on Veterans Affairs, 2004). In fact, the International Military Education and Training (IMET) program, established under the Foreign Assistance Act, alone spent $80 million in 2003 on training programs, including English-language training, flying training, observation/familiarization training, on-the-job/qualifications training (OJT), orientation tours (OT), professional military education, and technical training for foreign military personnel from countries who cannot financially support these types of training (Foreign Assistance Act, n.d.). Because of high costs associated with training, military leaders are increasingly interested in capitalizing on existing training techniques and minimizing training costs as the U.S. military confronts an increasing number of obligations around the world. Therefore, the military must continue to invest in and use cost-efficient, safe, and effective learning methodologies and training systems. One solution to this dilemma is the implementation of an instructional strategy that can make the acquisition and transfer of complex cognition, behaviors, and attitudes, necessary for military needs, more successful. One such strategy is scenario-based training (SBT), which is the focus of this chapter.

The Science of Training

The past 40 years has seen a great deal of progress made in the science of training. Particularly in the 1990s, the field has seen an explosion of training research, resulting in numerous training models, methods, and strategies (Salas & Cannon-Bowers, 2001). Training is defined as the systematic acquisition of the knowledge (i.e., K; cognitions and what you know), skills (i.e., S; behaviors and what you do), and attitudes (i.e., A; what you feel), with the goal being to develop the competencies necessary for effective performance in work environments (Salas & Cannon-Bowers, 2000). Effective training revolves around changing cognition, behaviors, attitudes, and, consequently, the way people do their jobs. However, change is not in and of itself enough; this change must focus on correcting deficiencies by targeting the right competencies (i.e., the competencies necessary to perform effectively on the job). Ultimately, it can be said that the systematic approach to the design, implementation, and evaluation of training is necessary for success.

Theoretical developments have driven empirical research on the systematic approach to training design and delivery, with the most influential theories of today evolving in the early 1990s (Salas & Cannon-Bowers, 2001). These theoretical developments often took the form of either general (e.g., Cannon-Bowers, Salas, Tannenbaum, & Mathieu, 1995; Kozlowski & Salas, 1997; Tannenbaum, Cannon-Bowers, & Mathieu, 1993) or more focused models (e.g., Cannon-Bowers, Burns, Salas, & Pruitt, 1998; Colquitt, LePine, & Noe, 2000; Ford, Kozlowski, Kraiger, Salas, & Teachout, 1997; Thayer & Teachout, 1995). General models typically focused on training as a whole, covering constructs that relate to pretraining, the training period, and evaluation. More focused models emphasized specific constructs related to training by cueing in on themes such as transfer of training, training motivation, practice, and individual characteristics. These models included the development of instructional strategies like the SBT life cycle (discussed in the next section; Cannon-Bowers & Salas, 1998a). As a result of these theoretical developments, multiple variables have been identified that can affect the design of effective training. Ultimately, it is important to acknowledge that there is a science of training that should guide the design, delivery, and evaluation of training. Training system design ought to be rooted in proven scientific principles. In the last decade, we have seen an increased amount of research on what leads to effective training (Salas & Cannon-Bowers, 2001). We now have new (and better) theories, evaluation approaches, strategies, and tools as a result.

The advancement of the training field revolves around a "systems approach" to training, realizing that more factors than the individuals involved in the training influence the effectiveness of training. Empirical and theoretical contributions in the last two decades have emphasized additional factors in training application—the effect of organizational factors (e.g., climate; reward systems) on training (e.g., Kozlowski, Brown, Weissbein, Cannon-Bowers, & Salas, 2000), issues in transfer of training (e.g., Ford et al., 1997), individual differences (e.g., motivation) and training (Mathieu & Martineau, 1997), and training evaluation strategies (e.g., Cannon-Bowers & Salas, 1997). The multiple variables threaded throughout the training literature are necessary for effective training and have often been integrated into training effectiveness models. Alvarez, Salas, and Garofano (2004) conducted a comprehensive review of the literature that revolves around training effectiveness and provides a model that encompasses the factors leading to the design of effective, systematic training, many of which will be discussed within the context of SBT. Alvarez and colleague's (2003) Integrated Model of Training Effectiveness and Evaluation (IMTEE) illustrates the multiple factors, often examined in isolation, that together contribute to training effectiveness (see Figure 3.1).

The accumulation of this research has led to scientists concentrating beyond the actual training itself. This is not to imply that the training program isn't central to successful training. However, findings support the importance of pretraining, during-training, and posttraining considerations that can make or break a training program (Tannenbaum et al., 1993).

Using the IMTEE (Figure 3.1) as a framework, pretraining considerations should include conducting a training needs analysis, which consists of an organizational analysis, job/task analysis, cognitive task analysis, and person analysis. This is the first layer (top box in Figure 3.1) of the model and informs the rest of the process. The information obtained from these analyses enable training designers to systematically and reliably develop training content, select training methods (e.g., information, demonstration) and instructional strategies (e.g., SBT), and determine training objectives and their relevant knowledge, skills, and attitudes (KSAs) during training. In addition, factors, such as the pretraining environment, organizational

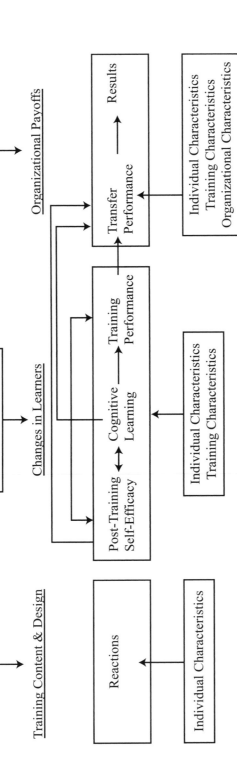

Figure 3.1
Integrated Model of Team Effectiveness and Evaluation

Source: Alvarez et al., 2004.

characteristics, and individual characteristics of trainees (seen at the bottom of the IMTEE in Figure 3.1), can have a significant impact on how training should be designed. During training, factors include the implementation of practice and feedback, a part of training content and design. Practice should be structured and paired with real-time feedback to make the implementation of training successful, a recurring theme in our discussion of SBT. Posttraining factors revolve around the issues of performance measurement, training evaluation, and transfer of training. Once training has been developed, its outcomes must be evaluated at multiple levels (i.e., reactions, learning, behavior, and organizational impact; Kirkpatrick, 1976; Kraiger, Ford, & Salas, 1993), and the transfer of acquired knowledge, skills, and attitudes to the job must be ensured (Baldwin & Ford, 1988).

What Is Scenario-Based Training?

SBT is a training strategy that uses several aspects of scientific, theory-based training, incorporating information, demonstration, and practice-based methods. It is a tool that was developed out of science-based research that can be applied in a number of settings. One thing that makes SBT so unique is that, unlike classroom or lecture training, the scenarios become the curriculum—meaning the events inserted in the scenarios constitute the learning objectives, the means to achieve the desired learning outcomes. So, careful consideration should be given to the design of scenarios. In addition, a key component that distinguishes SBT from other training techniques (e.g., lecture-based) is the incorporation of opportunities for practice and feedback using scenarios designed to elicit specific KSAs.

SBT is one of the most effective methods for applying practice and feedback systematically to promote the necessary KSAs. SBT uses scenarios that are defined a priori based on the training objectives identified in the training needs analysis. Typically referred to as scenario-based training (SBT), or event-based approach training (EBAT) (Prince, Oser, Salas, & Woodruff, 1993; Oser Cannon-Bowers, Salas, & Dwyer, 1999), this instructional strategy follows the tenets of the science of training through development (i.e., pretraining), application (i.e., during training), and evaluation (i.e., posttraining). Similar to the components of scientific training, there are steps that should be taken to ensure that SBT is applied within an appropriate learning environment. Factors influential to SBT learning environments include the audience, task requirements, training environment, methods, strategies, and tools. All of these components are further explained within the steps of the SBT life cycle.

Why Scenario-Based Training?

It is clear that the military requires a practice-based training system, with real-time measurement and feedback, in order to prepare its team and collectives (i.e., work groups, organizational units, departments, networks, or learning communities). So, we submit that scenario-based training is an optimal instructional strategy for training the knowledge, skills, and attitudes needed for accomplishing military tasks.

SBT has a number of benefits for the military. First, it establishes an environment that promotes learning and the acquisition of KSAs to ensure that training will promote more effective performance on the job. Second, SBT encourages emergence and is engaging. That is, scenarios within SBT allow trainees to interact with "realistic situations that will facilitate learning" (Oser et al., 1999, p. 454). This is not possible within classroom-based training in which information is presented in the form of a lecture. Essentially, SBT enables trainees to create a "microworld" that increases the psychological fidelity, experimental realism, and trainee experimentation (Bowers & Jentsch, 2001; Senge, 1990). Therefore, SBT provides "rich experiences" during training, which accelerate learning and the acquisition of expertise. Scenarios embedded within SBT allow trainees to see how different performance strategies can be applied across a number of situations and how those strategies work out (Johnston, Driskell, & Salas, 1997). Third, SBT enables dynamic trainee performance. Practice is vital in the acquisition of competencies. SBT allows trainees to practice these competencies by performing tasks when they must apply them (i.e., given a situation or event). Complex tasks, like those found in military operations, require trainee participation and practice (Salas et al., 2000). Fourth, SBT is diagnostic. By embedding triggers within scenarios, observers have the opportunity to anticipate and, therefore, more easily observe, record, and diagnose performance throughout training. The structure of SBT offers control of task content and the accurate diagnosis of performance in dynamic environments (Fowlkes, Dwyer, Oser, & Salas, 1998). Furthermore, SBT and event-based methods and tools have been shown to contain psychometrically sound measures and improved problem-solving performance across a variety of settings (Oser et al., 1999). With these benefits in mind, we provide some examples in the following section of how SBT has been successfully implemented within military settings.

Steps in Designing SBT

To best understand the components of SBT, Cannon-Bowers and colleagues (1998) provide a graphical representation of SBT's life cycle, which we have adapted for this chapter (see Figure 3.2). The SBT life cycle involves seven interrelated stages (each represented by a circle in Figure 3.2), which occur in succession. SBT methods and tools have been applied extensively with much success within complex environments like the military. A brief review of the literature cites several areas within this domain that have benefited from SBT-type training. For example, SBT has been applied in Combat Information Centers (CICs; Johnston, Smith-Jentsch, & Cannon-Bowers, 1997), military aviation cockpits (Fowlkes et al., 1998; Prince, Oser, Salas, & Woodruff, 1993), military operations on urbanized terrain (MOUT; Wilson, 2003), and other military settings (Dwyer, Oser, & Fowlkes, 1995) to train teams. To better illustrate these steps, we provide examples from real-world military training programs already in place that will be used throughout the following section.

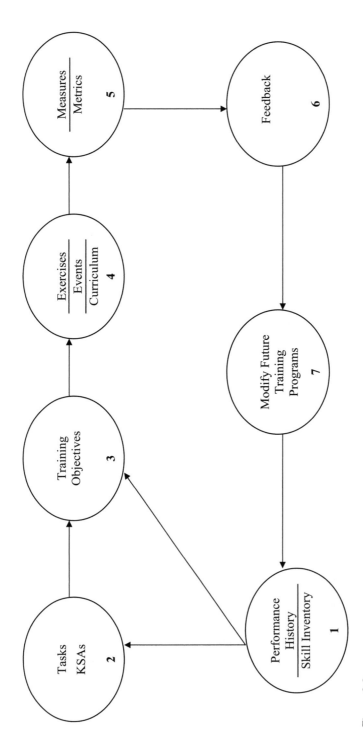

Figure 3.2
Components of Scenario-Based Training

Source: Adapted from Cannon-Bowers et al., 1998.

Step 1: Use Performance History and Conduct Skill Inventory

The SBT life cycle (shown in Figure 3.2) begins with determining what skills trainees currently hold and leveraging their previous performance data. This entails the incorporation of a number of resources. First, the current skills held by trainees must be determined. This can be done by conducting a skills inventory, usually conducted by looking at past training, consulting subject matter experts (SMEs), and conducting surveys to assess current skill levels (Oser et al., 1999). Second, training developers must examine past performance data of trainees. This will provide a starting point for developers so that they will address the needs of the organization (e.g., the military) and the individual trainees more effectively.

An example of this can be found in distributed mission training (DMT), which uses advanced computing and communication technologies to train soldiers in synthetic training environments (Bell, 1999). The goal of DMT is to develop mission-critical team performance. This is done by embedding targeted scenarios within synthetic environments to develop and measure team skills within realistic environments to provide contextual factors in training. DMT is systematically designed to increase situation awareness through the inclusion of contextual factors, present in the real world, in the training process, while being able to specify the KSAs needed to achieve the targeted performance (Bell, 1999). The development of DMT used a naturalistic perspective, targeting the training of processes in decision making that rest in "situational awareness and assessment, prioritization in dynamic task environments and action/feedback structures in event management" (Bell, 1999, p. 74). Building on what experts know about past performance and requirements on the battlefield, instructors use domain-specific knowledge; a set of cognitive skills, psychomotor skills, and processes; and the use of psychometric properties to evaluate the acquisition of competencies.

Step 2: Determine Tasks and Competencies

The second step of the life cycle is to determine the tasks and competencies to be targeted during the training. Competencies necessary for effective performance should be established early on, using SMEs, task lists, skill inventories, and historical performance data (see step 1). These tools can help establish targeted competencies, identify trainee and organizational deficiencies, and define the overall focus of the scenarios (Oser et al., 1999).

One way to do this is by conducting a training-needs analysis. There are four types of analyses that make up a training-needs analysis: (1) organizational analysis, (2) job/task analysis, (3) cognitive task analysis, and (4) person analysis. Organizational analysis is a useful tool for getting at the organizational system components, which can affect whether training is delivered effectively (Goldstein, 1993). The training methodologies and strategies available depend on the resources available within the organization. In addition, less tangible organizational factors, such as organizational climate and support from leaders, can help determine the effectiveness of training programs. While these factors should be considered pretraining, their impact is ongoing and can manifest themselves most obviously during training. Job or task analysis can be defined as a tool that is used to "determine the instructional objectives that will be related to performance of particular activities or job operations" (Goldstein, 1993, p. 54; Figure 3.3). There are essentially three steps to conducting a job/task analysis: (1) describing and clarifying the job/task needs, (2) detailing the specifications of the task, and (3) determining the competencies or KSAs needed for the task (e.g., communication, decision making, adaptability, performance monitoring; see Salas et al., 2000 for a description of these and other competencies).

However, within military settings, tasks may be particularly complex and require higher levels of cognitive processing (e.g., problem solving). In dealing with these tasks, the requisite KSAs are particularly important. To overcome the difficulty of identifying competencies and to encourage their inclusion, training researchers developed the cognitive task analysis (CTA; Klein & Militello, 2001). CTA is driven by the need to understand cognition and mental processes necessary for successful training. Overall, CTA is a tool for analyzing the mental processing requirements for carrying out a particular task (for more information see DuBois & Shalin 1995, 2000; Klein & Militello, 2001; Schraagen & Chipman, 2000). In addition to the analysis of the task and the organization, the members of the organization should be analyzed using person analysis. Person analysis is used to determine who needs to be trained and what training is needed by each individual (Goldstein, 1993; Tannenbaum & Yukl, 1992). The purpose of person analysis makes certain that the right people get the right training. This may be particularly important in the military, where needed skills often vary from person to person or division to division.

An example of this can be taken from the Office of Naval Research, which sponsored a program of research called the Tactical Decision Making Under Stress

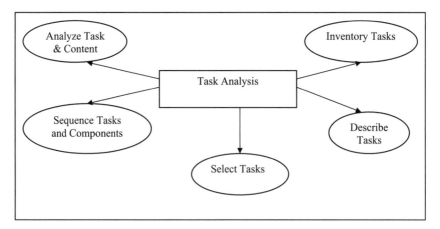

Figure 3.3
How to Conduct a Task Analysis

Program (TADMUS; Cannon-Bowers & Salas, 1998b). One of the goals of TAD-MUS was to address a typical shipboard CIC, which requires flexible training for complex environments that are inherently stressful. To train operators who will be asked to perform in these environments more effectively and efficiently, researchers developed team dimensional training (TDT) for the Navy. TDT contains a prebrief training session, where instructors must define TDT teamwork dimensions and underlying behaviors, focus the team on these objectives, present an outline of how TDT will progress, and establish a positive learning climate. These steps ensure that all TDT programs will have the necessary tasks and components to promote effective training. For a more thorough examination of TDT development and implementation, see Smith-Jentsch, Zeisig, Acton, and McPherson (1998).

Step 3: Develop Training Objectives

Based on the outcomes of the previous two steps, training objectives must be developed that should be based on the competencies needed to operate effectively. The competencies, or KSAs, provide the foundation for training goals and objectives in that to complete these objectives, individuals and team members must possess the appropriate KSAs for the task and/or situation. Furthermore, training objectives provide trainees with the learning outcomes that are expected from the training program (Oser et al., 1999). Thus, the training objectives should be explicit and measurable such that they drive scenario development and ensure training results in the acquisition of the knowledge and skills necessary to perform in complex environments.

Training objectives can be either task specific or task generic (Oser, Dwyer, Cannon-Bowers, & Salas, 1998). Task-specific training objectives revolve around a specific task to accomplish a specific organizational goal. For example, military troops fighting in Iraq are often faced with the task of searching homes of possible insurgents. To prepare future soldiers for these situations, trainees must learn how to "clear a room" under a specific set of circumstances. The training objectives for this situation should, therefore, specifically address the learning outcomes necessary for clearing a room. Conversely, task-generic training objectives entail general learning that transfers to a number of settings. For example, some situations require that troops operate and make decisions under various stressors (e.g., time pressure, workload, ambiguity). Therefore, trainees must learn to make decisions in each of these situations. The training objectives should, thus, revolve around general decision-making competencies that would compensate for deficiencies under stress.

TADMUS offers a good example of this step as well. While TADMUS, discussed in an example earlier, was an overarching program of research, included in the objectives of this program was the development of tools to systematically generate scenarios that can address such complex issues as rapidly developing ambiguous events, multicomponent decisions, information overload, threat, and adverse physical conditions, thus targeting the appropriate training objectives and competencies.

Step 4: Embed Carefully Crafted Scenarios

Traditional training generally consists of classroom-based lectures that provide trainees with the requisite knowledge to perform in a mission. However, classroom training alone is not sufficient for the requirements of most military missions. Rather, military forces must have the ability to apply the learned knowledge and skills in the field. Scenario-based training can be used to provide trainees with the opportunity to apply their knowledge and skills in context (e.g., training at the National Training Center [NTC]). This is the key difference between traditional training and SBT; scenarios must be carefully crafted and embedded in the training. Scenario events must be developed such that they target the desired competencies, promote training objectives, and provide meaningful practice opportunities for trainees. Scenario events should be scripted a priori, based on data gathered in the pretraining phase (i.e., steps 1 through 3). Furthermore, scenarios should be constructed based on sound methodology, which is representative of training objectives and desired KSAs (Stretton & Johnston, 1997). These scenarios (e.g., events, exercises) are thus embedded in the training and serve as the training's curriculum.

To further explain, we refer back to Figure 3.2. The skills inventory developed (step 1) drives the competencies (step 2) and training objectives (step 3). The training objectives that are developed, in turn, drive the development of the actual training scenarios embedded within the strategy and help develop the scripts associated with the scenarios. Within these scenarios, "triggers" are embedded a priori at multiple points, which are designed to elicit certain KSAs that are the focus of training. These triggers must be embedded with the training objectives in mind, so there are certain criteria to structuring such events. The development of scenarios should include events that target each training objective and vary in difficulty and occur at different points within a scenario (Oser et al., 1999). To be effective, multiple events should vary in difficulty, should be specified for each objective, should be introduced at several points during the exercise, and should serve as opportunities for trainees to practice and to exhibit the targeted KSAs.

This must be done systematically and requires the development of a master scenario event list (MSEL). The MSEL serves to organize events that occur within the scenario and can help developers ensure that all training objectives are addressed. Components of MSELs include the system requirements (e.g., hardware/software) for the scenario, relationships between events and learning objectives, timing of events, and links between events and performance measurement opportunities. For an example of an MSEL, see Oser and colleagues (1999).

Furthermore, the scenarios provide opportunities to practice. Practice is essential to the translation of knowledge into actual skill (Shute & Gawlick, 1995). Although "practice makes perfect" is a popular sentiment, it is not completely accurate. First, practice alone is not enough. It must be tied to what is being trained and used as a learning experience, not just free play. Second, while practice makes certain behaviors long-lasting, it does not necessarily make them perfect or even complementary to the task to be performed (Oser et al., 1999). Therefore, practice must be a recurring process in which trainees are guided and provided feedback. This will ensure that practice is useful, targets appropriate KSAs, and reinforces good behaviors.

Lastly, to be effective, scenarios must be crafted to promote realistic practice and promote the transfer of training. Therefore, these scenarios must be representative of what a soldier would be expected to experience in the field. As a result of the complexity of military environments, SBT scenario events must represent realistic routine and nonroutine events (Oser et al., 1999). By providing opportunities to practice routine and nonroutine events, SBT will promote effective, adaptive performance. There are several programs available to help training designers develop scenario-based training. For example, based on the Rapidly Reconfigurable Line Operational Evaluation (RRLOE) developed for the commercial aviation community (Bowers, Jentsch, Baker, Prince, & Salas, 1997), a computer-based system has been developed to support scenario-based training in the military (Anacapa Sciences, Inc., n.d.). This system, known as Scenario Design and Assessment Tool for Training (ScenDATT), takes a systems approach to developing training scenarios to improve mission performance. Specifically, ScenDATT walks training designers through the steps necessary (pre-, during, and posttraining) to design realistic scenarios in which training objectives can be linked to performance, which can then be evaluated and feedback provided. While ScenDATT has been designed to support U.S. Navy S-3B training simulations, plans to extend it to apply to other aircraft in the Navy are in progress.

Step 5: Develop Performance Measures

Step 5 of the SBT life cycle involves the development of performance measures, which will be used to diagnose whether the trained competencies are learned and being applied in either a simulated or real environment. Once training objectives (step 3) and SBT scenarios have been developed (step 4), you must evaluate the outcomes of the training at multiple levels (Kirkpatrick, 1976; Kraiger et al., 1993). Like scenario development, measures must clearly link training objectives, desired KSAs, and trainee performance. SBT is of no use unless it is training the desired KSAs and can clearly illustrate that through measurement. Therefore, the training scenarios and trainee performance should be evaluated during and after SBT to ensure that behavior has changed in the appropriate direction.

Following the creation of events and scenarios (step 4), measurement instruments are developed that will be used to assess task performance during each a priori-defined event establishing the explicit links mentioned above. These links also allow instructors to incorporate standardized measurement, which will reduce the workload for those in charge of observation and collection of performance data. For example, if measures embedded within SBT are tied to defined events, observers can offer near-real-time feedback to trainees and do not have to observe every instance of behavior (reducing their own workload).

The effective assessment of training is complex and should include multiple diagnostic measures. To address these multiple measurement levels, measurement tools are often employed to assess performance and training effectiveness during and following training interventions. It is important that all measurement tools be multi-dimensional (i.e., allow the assessment of both process and outcome level feedback). This is useful for both individuals and teams within organizations. Ultimately, measurement should be tied to learning objectives and scenario events to ensure the assessment of whether or not targeted competencies are learned (i.e., outcome) and why performance occurred as it did (i.e., process).

While measurement after the fact is useful and easier to provide, there are also some useful measurement techniques to capture performance as it happens within scenarios, one of the most meaningful benefits of SBT. Tools such as Targeted Acceptable Responses to Generated Events or Tasks (or TARGETs) can be integrated within the training environment to ensure that trainee performance is captured. TARGETS was developed to evaluate the behavioral components of the Navy's skill-based aircrew coordination training (ACT) program (Fowlkes, Lane, Salas, Oser, & Prince, 1992; Prince & Salas, 1993; Stout, Salas, & Fowlkes, 1997). The developers of ACT needed an evaluation technique that was both psychometrically sound and would be sensitive to targeted team constructs in order to diagnose performance deficiencies that would require program adjustments. Similar methods of performance measurement have been developed for commercial aviation, which can be adapted for military use, such as the Line Operational Safety Audits (LOSA; Klinect, Wilhelm, & Helmreich, 1999). Event-based training programs, such as SBT, are ideal for this, because they embed triggers to systematically evaluate performance and are embedded with strong psychometric properties. Often, performance measures are built into the simulation environment themselves. For example, following the steps of SBT, TADMUS also resulted in the development of an event-based performance criteria and measurement system for training systems aboard ships for the Navy, which was embedded in training programs like TDT. Specifically, TDT uses the Shipboard Mobile Aid for Training and Evaluation (Ship-MATE). ShipMATE enables instructors to prepare for, conduct, and debrief objective-oriented, scenario-based training, assisting the instructor in making pre- and postexercise briefings (Cannon-Bowers et al., 1998).

Step 6: Provide Constructive and Timely Feedback

Based on the information obtained from the performance data, constructive and timely feedback must be provided to trainees so that performance can be improved in the future (step 5). Practice within scenarios in SBT is not enough. Practice is much less effective when not paired with feedback. In fact, practice without constructive, immediate feedback can reinforce negative behaviors (Frese & Altman, 1989). Therefore, during SBT, practice and feedback should be well planned and should serve a specific purpose. Posttraining feedback and debriefings should accompany all SBT interventions. Feedback must also be structured around training objectives and targeted competencies to reinforce desired behaviors and correct undesirable behaviors, while employing the science of training. Furthermore, timing is equally important, so feedback should be provided as close as possible to practice sessions to ensure retention and learning. Furthermore, feedback can serve to inform future training (see step 7).

For example, the U.S. military currently uses a form of scenario-based training at the National Training Center located at Fort Irwin, California. Training at the NTC has been developed with the specific mission of providing "tough, realistic combined arms and services in accordance with operational doctrine for brigade/regiments in a mid-to-high-intensity environment while retraining the training feedback and analysis focus at the battalion/task force level" (Division Transportation Operations, n.d., National Training Center Section, para. 1). These realistic scenarios provide trainees with the opportunity to practice what they have learned in more traditional classroom-based training. Furthermore, practicing in a realistic environment allows trainees to develop a more accurate mental model of situations they may be facing in the future, while reinforcing what they learn with real-time feedback. These mental representations can help soldiers to better prepare for the mission that lies ahead.

Step 7: Modify Future Training Programs

The final stage of the SBT life cycle involves the modification of future training programs such that they build on the strengths of previous training while designing out weaknesses. To capitalize on past training, SBT should incorporate lessons learned into future training interventions. The practice sessions embedded within SBT provide an excellent opportunity to learn from mistakes being made by the trainees and the things they are doing right. Future SBT interventions can incorporate these factors into scenarios to reinforce the positive behaviors and correct negative ones. Past sessions are a valuable resource for trainers and trainees to learn from history. Drawing on the feedback from the measures and trainer observation of the effectiveness of the SBT in the current scenario, developers can modify future training interventions. Like performance history and skill inventory, feedback from SBT can give training developers insight in how to design (and how not to design) future training for similar tasks. For example, if trainee feedback indicates a certain KSA (e.g., situational awareness) was not increased during SBT, future scenarios can be adapted to better target that particular competency. In this capacity, feedback can serve as "lessons learned" for designers of future training. In addition, both trainees and trainers can offer perspectives on their lessons learned after completing SBT. It is important to learn what works and what doesn't to ensure that future SBT is effective and appropriate to future tasks.

Tips for Making SBT Effective

To effectively use SBT, the design of training must follow certain guidelines founded in science (Fowlkes et al., 1998). These guidelines have been applied in a number of research arenas (e.g., aviation) and have proven their validity through their repeated applications. A comprehensive listing of guidelines can be found in

Table 3.1
Guidelines for SBT

SBT Guidelines
1.	Scenarios should be developed to ensure: (1) an end-to-end system design that links systematically the major components of the learning methodology; (2) the incorporation of learning principles; (3) architecture that supports the linkages; (4) system capabilities that are based on human-centered design; (5) technologies that support learning-based system performance; and (6) capabilities that permit distributed scenario planning, preparation, execution, and analysis.
2.	Define and document the overall focus of the scenario from the skill inventory and historical performance data.
3.	Determine and document the tasks to be trained based on the skill inventory and historical performance data.
4.	Develop and document clear objectives for scenarios.
5.	Develop scenario events and scenario scripts based on realistic, real-world conditions.
6.	Develop performance measurement tools and standards around the scenario events, clearly linking objectives and performance.
7.	Develop a strategy and tools for diagnosing performance trends based on performance measures designed a priori.
8.	Conduct feedback based on the learning objectives.
9.	Prepare and conduct prescenario briefings and training for scenario participants.
10.	Develop and implement a scenario management plan for control of scenarios.

Source: Oser et al., 1999.

Oser et al. (1999); see Table 3.1). As a companion to these guidelines, this section is provided to serve as supplemental tips to designing effective SBT (see Table 3.2).

Tip 1. Use What We Know about the Science of Training... and We Know a Lot

SBT must rely on the science of training developed over the past four decades. This includes factors involved in pre-, during-, and posttraining. Factors affecting the development and implementation of SBT, including organizational support, pre-practice environments, and transfer of training, should be appropriately addressed, using theoretically based and, when available, empirically tested methods. Implementing SBT scientifically entails the application of (1) tools (e.g., task analysis), (2) competencies (i.e., KSAs), (3) delivery methods (e.g., practice based), and (4) instructional strategies (e.g., cross training, SBT), which are driven by a set of training objectives (Salas, Cannon-Bowers, & Smith-Jentsch, 2001).

Table 3.2
Tips for SBT

Tip 1:	Use what we know about the science of training...and we know a lot.
Tip 2:	Subject-matter experts and learning experts must work together...create partnerships.
Tip 3:	Use what works...incorporate other training strategies into SBT.
Tip 4:	Guide trainee learning...practice does not necessarily make perfect!
Tip 5:	Apply scenario-based training experientially...

Source: Adapted from Oser et al., 1999.

Tip 2. Subject-matter Experts and Learning Experts Must Work Together... Create Partnerships

When designing SBT, it is important to remember that learning is not just about domain knowledge. Learning is both a behavioral and cognitive event. Therefore, effective learning within SBT requires a partnership between subject matter experts, who know the task and military environment, and learning experts, who know the science of learning, including practice, assessment, diagnosis, remediation, and reinforcement. Because you cannot expect SMEs to know how to effectively design SBT and learning experts to know the intricacies, tasks, or culture of the military, both experts are necessary to design effective SBT—neither is wholly effective alone. A balance between the two will ensure that trainees show long-lasting changes in KSAs that can be applied in and are relevant to their domain (e.g., military operations). Therefore, this partnership is vital to the success of SBT.

Tip 3. Use What Works...Incorporate Other Training Strategies into SBT

Throughout this chapter, we have discussed how SBT can be used as a single training strategy to improve mission performance. However, there are some situations in which the use of SBT in conjunction with other proven strategies may be beneficial to enhance training and learning. The premise behind SBT training will remain the same, and thus, all of the elements discussed previously are still essential for training to be effective. We will next briefly discuss two training strategies relevant to the military community (i.e., stress exposure training and error training) that can be used in combination with SBT.

Stress Exposure Training

The first training strategy that is relevant to the military community and that can be beneficial in conjunction with SBT is stress exposure training (SET), which provides trainees with tools and competencies that will enable them to perform more effectively in stressful and ambiguous environments (Driskell & Johnston, 1998;

see also Thompson & McCreary, this volume). The goal of SET is to decrease the likelihood of errors when individuals or teams are in high-stress situations, because these situations increase the likelihood that errors will occur in the first place. By incorporating this strategy with SBT, trainees will be able not only to learn what stress is and how it may affect performance, but also that they can experience the relevant stressors and learn strategies to mitigate the consequences of them. There are three critical steps to SET: (1) trainees are provided with information regarding the stressors that may be present in their work environment and how these stressors may affect them (i.e., create awareness), (2) trainees learn the skills (behavioral and cognitive) that will help them adapt to these stressors, and (3) trainees are provided with practice opportunities where they can apply what they know. While SET is often provided to target a specific stressor, depending on the task (e.g., time pressure), it often generalizes to other stressors (e.g., high workload), preparing trainees for a number of differing situations (Driskell, Johnston, & Salas, 2001). This is particularly important for military personnel who more often than not find themselves operating in high-stress environments.

Error Training

Error training is another strategy that can be used in conjunction with SBT to improve performance and reduce errors. Error training provides trainees with strategies for avoiding errors and minimizing their damage when they do occur, opportunities to practice these strategies and see their consequences, and feedback to improve learning (Frese et al., 1989; Heimbeck, Frese, & Sonnentag, 2003; Karl, O'Leary-Kelly, & Martocchio, 1993; Lorenzet, Salas, & Tannenbaum, 2003). Scenarios can thus be developed to elicit the potential errors so that they will be more readily recognized and mitigated in the future. There are two basic components of error training: (1) error occurrence, and (2) error correction. The first component refers to how errors occur during training. Training can be designed such that errors are avoided (i.e., no errors occur), allowed (i.e., errors may or may not occur; depends on trainees' actions), induced (i.e., errors are evoked), or guided (i.e., trainees are led to make errors). Error correction refers to how trainees deal with the errors they encounter within training. There are two approaches to error correction that can be incorporated in error training: (1) self-correction (i.e., trainees work through errors alone), and (2) supported correction (i.e., trainees are provided with support and feedback from trainers or SMEs). Research suggests that training incorporating guided error occurrence and supported error correction leads to superior performance over error free training (Lorenzet et al., 2003).

Tip 4. Guide Trainee Learning...Practice Does Not Necessarily Make Perfect

If trainees are allowed to practice without guidance, this can lead to unintended consequences. For example, without guidance, trainees may spend too much time focusing on one competency or skill, while ignoring other critical ones. This may result in ineffective training and a failure to transfer training to real-world environments (Salas & Burke, 2002). To reduce the likelihood of this occurring, trainees must be guided through practice in order to make sure they learn the appropriate lessons.

For example, when incorporating error training into SBT, you have the option of structuring it as avoiding, allowing, inducing, or guiding error occurrence (see tip 3). Guided error occurrence refers to the method of presenting error so that trainees can be guided to errors to encourage learning. Lorenzet and colleagues (2003) recommend the use of guided error training with supported correction (i.e., trainees are provided with support and feedback from trainers or SMEs) for optimal learning. Ultimately, guiding trainees through scenarios can ensure that all targeted competencies are addressed.

Tip 5. Apply Scenario-Based Training Experientially...Once Is Not Enough

One session of SBT is simply not enough. A team evolves and changes throughout its life span as does an individual throughout his or her period of service. This may lead to the development of other counterproductive habits and may result in a lessening of effective performance. Therefore, SBT should be applied experientially, targeting additional competencies, while reinforcing previously learned behaviors. Repeated exposure to SBT will ensure that soldiers are more effective in the field, increasing their experience level and providing a wider array of competencies from which they can draw.

Conclusion

With the advancement of technology and an increasingly ambiguous and "hard to predict" enemy, the military must train soldiers to be more adaptive, think on their feet, and perform as experienced soldiers. They are increasingly required to make decisions, problem solve, coordinate, and negotiate in environments where they may not have expertise. Therefore, training must provide the opportunity to gain expertise, to practice KSAs, and receive feedback they can apply in the field. This is difficult, but not impossible, using scientifically valid means of training (i.e., SBT). By providing soldiers with practice and feedback, while targeting specific and important knowledge, skills, and attitudes, soldiers will be better prepared, safer, and more effective in ambiguous, stressful environments.

SBT is an essential strategy to train modern and future soldiers. SBT is scientifically grounded and employs training methodologies that provide a means for training competencies of interest to the military. However, it is important to reemphasize the value of the systematic design and application of SBT, which uses structured, guided practice, and provides useful, immediate feedback. By following the steps of the SBT life cycle, the guidelines cited, and the tips provided within this text, training developers can provide an applicable, practical strategy for training the requisite competencies.

References

Alvarez, K., Salas, E., & Garofano, C. M. (2004). An integrated model of training evaluation and effectiveness. *Human Resources Management Review, 3*(4), 385–416.

Anacapa Sciences, Inc. (n.d.). *Current projects: Scenario design and assessment tool for training (ScenDATT).* Retrieved October 15, 2005, from http://www.anacapasciences.com/projects/scendatt/index.html

Baldwin, T. T., & Ford, J. K. (1988). Transfer of training: A review and directions for future research. *Personnel Psychology, 41,* 63–105.

Bell, H. H. (1999). The effectiveness of distributed mission training. *Association for Computing Machinery: Communications of the ACM, 42*(9), 73–78.

Bowers, C. A., & Jentsch, F. (2001). Use of commercial, off-the-shelf, simulations for team research. In E. Salas (Ed.), *Advances in human performance* (Vol. 1, pp. 293–317). Amsterdam: Elsevier Science.

Bowers, C. A., Jentsch, F., Baker, D., Prince, C., & Salas, E. (1997). Rapidly reconfigurable event-based line operational evaluation scenarios. *Proceedings of the 41st annual meeting of the Human Factors and Ergonomics Society* (pp. 912–915). Santa Monica, CA: HFES.

Brown, R. H. (2003, May–June). Developing agile, adaptive soldiers. *Military Review.* Retrieved on June 1, 2004, from http://www.findarticles.com/p/articles/mi_m0PBZ/is_3_83/%20ai_109268906/print

Cannon-Bowers, J. A., Burns, J. J., Salas, E., & Pruitt, J. S. (1998). Advanced technology in scenario-based training. In J. A. Cannon-Bowers and E. Salas (Eds.), *Making decisions under stress: Implications for individual and team training* (pp. 365–374). Washington, DC: American Psychological Association.

Cannon-Bowers, J. A., & Salas, E. (1997). A framework for developing team performance measures in training. In M. T. Brannick, E. Salas, & C. Prince (Eds.), *Team performance assessment and measurement: Theory, research, and applications* (pp. 45–62). Mahwah, NJ: Erlbaum.

Cannon-Bowers, J. A., & Salas, E. (1998a). Team performance and training in complex environments: Recent findings from applied research. *Current Directions in Psychological Science, 7,* 83–87.

Cannon-Bowers, J. A., & Salas, E. (Eds.) (1998b). *Making decisions under stress: Implications for individual and team training.* Washington, DC: American Psychological Association.

Cannon-Bowers, J. A., Salas, E., Tannenbaum, S. I., & Mathieu, J. E. (1995). Toward theoretically based principles of training effectiveness: A model and initial empirical investigation. *Military Psychology, 7*(3), 141–164.

Colquitt, J. A., LePine, J. A., & Noe, R. A. (2000). Toward an integrative theory of training motivation: A meta-analytic path analysis of 20 years of research. *Journal of Applied Psychology, 85,* 678–707.

Division Transportation Operations. (n.d.). *Section I: Peacetime support* (Chap. 2). Retrieved October 15, 2005, from http://www.transchool.eustis.army.mil/pcc/DTO/DTO_Guide_Chapter2.htm

Driskell, J. E., & Johnston, J. H. (1998). Stress exposure training. In J. A. Cannon-Bowers & E. Salas (Eds.), *Making decisions under stress: Implications for individual and team training* (pp. 191–217). Washington, DC: American Psychological Association.

Driskell, J. E., Johnston, J. H., & Salas, E. (2001). Does stress training generalize to novel settings? *Human Factors, 43*(1), 99–110.

DuBois, D., & Shalin, V. L. (1995). Adapting cognitive methods to real-world objectives: An application to job knowledge testing. In P. D. Nichols, S. F. Chipman, & R. L. Brennan (Eds.), *Cognitively diagnostic assessment* (pp. 189–220). Hillsdale, NJ: Erlbaum.

DuBois, D., & Shalin, V. L. (2000). Describing job expertise using cognitively oriented task analyses (COTA). In J. M. C. Schraagen & S. E. Chipman (Eds.), *Cognitive task analysis* (pp. 317–340). Mahwah, NJ: Erlbaum.

Dwyer, D. J., Oser, R. L., & Fowlkes, J. E. (1995). A case study of distributed training and training performance. In *Proceedings of the Human Factors and Ergonomics Society 39th Annual Meeting* (pp. 1316–1320). Santa Monica, CA: HFES.

Ford, J., Kozlowski, S. J. W., Kraiger, K., Salas, E., & Teachout, M. (Eds.) (1997). *Improving training effectiveness in work organizations*. Hillsdale, NJ: Erlbaum.

Foreign Assistance Act. (n.d.). *International Military Education and Training (IMET)*. Retrieved October 1, 2005, from http://www.fas.org/asmp/campaigns/training/IMET2.html

Fowlkes, J. E., Dwyer, D. J., Oser, R. L., & Salas, E. (1998). Event-based approach to training (EBAT). *International Journal of Aviation Psychology, 8*(3), 209–221.

Fowlkes, J. E., Lane, N. E., Salas, E., Oser, R. L., & Prince, C. (1992). Targets for aircrew coordination training. *Proceedings of the 14th Interservice Industry Training Systems Conference* (pp. 342–352). San Antonio, TX: Interservice Industry Training Systems.

Frese, M., & Altman, A. (1989). The treatment of errors in learning and transfer. In L. Bainbridge & S. A. Quintanilla (Eds.), *Developing skills with new technology* (pp. 65–86). Chichester, UK: Wiley.

Goldstein, I. L. (1993). *Training in organizations: Needs assessment, development, and evaluation* (3rd ed.). Pacific Grove, CA: Brooks/Cole.

Heimbeck, D., Frese, M., & Sonnentag, S. (2003). Integrating errors into the training process: The function of error management instructions and the role of goal orientation. *Personnel Psychology, 56*(2), 333–361.

House Committee on Veterans Affairs. (2004, March 24). *Employing veterans of our armed forces: Hearing* (Serial No. 108-33). Retrieved October 24, 2005, from http://veterans.house.gov/hearings/schedule108/mar04/3-24-04/3-24f-04.pdf

Johnston, J. H., Driskell, J. E., & Salas, E. (1997). Vigilant and hypervigilant decision making. *Journal of Applied Psychology, 82*(4), 614–622.

Johnston, J. H., Smith-Jenstch, K. A., & Cannon-Bowers, J. A. (1997). Performance measurement tools for enhancing team decision making. In M. T. Brannick, E. Salas, & C. Prince (Eds.), *Team performance assessment and measurement: Theory, methods, and applications* (pp. 311–327). Hillsdale, NJ: Erlbaum.

Jonassen, D. H., & Hannum, W. H. (1995). Analysis of task analysis procedures. In G. J. Anglin (Ed.), *Instructional technology, past, present, and future* (pp.197–214). Englewood, Colorado: Libraries Unlimited.

Karl, K. A., O'Leary-Kelly, A. M., & Martocchio, J. J. (1993). The impact of feedback and self-efficacy on performance in training. *Journal of Organizational Behavior, 14*(4), 379–394.

Kirkpatrick, D. L. (1976). Evaluation of training. In R. L. Craig (Ed.), *Training and development handbook: A guide to human resource development* (2nd ed., pp. 1–26). New York: McGraw-Hill.

Klein, G., & Militello, L. (2001). Some guidelines for conducting a cognitive task analysis. In
    E. Salas (Ed.), *Advances in human performance and cognitive engineering research* (Vol. 1,
    pp. 163–199). London: Elsevier Science.

Klinect, J. R., Wilhelm, J. A., & Helmreich, R. L. (1999). Threat and error management:
    Data from line operations safety audits. In *Proceedings of the Tenth International Symposium
    on Aviation Psychology* (pp. 683–688). Columbus: The Ohio State University.

Kozlowski, S. W. J., Brown, K., Weissbein, D., Cannon-Bowers, J., & Salas, E. (2000). A mul-
    tilevel approach to training effectiveness: Enhancing horizontal and vertical transfer. In
    K. Klein & S. W. J. Kozlowski (Eds.), *Multilevel theory, research and methods in organization*
    (pp. 157–210). San Francisco, CA: Jossey-Bass.

Kozlowski, S. W. J., & Salas, E. (1997). A multilevel organizational systems approach for the
    implementation and transfer of training. In J. K. Ford (Ed.), *Improving training effectiveness
    in work organizations* (pp. 247–287). Mahwah, NJ: Erlbaum.

Kraiger K., Ford, J. K., & Salas, E. (1993). Application of cognitive, skill-based, and affective
    theories of learning outcomes to new methods of training evaluation. *Journal of Applied
    Psychology, 78,* 311–328.

Lorenzet, S. J., Salas, E., & Tannenbaum, S. I. (2003). *The impact of guided errors on skill
    development and self-efficacy.* Manuscript submitted for publication.

Machamer, R. (1995, April). Force XXI: Welcome to the 21st century [Electronic version].
    Soldiers, 50(4), 36–40.

Mathieu, J. E., & Martineau, J. W. (1997). Individual and situational influences in training moti-
    vation. In J. Ford, S. J. W. Kozlowski, K. Kraiger, E. Salas, & M. Teachout (Eds.). *Improving
    training effectiveness in work organizations* (pp. 193–222). Hillsdale, NJ: Erlbaum.

Oser, R. L., Cannon-Bowers, J. A., Salas, E., & Dwyer, D. J. (1999). Enhancing human per-
    formance in technology-rich environments: Guidelines for scenario-based training. In
    E. Salas (Ed.), *Human/technology interaction in complex systems* (pp. 175–202). Stamford,
    CT: JAI Press.

Oser, R. L., Dwyer, D. J., Cannon-Bowers, J. A., & Salas, E. (1998). Enhancing multi-crew
    information warfare performance—An event-based approach for training. In *Proceedings
    of the 1st Symposium of the Human Factors and Medicine Panel of the North Atlantic Treaty
    Organization* (pp. 40.1–40.8). Edinburg, UK.

Prince, C., Oser, R., Salas, E., & Woodruff, W. (1993). Increasing hits and reducing misses in
    CRM/LOS scenarios: Guidelines for simulator scenario development. *International Journal
    of Aviation Psychology, 3*(1), 69–82.

Prince, C., & Salas, E. (1993). Training and research for teamwork in the military aircrew.
    In E. L. Wiener, B. G., Kanki, & R. L. Helmreich (Eds.), *Cockpit resource management*
    (pp. 337–366). Orlando, FL: Academic Press.

Salas, E., & Burke, C. S. (2002). Simulation for training is effective when…*Quality Safety
    Health Care, 11,* 119–120.

Salas, E., & Cannon-Bowers, J. A. (2000). The anatomy of team training. In S. Tobias & J. D.
    Fletcher (Eds.), *Training and retraining: A handbook for businesses, industry, government and
    military* (pp. 312–335). New York: Macmillan Reference.

Salas, E., & Cannon-Bowers, J. A. (2001). The science of training: A decade of progress.
    Annual Review of Psychology, 52, 471–499.

Salas, E., Cannon-Bowers, J. A., & Smith-Jentsch, K. A. (2001). Principles and strategies for
    team training. In W. Karwoski (Ed.), *International encyclopedia of ergonomics and human
    factors* (Vol. 2, pp. 1296–1298). Louisville, KY: Taylor & Francis.

Schraagen, J. M. C., & Chipman, S. E. (Eds.) (2000). *Cognitive task analysis*. Mahwah, NJ: Erlbaum.

Senge, P. M. (1990). *The fifth discipline: The art and practice of the learning organization*. New York: Doubleday.

Shute, V. J., & Gawlick, L. A. (1995). Practice effects on skill acquisition, learning outcome, retention, and sensitivity to relearning. *Human Factors, 37*(4), 781–803.

Smith-Jenstch, K. A., Zeisig, R. L., Acton, B., & McPherson, J. A. (1998). Team dimensional training: A strategy for guided team-self correction. In J. A. Cannon-Bowers and E. Salas (Eds.), *Making decisions under stress* (pp. 271–298). Washington, DC: American Psychological Association.

Stout, R. J., Salas, E., & Fowlkes, J. E. (1997). Enhancing teamwork in complex environments through team training. *Group Dynamics: Theory, Research, and Practice, 1*, 169–182.

Stretton, M. L., & Johnston, J. H. (1997). Scenario-based training: An architecture for intelligent event selection. In *Proceedings of the 19th Annual Meeting of the Interservice/Industry Training Systems Conference* (pp. 108–117). Washington, DC: National Training Systems Association.

Tannenbaum, S. I., Cannon-Bowers, J. A., & Mathieu, J. E. (1993). *Factors that influence training effectiveness: A conceptual model and longitudinal analysis* (Rep. 93-011). Orlando, FL: Naval Training Systems Center.

Tannenbaum, S. I., & Yukl, G. (1992). Training and development in work organizations. *Annual Review of Psychology, 43*(1), 399–441.

Thayer, P. W., & Teachout, M. S. (1995). *A climate for transfer model* (Rep. AL/HR-TP-1995-0035). Brooks Air Force Base, TX: Air Force Mat. Command.

Virtual Training Solutions Group (2004). VTSG delivers STRATA project F/A-18 CAS mission trainer. Retrieved November 10, 2004, from http://www.vtsginc.com/News.html

Wilson, J. (2003). Army expands home-based MOUT training. *Military Training Technology, 8*(5). Retrieved November 2, 2004, from http://www.military-training-technology.com/article.cfm?DocID=361

CHAPTER 4

ENHANCING MENTAL READINESS IN MILITARY PERSONNEL

Megan M. Thompson and Donald R. McCreary[1]

The scope of military missions has evolved considerably over the past 50 years (Breed, 1998; Hotopf, David, Hull, Palmer, Unwin, & Wessley, 2003), ranging from traditional combat to peace support and humanitarian operations. There is no doubt that the wider spectrum and faster pace of modern military operations requires a high level of technical competence. However, while technical proficiency is necessary, it is not sufficient to guarantee operational effectiveness. Indeed, psychological injuries typically account for between 10 percent and 50 percent of operational casualties, regardless of the mission (Armfield, 1995; Hoge, Castro, Messer, McGurk, Cotting, & Koffman, 2004; Litz, Orsillo, Friedman, Ehlich, & Batres, 1997; Marshall, 1947; Orasanu & Backer, 1996; Orsillo, Roemer, Litz, Ehlich, & Friedman, 1998; Weerts et al., 2002). Despite considerable efforts (e.g., Hogan & Lesser, 1996), to date military screening programs have largely been ineffective in determining the personality factors that are associated with resiliency or vulnerability in the face of combat stress (Jones & Belenky, 1995). Thus, the onus has long been on military training programs to develop the potential of each soldier.

In this chapter we explore how the psychological literature on stress and coping might inform military training programs to enhance the "mental readiness" (Armfield, 1995, p. 743) or the baseline psychological resiliency of military personnel. We begin with brief summaries of the spectrum of modern military operations and military training programs, including those current training programs that address stress awareness and education. We then discuss the potential limitations of these

---

The views expressed in this chapter are those of the authors and do not reflect the official policy or position of the Canadian Department of National Defence.

programs in the approach by which they attempt to prepare soldiers for the psychological stresses associated with military operations. Next, we present overviews of the major theoretical foundations that guided our thinking, specifically the transactional model of stress and stress inoculation training (SIT). While SIT has been the mainstay of stress management programs, it has not been routinely used in military contexts. Thus we present additional studies that may provide important modifications to traditional military stress training programs. To foreshadow, we advocate an increased, more seamless integration of psychological coping principles into dynamic military training environments, ideally beginning during recruit training. In this way, the lessons and training points associated with mental readiness are more intrinsically applicable and salient to soldiers on both physiological and psychological levels, the techniques more contiguously practiced, and the benefits of these techniques more immediately experienced in operationally relevant contexts.

The Psychological Spectrum of Modern Military Operations

Military operations are characterized by multiple sources of stress (Novaco, Cook, & Sarason, 1983; Orasanu & Backer, 1996). Traditionally this has meant harsh physical circumstances, including extremes of temperature and noise, as well as both primitive living and poor hygienic conditions. When coupled with inadequate diet and limited medical care, these factors contribute to an increased prevalence of disease and non-battle-related injuries. There also are a wide variety of more purely psychological stressors at play. For example, military personnel often are called on to make decisions and take actions under considerable time pressure and in the absence of essential information, and, because of recent advances in battlefield technology, under conditions of information overload. These decisions and actions may involve life-threatening or life-altering consequences (Orasanu & Backer, 1996), which can significantly increase the stress levels of the people making those decisions.

Soldiers also must navigate "the threatening psychological ambiance of combat" (Novaco et al., 1983, p. 381), including the loss of friends, the recognition of one's own destructive capacity, and concern about failing one's comrades. (See also Orasanu & Backer, 1996.) Perhaps the most axiomatic psychological combat stressor with which soldiers must deal is the fear of death and injury (Horne, 2004). The presence of fear can seem to clash with the traditional military values of strength and stoicism. As such, it is often not admitted to, or if admitted to, it can be associated with weakness in the individual (Horne, 2004). However, research suggests that fear is a reality of combat that soldiers must acknowledge and control in order to remain effective (Dollard, 1944; Janis, 1949).

Modern peace support operations are often characterized by intense ethnic violence in which belligerents often abandon traditional laws of armed conflict (Breed, 1998). Shifting rules of engagement and role ambiguity (Adler, Litz, & Bartone, 2003) can add the powerful psychological dimensions of helplessness and frustration to soldiers, who, already constrained by rules of engagement (ROEs), often can do little but watch the atrocities and suffering unfold (e.g., Dallaire, 2002; Everts,

2000; Off, 2004; Thompson & Gignac, 2002; Weisaeth, 2002). These types of missions require knowledge and skills beyond those of traditional war fighting, including a greater understanding of the regional culture and the history of the conflict, negotiation and mediation skills, as well as the ability to diffuse threats and to tolerate frustration, hostility, and provocation (Franke, 2003; Johannsen, as cited in Weisaeth, 2003). In particular, peace support operations can demand a degree of restraint that can also appear to be at odds with traditional military roles (Litz, King, King, Orsillo, & Friedman, 1997). Indeed, the "task of peacekeeping is most psychologically challenging to soldiers in the combat arms [as]…anger control is necessary…to abstain from retaliation when threatened or harassed" (Jones & Belenky, 1995, p. 219). Even stable, low-intensity missions have their own share of stresses to be dealt with, including boredom and a lack of challenge and meaning (Adler et al., 2003).

Despite the doctrinal and tactical differences associated with the spectrum of modern military operations, the preceding discussion makes clear that there are fundamental psychological similarities in every military operation: all require emotional, cognitive, and behavioral control. Traditional combat primarily involves the control of fear and fear-related thoughts, but also the control of reckless behavior (that may endanger self and/or comrades) in order to maintain operational effectiveness (Driskell, Salas, & Johnston, Volume 1, this set; Marshall, 1947). Peace support operations also include controlling anger and frustration, in addition to the control of fear.

Beyond the psychological costs to soldiers, empirical results also indicate that the stressors found in military contexts can reduce operational effectiveness. Both the physiological and psychological stressors enumerated above can result in attentional lapses, the narrowing of perceptual focus, short-term memory impairment, and biased information processing, each of which can contribute to errors in judgment and performance (Driskell et al., Volume 1; Leach, 1994; Orasanu & Backer, 1996; Wickens 1987; Wickens & Flach, 1998). Finally, these various stressors can interact with each other "summat[ing] over time to increase the risk of psychological impairment" (Novaco et al., 1983, p. 382). Indeed, cumulative stress is an increasingly significant factor, given that many militaries have downsized their numbers but have increased their operational tempo, which has led to shorter intervals for recovery between missions (Jones & Belenky, 1995). Thus, training programs that successfully prepare personnel for the physical, and also the psychological, rigors of operations are important for operational effectiveness in addition to the improved health and well-being of individual military personnel.

Military Training Programs

Traditionally, military training has focused on skills development (Driskell et al., Volume 1; Keinan & Friedland, 1996), beginning with a knowledge component that is provided during lectures and briefings (Thompson & Pastò, 2003). Demonstrations and drills emphasize technical proficiency, discipline, strength, endurance, and teamwork (Novaco et al., 1983; Orasanu & Backer, 1996; see also Hytten, Jensen & Skauli, 1990). Practical exercises that incorporate increasingly realistic stressors also emphasize technical skills and procedural training. Implicit in this approach is a philosophy "that general training…will suffice to protect the worker from both the physical and the mental trauma that may be suffered" (Dunning, 1980, p. 91).

Certainly there is value in this approach. Practice, particularly the overlearning involved in repeated drills, can reduce the novelty of, and uncertainty associated with, the technical aspects of these tasks, resulting in an increased confidence in one's abilities. Thus, overlearning can decrease soldiers' psychological and physiological reactivity from competing responses (Driskell et al., Volume 1; Driskell & Salas, 1991; Thompson & Pastò, 2003) and may be particularly important in complex tasks (Keinan & Friedland, 1996). Nonetheless, there are costs when the psychological lessons are implicit and stress resiliency is largely predicated on individual and unit technical proficiency (Orasanu & Backer, 1996). "Too often…the individual is left to his own devices in learning to control thoughts and emotions. Yet it is evident that emotions and thoughts can affect behavior and may be elements critical to the acquisition of proficiency" (Epstein, 1983, p. 53). While many individuals may learn these valuable mental lessons through a natural or "implicit stress inoculation" process (Epstein, 1983, p. 39), other people will have some degree of difficulty acquiring these psychological skills. This deficit will, at best, delay their acquisition of technical competency, and at worst will undermine their operational effectiveness. A further subgroup of people will fail to develop these skills at all, developing a stress vulnerability rather than resiliency (Updegraff & Taylor, 2000). This latter subgroup is especially disadvantaged, leaving them (and their colleagues) consistently at risk and potentially limiting their ability to remain in the military at all (Cook, Novaco, & Sarason, 1982; Novaco et al., 1983).

Some militaries have started providing stress management programs in a more detailed and explicit fashion. Routinely provided in sessions distinct from military skills training, these stress management programs have tended to use a lecture format, varying between one and four hours in duration (Deahl, Srinivasan, Jones, Thomas, Neblett, & Jolly, 2000; Thompson & Pastò, 2003). The information covered includes general principles of stress, common deployment stressors, and general information on various effective and ineffective coping strategies. Typically, mental health professionals deliver these lectures.

Despite good intentions, the effectiveness of these programs can be hampered by several factors. First, most of these briefings adopt an academic lecture format that is often not engaging for soldiers and makes these lessons seem to be of little relevance (Thompson & Pastò, 2003). Second, similar to the civilian population, military personnel often hold the stereotype that psychological problems are ultimately the result of a weakness in character (Britt, 2000; Corrigan, 2004). Indeed, this mind-set may be particularly prevalent in the military, because the military explicitly values physical fitness, toughness, and courage. Not surprisingly, these attitudes affect help-seeking rates among soldiers (Manning & Fullerton, 1988; Noy, 1991). Indeed, recent research (Hoge et al., 2004) revealed that those soldiers returning from tours in Afghanistan and Iraq who reported significant mental health problem symptoms were twice as likely to report concerns about stigmatization and other barriers to mental health care. Indeed, only 20–40 percent of those soldiers who screened positively for psychological issues had subsequently sought mental health assistance. Similarly, a second study found that 61 percent of a sample of U.S. soldiers returning from Bosnia believed that admitting to a psychological problem would hurt their career progression, and 45 percent of these soldiers believed that admitting to a psychological problem would cause them to be ostracized by their coworkers (Britt, 2000). This study also showed that the perceived stigma associated with mental health problems was a significant deterrent to help-seeking among soldiers who were at risk. Beyond influencing the rate of mental health care use, these cultural and attitudinal factors may also contribute to a more general resistance to (or denial of) the personal relevance of this information.

Third, any resistance to mental health information may actually be fostered by the use of mental health professionals who typically deliver these lectures. As important as their skills are in terms of ensuring operational readiness and effectiveness, the primary role of the mental health professional is seen as treating the injured, not providing training that enhances operational effectiveness. Thus, stress management lessons may be more easily rejected if not given by training personnel who are perceived to have applicable operational experience. Fourth, the lecture/briefing approach does not provide training on the techniques that could be put to effective use during stressful situations, or if they do, they are only demonstrated quickly during the lecture, limiting the person's ability to generalize these practical techniques to real-world settings.

Notwithstanding these formidable obstacles, militaries must address the issue of developing psychological resiliency in their personnel. On the one hand, there is consistent evidence that psychological resilience is a vital operational requisite; on the other hand, there are a multitude of individual and cultural pejoratives that undermine the acceptance of this training. We now turn to the psychological theory and research in stress and coping that may address these obstacles and facilitate the effectiveness of military stress training programs.

Theoretical Foundations

The foundation of our thinking is the cognitive–behavioral paradigm that emphasizes the importance of each individual's appraisals of a stressful event instead of simply the presence or absence of the stressor itself. One of the most influential theories within this paradigm is the Transactional Model, in which stress is defined as the result of an imbalance between environmental demands and the perceived coping resources of the individual (Folkman & Lazarus, 1980, 1985). A key precept of the Transactional Model is that people are not merely passive observers of stressful events, but that they also can actively contribute to and shape how events unfold. On a fundamental level, then, the Transactional Model emphasizes the influence of cognitive factors, such as appraisals of current situations and expectations regarding future events, as well as the role of choice. Specifically, the model links adaptive cognitions and coping choices to the subsequent positive outcomes (e.g., better mental and physical health) that are implicated in resilience or growth in the face of stress (Paton, Smith, Viulanti, & Eranen, 2000; Taylor, 1983).

Although fundamentally cognitive in nature, physiological and emotional components are also integral to the Transactional Model. Accordingly, when the perceived mismatch between psychological resources and environmental demands is high, physiological (e.g., heart and breathing rate, sweating, etc.) and psychological (e.g., attention, anxiety, etc.) arousal increases (Epstein, 1983; Novaco et al., 1983). As interactive systems, increased physical, emotional, or cognitive arousal can increase arousal in the remaining systems through feedback loops (Mischel, 2004). In response to this nascent arousal, an individual will make an initial or primary appraisal that the event is either challenging (and thus is perceived as neutral or positive) or threatening (and is thus perceived negatively). If perceived as threatening, a secondary appraisal process then determines the extent to which the person believes that he or she has the coping resources to successfully manage and prevail in the situation (Folkman & Lazarus, 1985).

Within limits, people are able to cope with the increased arousal associated with the imbalance between perceived resources and environmental demands. Indeed, these circumstances are integral to the learning and mastery of new behaviors (Epstein, 1983). However, when the imbalance between events and resources becomes too great, a person's arousal exceeds his or her optimum threshold. In this case, they are most immediately focused on decreasing their arousal through means that may inhibit and interfere with effective learning, mastery, and adaptation to stressful environments.

The Transactional Model has been supported by a wide variety of evidence, including evidence from military contexts. For instance, the role of appraisals and coping strategies have been shown to be key factors influencing the mental health outcomes of military veterans (Litz et al., 1997; Orsillo et al., 1998; Solomon, Margalit, Waysman, & Bleich, 1991; Solomon, Mikulincer, & Benbenishty, 1989). The model is closely reflected in Gal's (1987) model of combat stress, which specifies that soldiers' cognitive interpretations and assessments of the combat situation mediate individual, unit, and mission-related antecedents. These assessments, in turn, determine individual differences in soldiers' cognitive, emotional, and behavioral responses to combat. It is also consistent with the more recent soldier adaptation model (SAM) (Bliese & Castro, 2003), which identifies individual-level factors (e.g., coping styles) as an important moderator in the stress versus well-being relation for soldiers.

One of the most commonly used cognitive–behavioral psychological training techniques is Meichenbaum's *Stress Inoculation Training* (SIT; Meichenbaum, 1985; see also Meichenbaum & Cameron, 1983, or Meichenbaum & Deffenbacher, 1988, for excellent overviews of the SIT process). While the term "inoculation" suggests that simple exposure to lower levels of stress will protect people from the adverse effects of more potentially debilitating stressors, the process and outcome of SIT is much more complex than this simple vaccine analogy implies. In fact, this technique is an intensive, multistage process, of which there are three ultimate goals (Meichenbaum & Cameron, 1983). The first goal is to change people's maladaptive behaviors in stressful situations (via changes in cognitions and behaviors). For example, SIT in a military context should lead to improved performance in an operational setting, such as increased marksmanship and improved decision making; a secondary outcome may be increased operational readiness, measured in the form of lower levels of attrition and fewer health problems. The second goal is to improve what Meichenbaum and Cameron (1983) refer to as "self-regulatory activity." That is, SIT hopes to make people more aware of their cognitive processes. Decreasing the intensity and frequency of negative thoughts (e.g., "I'll never be able to get through this") and disruptive feelings (e.g., anxiety, fear), while increasing the use of adaptive thoughts (e.g., problem solving, optimism), is believed to markedly improve people's ability to cope effectively in a stressful situation. The third goal for SIT involves increasing people's ability to cope with situations by attenuating the cognitive sets or habits that may be handicapping them. For example, through training and experience, people may learn that they have difficulty reading situations or that they handicap themselves by using maladaptive coping strategies, such as alcohol. New coping strategies are developed and taught to them. Through graduated exposure to more and more stressful situations, people learn that these new strategies are more effective and adaptive than their previous ones. They are then adopted on a more frequent or persistent basis.

With these goals in mind, SIT follows a three-stage intervention process. First, an educational phase is designed to help the trainee better understand the situational stressors to which they are reacting, the nature of stress (both generally and specific to their situation), and their physiological and psychological responses to those stressors. Here, trainees are taught a framework for an understanding of the nature of stress and people's responses to it. This framework provides a coherent conceptual system that promotes understanding and facilitates the assimilation of these new experiences (Epstein, 1983; Meichenbaum, 1985) and enhances motivation to complete the training (Meichenbaum & Cameron, 1985; Pierce, 1995).

Second, a specifically tailored skills-acquisition and rehearsal phase teaches the trainee strategies for coping with the environmental stressors and provides him or her with opportunities to practice those strategies. Two major classes of coping techniques are presented. Instrumental coping strategies largely focus on active problem solving—for instance, specific behavioral skills (e.g., time management and communication skills, or other situation-specific competencies), breaking a problem into its component parts, and talking with others about their coping strategies. Palliative coping strategies (Meichenbaum, 1985) such as perspective taking, the development and use of social support networks (Taylor, 1991), as well as some form of relaxation training to ameliorate the main physical symptoms of stress, often are taught for use in situations that the individual can neither change nor realistically avoid.

Third, an application and follow-through phase provides the trainee opportunities to undergo graduated exposure to the stressors he or she is being inoculated against, using the skills taught as part of the training. In this way, the trainee develops proficiency in applying the new coping strategies, especially in the face of setbacks that provide important additional information in subsequent successful coping. Although the SIT stages are described as discrete components, clearly they overlap. For example, while in the initial education phase, the trainee may also be acquiring and practicing better coping skills. Similarly, problem identification that begins in the first phase continues throughout SIT programs and beyond. Importantly, SIT is not intended to be an "off-the shelf" program, but rather outlines procedures that the trainer uses to build tools that are *specialized* to the training that the individual or group specifically needs.

Two large-scale reviews support the general effectiveness of SIT-based programs (Johnston & Cannon-Bowers, 1996; Saunders, Driskell, Johnston, & Salas, 1996). For instance, Saunders and colleagues (1996) concluded that SIT was most effective at reducing performance anxiety, followed by state anxiety, and lastly increasing performance, in both controlled clinical and field studies. The results of a second narrative overview of this literature (Johnston & Cannon-Bowers, 1996) confirmed these outcomes, also showing that SIT performed as well as, or better than, the other treatment modalities in 70 percent of the cases.

Nonetheless, there are several concerns of which trainers need to be aware when they are developing and implementing programs of this nature. First, to date, there have been relatively few attempts to implement SIT in a proactive or preventive manner (e.g., to increase performance under future stress), rather than to ameliorate the effects of already-apparent maladaptive coping responses (i.e., reactive programs) (Johnston & Cannon-Bowers, 1996; Saunders et al., 1996). To date, the effectiveness of training on potential outcome benchmarks and the equivalence of procedures have not been established in a training context. Second, program length influences the effectiveness of SIT interventions, with programs of at least 6.5 hours leading to better performance and psychosocial outcomes (Johnston & Cannon-Bowers, 1996; see also Saunders et al., 1996). Third, group interventions with fewer people are more effective at reducing a state of anxiety and increasing performance, but may actually increase performance anxiety (Saunders et al., 1996). This has implications for training in larger organizations, such as a military service, where small group classes are often impractical. Fourth, although Saunders and colleagues (1996) concluded that trainer education level did not influence the effectiveness of these programs (see also Johnston & Cannon-Bowers, 1996), these findings should be interpreted with some caution. In the reviewed cases, the "untrained" leaders were usually masters-level psychology graduate students who were under the direct supervision of a doctoral-level clinical psychologist. It may be that SIT can be implemented by lay persons, with program development and monitoring by doctoral-level clinical psychologists. This, however, is an empirical question that needs to be addressed by future research.

Despite these encouraging literature reviews (Saunders et al., 1996; Johnston & Cannon-Bowers, 1996), to date, applications of SIT in military contexts have largely been experimental in nature and have yielded mixed results. Furthermore, some studies have suffered from notable methodological problems, such as nonrandom assignment and limited power because of small sample sizes (e.g., Crago, 1995; Nair, 1989). Other studies have shown positive effects of SIT-based programs on military personnel, most notably in terms of higher perceived control and success appraisals as well as improved emotional outcomes in recruits and soldiers (e.g., Gerwell & Fiedler, as cited in Cigrang, Todd, & Carbone, 2000; Israelashvili & Taubman, 1997) and in veterans with posttraumatic stress disorder (PTSD; e.g., Bolton, Lambert, Wolf, Raja, Varra, & Fisher, 2004; Chemtob, Novaco, Hamada, & Gross, 1997; Sherman, 1998). Studies that have specifically assessed performance outcomes also have produced mixed results. For instance, in one study (Cigrang et al., 2000), Air Force recruits at risk for discharge participated in a two-session, SIT-based stress management group that focused on information coping skills and practice in relaxation techniques. A similar at-risk control group underwent standard care, consisting of a short discussion with a health care provider that focused on encouraging the recruit and offering limited problem-solving and coping advice. Results showed that the SIT-based sessions had no effect on graduation rates relative to trainees in the control condition. (See also Backer, 1987, for similar results.) Conversely, Swedish recruits who were taught mental-training techniques, relaxation, meditation, and imagery rehearsal scored higher on task exams (Larsson, 1987). A further study indicated that stress training targeting respiration control led to lower heart rates during night jumps and higher performance scores for a group of jumpmasters (Burke, 1980, as cited in Orasanu & Backer, 1996).

Earlier in this chapter we also identified other factors that may limit the effectiveness of many traditional military stress-training programs. A significant issue is the general stigma associated with mental health issues, a factor that may inadvertently be exacerbated by the use of mental health workers as the primary lesson deliverers. Second, these presentations often begin with a fairly academic discussion of a generic stress model that may seem unrelated to soldiers' experiences. Third, most military SIT-based programs fall far short of the minimum of 6.5 hours recommended by Johnston and Cannon-Bowers (1996) (although this limited time is understandable, given the pressures to reduce training times and costs, Driskell et al., Volume 1; Orasanu & Backer, 1996). Fourth, there is virtually no practical training associated with stress-management briefings. Current military stress training, then, may be too limited and out of a relevant context for many personnel. Novaco and colleagues (1983, p. 417) cogently underscore the challenges in applying traditional SIT to nonclinical applied settings in general, and perhaps particularly to military training settings. "Far too often...attempts to implement the stress inoculation approach have consisted of little more than the use of coping self-statements anteceded by some didactics about the problem state." (See also Orasanu & Backer, 1996.)

This state of affairs is especially frustrating when many aspects of general military training are natural venues for the application of SIT-based principles. For instance, many of the more challenging military courses already involve a graduated exposure to more and more realistic training scenarios. What appears to be lacking, and what we are advocating here, is an effective integration of, and practice in, the psychological principles of stress and coping (or what we are referring to as mental readiness) into these preexisting training settings. The challenge, then, is to incorporate into training the important aspects of the Transactional Model in ways that are engaging and relevant to military audiences and that do not cause psychological reactance as a result of stigma-related attitudes. To address this challenge, we next explore other literature for ideas and methodologies that might be particularly relevant to mental readiness training for military contexts and, just as important, that will resonate with military personnel.

Stress Exposure Training

Stress Exposure Training (SET; Johnston & Cannon-Bowers, 1996; see also Driskell et al., Volume 1) was designed to expand the scope of SIT beyond its traditional clinical applications and to enumerate a conceptual framework that integrates relevant organizational and task stressors and coping-skills training appropriate to complex cognitive tasks. Thus, SET is specifically designed to enhance the performance of "normal" people in stressful working environments versus eliminating the nonadaptive responses of anxious people to benign environments, as is the case in the majority of SIT programs. The stated goals of SET also reflect this focus on training techniques applicable to nonclinical populations. Accordingly, the three goals of SET are "(a) to build skills that promote effective performance under stress, (b) to build performance confidence, and (c) to enhance familiarity with the stress environment" (Johnston & Cannon-Bowers, 1996, p. 225).

Despite these philosophical distinctions, the SIT and SET interventions have much in common. SET also involves three developmental stages. Similar to SIT, in the first phase of SET, typical reactions to stress are discussed, and the trainees' own reactions to the situational stressors that are the target of the specific SET intervention are identified. The second stage is devoted to the development of specific skills required to ameliorate the effects of the stress. Consistent with SIT, the goal of this phase of SET is to develop the ability to maintain awareness of stress reactions and, via feedback from the trainer, develop cognitive, emotional, and behavioral control strategies specific to the stressful environment. The third stage of SET involves the practice of the new control strategies in situations that simulate the stress operational context.

One of the benefits of SET is the conceptual framework that specifically places an emphasis on the role of environmental/occupational stressors in stress responses. Moreover, the proactive nature of SET, with its explicit focus on optimizing the performance/operational effectiveness of military personnel, should increase its acceptance by trainers in a military setting. However, applications of SET have been largely experimental in nature and have not been routinely adopted by militaries. Johnston and Cannon-Bowers' (1996) review of the SET literature concluded that there was justifiable evidence to support its efficacy. However, an examination of the results of those studies and samples most relevant to military contexts (e.g., Marine recruits, scuba divers, off-shore oil workers, police) again produced mixed results in terms of the psychological and performance measures.[2] Thus, many of the same issues and empirical questions relevant to SIT are equally applicable to SET programs.

A Natural Process of Graded Stress Inoculation

Also germane to the challenge of integrating stress management principles into military training is Epstein's seminal research on the natural process of graded stress inoculation (for an excellent review of this work see Epstein, 1983). Using the natural stress and coping laboratory of skydiving training, Epstein and colleagues (Epstein 1962; Epstein & Fenz, 1965; Fenz & Epstein, 1967) conducted a series of ingenious studies demonstrating the distinct patterns of physiological and psychological reactivity in novice versus experienced parachutists. In one study (Epstein & Fenz, 1965), a word-association task containing items with varying degrees of relatedness to jumping was presented to parachutists on jump and nonjump days. On nonjump days, both novices and experienced parachutists produced the lowest galvanic skin response (GSR) reactivity to neutral words, with increasing degrees of reactivity to words more associated with skydiving. Novices produced a similar, although much more elevated, pattern on jump days.

Experienced parachutists, however, showed a very different pattern of reactivity on jump days. When tested shortly before a jump, they showed the greatest reactivity to words of *intermediate* relevance to parachuting with less reactivity to words of both low and high relevance, demonstrating an inverted-V response. The pattern was developmental: as parachutists increased their number of jumps, their GSR reactivity was increasingly displaced from the most jump-related words toward the more neutral words, indicating that this reactivity was associated with experience, rather than merely a function of self-selection (Epstein, 1962). Importantly, these effects were only seen on jump days; on control days, experienced parachutists reacted in a manner similar in shape to that of novices. Similarly, experienced parachutists showed highest levels of GSR reactivity early in the actual jump sequence (e.g., arriving at the airport and just after takeoff, for fear and GSR ratings, respectively); novices' reactivity levels peaked immediately before stepping out of the airplane (Epstein & Fenz, 1965; Fenz & Epstein, 1967).

Most compellingly, experienced jumpers did not consistently produce this inverted-V pattern of reactivity. For instance, the novice arousal pattern reappeared after experienced parachutists read a report of other parachutists being injured during a jump, when there was a possibility of a main chute malfunction during a jump,[3] or when viewing a film of other parachutists making a jump. A further case of this reversion to a novice pattern of reactivity occurred when one experienced jumper fell asleep on the plane's ascent, waking just before the plane reached the jump zone (Epstein, 1983). These departures in the pattern of reactivity are critical in that an automatic process of stress habituation could not account for this pattern of experienced reactivity. Rather, these effects were clearly a consequence of an active coping process that prepare[d] the [experienced] individual for the upcoming jump…[wherein their] anxiety…[was] controlled by an active mental process developed by experience…[that] effectively constrained the effects of disruptive emotions on essential cognitive preparation and behavioral maneuvers. (Epstein, 1983, p. 48)

We believe these studies hold potential importance for the development of mental readiness in military training programs in several ways. First, they detail the stress-coping relation in an environment that involves high risk, technical proficiency, and the control of arousal (i.e., parachuting), all features of the prototypical military context. Second, the participants were physically fit, highly motivated people, in contrast to people with identified psychological issues (phobics, people diagnosed with PTSD) who are the typical subjects of the majority of traditional SIT programs. Third, these studies explored the development of coping adaptation in a proactive setting, rather than after a significant coping deficit had been identified. Fourth, these results are consistent with the Transactional Model of stress. Novice parachutists perceive a greater gap between the event and their coping resources, leading to a greater degree of arousal. Their focus then is on coping with their emotional and physical arousal, providing them less capacity to systematically attend to the immediate practical requirements and potential realistic dangers at the critical moments of the jump. Experienced parachutists, in contrast, have developed a set of technical skills that enable them to perceive less of a gap between event requirements and their coping resources. They also have strategies that enable them greater control of their arousal levels, leaving them more cognitive resources for the technical aspects and any relevant danger signs during the jump. Thus, as parachutists gain experience, they appear to be active agents in the construal of events and their cognitive, emotional, and physiological control.

These findings teach the stress–outcome relationship and the important relations among cognitive, emotional, and physiological control in a context that should not trigger negative attitudes and psychological reactance to these stress management principles. The research findings could easily be integrated into an involving and relevant educational phase of military training programs. Just as important, however, Epstein's work offers a potential methodology for extracting the self-statements of experienced personnel and feeding these into training programs to promote and accelerate the development of coping skills under stress for novices.

Modeling Adaptive Coping

Just such an innovative application was undertaken by Novaco and colleagues (1983) in the context of U.S. Marine recruit training. These researchers developed an experimental training film that followed the first days of training of a small group of recruits. The recruits subsequently provided the film's voiceovers, focusing on what they thought, how they felt, and how they learned to cope with the demands of basic training. Consequently, while the videos validated feelings of uncertainty and lack of control in this new demanding setting, they also modeled potential adaptive cognitions (e.g., reappraisals of the demanding training staff and ways to control self-defeating emotions and cognitions). Moreover, the filmed recruits provided especially effective and credible models of successful coping techniques, self-statements, and behaviors.

The training videos then were incorporated into the first days of training of a second cadre of recruits. Specifically, one group of Marines viewed the experimental coping skills video, while a second group saw a film that simply detailed the coming recruit training period. Two additional groups saw the two films in counterbalanced order, and a final group saw no film at all. Results showed that viewing the coping skills films led to higher expectations of efficacy in relation to a number of specific tasks to be mastered during basic training (e.g., marksmanship, stress endurance, controlling emotions). Hence, the training film provided new recruits with three relevant types of information: procedural information on what to expect, sensory information on what they would feel (and what feelings were normal to experience), and instrumental information on effective means to cope with the experience (Keinan & Friedland, 1996; see also Driskell et al., Volume 1). Moreover, all this information was provided to the new recruits by credible sources; that is, people just recently, and successfully, completing the same training.

Importantly, the strongest increases in expectations were evident for recruits with an external locus of control (compared to recruits with an internal locus of control, who showed no changes in their expectations). A similar pattern of results was evident for recruits' perceptions of control in training success. In the groups not viewing the coping skills training video, control perceptions for those with an internal locus of control increased across the training period, but they remained unchanged for those with an external locus of control. This finding is especially notable in that it suggests that this approach may offer an effective intervention for individuals who are not inherently equipped with the adaptive coping skills required for Epstein's (1983) natural stress inoculation process.

The Organizational Context

The work conducted by Epstein and Novaco focused primarily on the trainees' reactions and effective means to control these reactions. However, in a hierarchical institution such as the military, informal social and formal organizational factors should also play a significant role in individuals' assessment of situations and coping strategy selection. These are tenets integral to a variety of social psychological theories addressing social motivation (Forgas, Williams, & Laham, 2005), self-regulation (Michel & DeSmet, 2000; Wyer, 1999; Zalazo, Astington, & Olson, 1999), the attitude–behavior relation (Ajzen & Fishbein, 2000), and organization psychology (see Kanfer, 1990).

One of these, Action Theory (Young & Valach, 1994; Valach, 1990), is particularly relevant in that it specifically applies these notions to decision making and behavior in an individual's career, explicitly addressing the social or organizational context in which an action or behavior occurs. Accordingly, all action is hypothesized to be context dependent and meaningful (Chen, 2002). Based on SIT, in that it focuses on cognitive, social, and behavioral reactions to stress, Action Theory is intended to improve individual problem-solving abilities and skills in an organizational context (Boog, 2003). Directed by social rules, conventions, norms, representations, and processes of social control (Valach, 1990), individual actions are considered as part of long-term, goal-directed systems (Valach & Young, 2002). These notions are underscored via the development of coping skills in a group setting, which better allows for the discussion of people's differing perspectives on stressors and potential coping strategies, as well as for the reliance on each other to develop appropriate responses to stress.

Action Theory principles were integrated into a program to prepare Israeli high school students for mandatory military service (Israelashvili, 2002). An initial presentation provided a realistic preview of military training and life, refocusing recruits' initial concerns about danger and death onto the daily hassles that are the larger part of military life. Several days later, the trainees met as a group to discuss all possible coping responses to the daily hassles they had generated. This format helped the recruits understand that people experience similar problems and concerns, that others form an excellent source of support and insight, and that other people's perspectives should be taken into account. Indeed, trainers provided only minor interventions in the discussions, primarily underscoring that the appropriateness of a response is embedded within the social context (e.g., the unit, or the military goals) and in whether a potential response furthered goals in that context. Trainers also introduced the notion of behavioral and emotional restraint as viable responses in certain situations. Interestingly, restraint was not a response that was often spontaneously proffered by the recruits.

A second important influence of organizational factors on coping and performance was highlighted dramatically in a study of Marine recruits, who were followed from in-clearance to graduation from training (Cook et al., 1982). Initial archival data revealed that training units had consistently different attrition rates, suggesting that there were important differences in the social environments of the units supervised by different drill staff. Notably, these environments interacted with the natural coping abilities of the recruits. Specifically, recruits who scored high on external locus of control at intake were much more likely to be discharged when they had been assigned to a unit that had a high attrition rate than when they were assigned to a low- or medium-attrition unit.[4] Subsequent assessment revealed that the control expectancies of recruits with an internal locus of control, but who were in the high-attrition units, became significantly more external as training progressed. Just as important, the control expectancies became more internal for recruits with initially external locus of control scores who were assigned to low-attrition units. This finding is significant, because it underscores the crucial impact of the trainer in the development of all aspects of the trainee.

Applications of Mental Readiness Training

We have proposed that mental readiness training needs to be integrated into military training contexts. However, certain training situations lend themselves particularly well to the integration of mental readiness training; two examples from the cited research are parachuting and basic training. Indeed, recruit training is the perfect place to start this type of training (e.g., Israelivili, 2002; Novaco et al., 1983). First, this is the initial "natural stress laboratory" that people entering military life encounter, typically at an age where they are still quite malleable. Second, recruit training is the perfect setting to begin to integrate social and organizational goals into situation assessment and selection of optimal coping strategies. Third, it would encourage the early development of social networks and the use of colleagues for reality checks, as well as the exchange of coping strategies. Indeed,

> [i]f conditions can be specified and structured such that recruits have the opportunity to overcome learning that has resulted in failure [and] a negative self-concept,…not only might the military have better personnel, but society might receive individuals who are better able to cope with the demands of life. (Cook et al., 1982, p. 426)

Other military training also would be ideal for the review of key mental readiness principles and techniques. Just some of these include nuclear, biological, chemical, and radiological hazards training and house-to-house assaults in combat settings, as well as human rights violations and hostage-taking scenarios in peacekeeping and military observer training. In each of these cases, the instructor would note the physiological responses and how they may affect soldiers' reactions, and potentially the decisions made and the course of action taken, as well as how these factors interact. The key here is that training opportunities appropriate to the infusion of mental readiness training require somewhat higher stress levels in order to make training points and techniques salient.

One theme of the studies summarized in this chapter is the setting of realistic expectations about experiences, including what military members can expect to feel and think, as well as the optimal ways of thinking about (i.e., ways to cope with) coming events. This information was used to particularly good effect in the cited studies involving recruit training (Israelivili, 2002; Novaco et al., 1983). However, these techniques could be easily transferred to the initial stages of other training situations. For instance, in Epstein's (1983) program of research, such an introduction could have been used to acquaint novice paratroopers with the reality of, as well as ways to mentally cope with, their first jump. Similar introductions naturally lend themselves to the other forms of training cited in the previous paragraph. As we noted earlier, and we believe cannot be emphasized enough, this information needs to be delivered by individuals with operational credibility (e.g., previous recruits, training staff, veterans of operations; Armfield, 1995). Similarly, deployment-specific training should emphasize the setting of realistic expectations to address a range of issues, including the geography and history of the area and the conflict, awareness of cultural differences and customs, and an overview of potential stressors, threats, and dangers (see Weerts et al., 2002). Preparatory information of this sort reduces novelty, increases predictability and a sense of control, and has been shown to decrease self-reports of anxiety and increase confidence and performance in military personnel (Inzana, Driskell, Salas, & Johnston, 1996). An important caveat to the positive effects of information is that it must provide an effective means of coping with the military stressor (Keinan & Friedland, 1996). Indeed, information of this sort may be especially useful in peace support operations that have traditionally required a greater knowledge of these topics and that have also been characterized by greater role ambiguity (Britt, 1998).

Peace support operations also tend to require different skills than war fighting. For example, restraint and not responding are often at odds with a great deal of traditional military training. Yet, there are some situations in peace support operations in which control may be optimal; for instance, dealing with provocation attempts (sometimes undertaken for publicity/media value) by belligerents or local populations. In these contexts, it might be particularly instructive for training staff to bring attention to the physical, emotional, and cognitive components that are linked to anger and frustration, the ways in which these factors can affect decisions, and behavior and methods to diffuse these personal reactions (see Novaco, 1977).

In fact, explicitly making people aware of, and training them for, the use of restraint as a viable reaction in certain situations increases the range and flexibility of the response repertoire of military personnel. Certainly, one example of the effectiveness of restraint occurred in a well-publicized incident in which a U.S. infantry company was tasked to protect a mosque. The Iraqi crowd misinterpreted the troops intentions and began to get angry. The situation was likely to escalate into a riot. However, rather than continuing on with their stated mission to protect the mosque, the U.S. company commander gave orders to his troops to deliberately lower their weapons, smile, turn their backs on the crowd, and back down the road. This was a remarkable feat of restraint for battle-trained troops in a volatile situation, but this restraint also ensured the safety of all involved.

Training Issues Relevant to Mental Readiness Preparation

The mental readiness training approach means instructors must pay increasing attention to incorporating cognitive and emotional control and readiness, in addition to technical and physical performance, as part of their teaching. This involves some training in these proficiencies. Mental health personnel should clearly play an important consultation role in the provision of the information relevant to the stress–reaction relation, as well as in the techniques to counteract these effects. Our intent is not to eliminate the benefits of the expertise of mental health professionals. However, these important mental readiness lessons will have the most impact and chance of being absorbed if they are taught by someone who has operational credibility with trainees; that is, someone who has been there, done that, and has clearly "got the T-shirt." We realize that our suggestions add a burden to trainers' tasks of developing technical skills, especially in the face of organizational pressures to reduce training time. Nonetheless, "it is both prudent and logical that [training staff] be given an active part in the stress-coping interventions" (Cook et al., 1982, p. 415). These fundamental principles will almost certainly fail if trainers do not endorse them implicitly and explicitly.

We also hasten to note that a proportion of military trainers/instructors will have already intuitively adopted these techniques; for instance, encouraging trainees to monitor their physiological, cognitive, and emotional reactions, as well as modeling task focus and control. Our point here is that these trainers are the ideal, explicitly embedding mental readiness principles within training scenarios. We are advocating that these procedures be systematically incorporated within relevant military training courses and scenarios, in addition to traditional procedural and technical aspects of a maneuver.

Although they found evidence of the effectiveness of videos as a means of modeling coping strategies, Novaco and colleagues (1983) raised an important issue with respect to the exclusive reliance on the use of videotapes. In this methodology, recruits take a passive role so there are no opportunities to try out these methods or to receive feedback from peers or instructors. Similarly, technical proficiency can be, and increasingly is being, accomplished via computer simulations. However, these simulations must be realistic and focused on tactical-level decision making, not merely on technical proficiency (Yardley & Newman, 1986). More research needs to be conducted on measures of involvement and the "realism" of these teaching approaches, as well as on the ability to generalize psychological training points to operational environments. Simulations and videos probably cannot supersede traditional, behavioral exercises. Rather, these methods must be used in concert with instruction in coping and problem solving to maximize the internalizing of such training interventions; if not as the scenario unfolds, then immediately afterward, to underscore teaching points and maximize learning. Therefore, in situ teaching and practice must reinforce the lessons of the videotapes and simulations. There should be opportunities to provide feedback to recruits on the efficacy of various cognitive strategies or behaviors and to suggest alternatives based on their personal experiences.

Especially powerful would be training scenarios taken from, or combining elements from, actual after-action reports. Such scenario-based training is often quite emotionally and physiologically involving (Novaco, 1977). A continuing challenge for military training systems will be to determine how to make the best use of simulators of varying degrees of fidelity, or virtual reality techniques, to simulate high-stress combat scenarios for training purposes (Orasanu & Backer, 1996). Importantly, scenario-based training must offer the opportunity for debriefing on all aspects of student experience and its potential impact on the decisions made and courses of action chosen by the student. (See Salas, Priest, Wilson, & Burke, this volume.)

Some of the research summarized in this chapter has suggested that individual differences play a significant role in stress training outcomes. For instance, the work of Novaco and colleagues (Cook et al., 1982; Novaco et al., 1983) suggested that external locus of control was related to positive changes in expectations of efficacy and control over events. Similarly, Hytten, Jensen, and Skauli (1990) found evidence of the impact of individual differences in psychological defensiveness (e.g., neuroticism) and physiological arousal (although defensiveness was unrelated to psychological variables such as efficacy and anxiety level). Other individual difference measures that should prove useful to pursue in this context would be psychological hardiness (see Bartone, 2003), coping flexibility or adaptability (Kohn, O'Brien-Wood, Pickering, & Decicco, 2004; Ployhart & Bliese, in press), and anxiety sensitivity (Taylor, 1999). One potential application of these sorts of results would be to refine individual difference criteria in military selection. However, an even more hopeful use of these results would be to develop those training techniques that provide their greatest value and provide the greatest benefits for those individuals who enter military service with a less-than-optimal range of coping responses.

The recent combination of higher operational tempo and reduced regular force sizes has seen the increasing participation of reservists and national and home guard members as augmentees to military operations. With this increased participation comes a concomitant increased risk for stress-related injuries. Indeed, operational stress can be especially high for soldiers who "have not had a career of active duty military service and thus lack both the professional identification and the [prolonged] intense preparation for combat" (Armfield, 1994, p. 740). Thus, these mental readiness principles and techniques could be particularly useful for these soldiers. Similarly, these techniques also may be quite helpful for those regular force soldiers who are serving as augmentees in formed units, because they may be less able to make use of the strong cohesion that serves as a protective factor for formed units both during a deployment and afterward.

The training principles and approaches discussed here also could be readily applied to other high-risk occupational groups, including police, firefighters, and other first responders. For instance, Novaco (1977) proposed using a SIT framework to address the issue of anger and aggression control among police officers. Indeed, a similar program might be an extremely valuable addition to scenario-based training for traditional peacekeeping and some humanitarian relief operations in which military personnel are often required to undertake policing and crowd control functions within the mission. For instance, in one study, half of a group of 54 police recruits in the final weeks of basic training attended a one-hour session in which they were instructed in visuo-motor behavioral rehearsal (VMBR), consisting of relaxation techniques and skill-based imagery rehearsal. Pairs of recruits then participated in a night training scenario that began with a routine pursuit of a speeding van. As the recruits approached the pulled-over van, however, the "assailants" drew weapons (using simulated ammunition) and began firing on the recruits. Results showed that recruits who had undergone the single-session VMBR training performed more effectively and evidenced lower levels of cognitive state anxiety than did recruits in the control group during the scenario (Shipley & Baranski, 2002). These results, although preliminary, are encouraging, suggesting the effectiveness of such interventions, especially in light of the short duration of the training and the performance measures affected. Overall, much more could and should be done for the larger world of first responders, who are often quickly mobilized and dispersed after a disaster with little or no provision for preventative or after care (Dunning, 1990).

Mental Readiness Training within the Continuum of Therapeutic Techniques

Mental readiness training should not be considered a panacea for all forms of operational stress, in particular those associated with extreme trauma (e.g., personal injury or maiming, massacres, death of friends), nor are they meant to supplant the important clinical interventions that address such traumas. Nonetheless, incorporating the mental readiness training principles outlined here may provide a higher baseline resiliency level for military personnel and also may reduce the impact of chronic sources of operational and organizational stress. Moreover, as cognitive–behavioral interventions such as SIT programs are major modalities used to treat military veterans with PTSD (Foa, 1997; Sherman, 1998), building a proactive training foundation out of these principles is certainly appropriate.

Similarly, despite the potential benefits of these training methods to increase operational effectiveness, the hard-won lessons of essential combat psychiatry must be kept in mind and practiced. Rest, basic health, and hygiene must be attended to. Further, when stress reactions seem to be appearing, they must be dealt with early; in other words, the PIES principle (proximity, immediacy, expectancy) is still an important complement to the preventative strategies outlined here (Jones & Belenky, 1995; see also Lewis, this volume). Interestingly, the technologically advanced modern battlefield of highly mobile, distributed units may not allow for the safe forward-treating area so integral to traditional PIES. Therefore, new approaches that rely more heavily on unit resources (e.g., unit cohesion, monitoring of stress levels by unit members) to prevent vulnerabilities from emerging must be refined; for instance, progress should be made toward the development of "buddy aid" (Jones & Belenky, 1995). In general, then, the mental readiness training approach outlined in this chapter may serve as an important precursor to clinical interventions.

Nor should these preventive training programs replace the importance of leadership, which is among the strongest mediating factors in preventing psychological breakdown and increasing operational effectiveness (Gal & Manning, 1987; Jones & Belenky, 1995; see also Murphy & Farley, 2000). In particular, leaders must be seen to be technically competent, and "to partake of dangers and hardships, display concern for [their] soldiers" (i.e., not just be concerned, but communicate that concern) (Jones & Belenky, 1995, p. 477). In line with our thinking in this chapter, leaders are important models for soldiers. Leaders' operational briefings need to be realistic, but not pessimistic, and after-action reviews must "allow recognition of misunderstandings, recognition of performance, and consolidation of lessons learned" (Jones & Belenky, 1995, p. 477). Furthermore, the more thorough integration of these training methods into regular operational training programs is, the more is underscored that the "prevention of combat stress casualties is primarily a command responsibility" (Jones & Belenky, 1995, p. 484), with medical and mental health personnel playing an important consultation role to commanders during both training and operations. Mental readiness training then is but one of the many tools available to military personnel to proactively weather the stress of operations and military life.

Conclusions

Throughout this chapter we have advocated that the psychological principles of mental readiness must be introduced and practiced in context in order to have maximal impact. That is, the important lessons of stress awareness and physiological, cognitive, and emotional control need to be incorporated into all relevant operational training. Consequently, we have deliberately chosen and used the term "mental readiness" throughout the chapter to describe this approach. This is because the basic tools of stress management must not be parsed out and put on a shelf, separate from "normal" responses to "normal" military situations—to be used only after traumatic events occur and stress symptoms emerge. Rather, they should be integrated into all relevant training opportunities so that they become reflexive in the same way that technical proficiencies are reflexive. Similarly, the notion of mental readiness should be thought of as a trainable skill that can be acquired and developed, much like physical fitness, as opposed to the lay view of psychology as involving static aspects of personal strength and character. These goals can only be accomplished if the techniques to develop mental readiness are fully integrated and ingrained in the overarching arsenal of responses available to military personnel.

In the final analysis the

> [f]easibility in administering the various types of training may become the deciding issue in the military. Stress-reduction techniques take time and effort and the military is always seeking ways to reduce training time and costs…techniques like SIT, are probably the most cumbersome to administer, but may be most beneficial for certain combat situations.…Stress is not going to go away and may be exacerbated by the high-tech battlefield of the future. Military effectiveness may depend on how well the services prepare their personnel to perform under the stressful conditions that they are certain to face. (Orasanu & Backer, 1996, p. 116)

In the present chapter we have proposed a potential mechanism to resolve some of the issues that have hindered the successful employment of stress management techniques. We have advocated that these principles be better integrated into existing stressful military training programs within the context of mental readiness for operations, similar to the notion of physical and technical operational readiness. All the suggestions we offer are designed to maximize the likelihood that these important mental readiness techniques will be made maximally accessible and relevant, and thus adopted and successfully used, thereby increasing the individual well-being and resiliency and the operational effectiveness of military personnel.

Notes

1. We would like to extend our gratitude to the staff of the Peace Support Training Centre, Canadian Forces Base Kingston. The extremely productive research collaboration between the first author and the PSTC staff has significantly informed and influenced our thinking about the infusion of mental readiness concepts into operationally relevant training contexts. Our sincere thanks also goes to Stewart Harrison, head of the Scientific Information Centre, DRDC Toronto, for his ready assistance and patience in responding to our many requests to track down relevant articles and providing them to us so quickly. Finally, we are most grateful to our editors for providing us an opportunity to consolidate our ideas concerning mental readiness training, and for their support in the development of this chapter.

2. A summary of these studies is provided in Johnston and Cannon-Bowers (1996), Table 7.3.

3. In this case, an experienced parachutist volunteered to have a malfunction of his main chute that would necessitate the use of his reserve chute at some point during one of ten jumps. Arousal was assessed, but in actuality no malfunction ever occurred.

4. Locus of control scores were evenly distributed across units at the beginning of training.

References

Adler, A. B., Litz, B. T., & Bartone, P. T. (2003). The nature of peacekeeping stressors. In T. W. Britt & A. B. Adler (Eds.), *The psychology of the peacekeeper* (pp. 149–168). Westport, CT: Praeger.

Ajzen, I., & Fishbein, M. (2000). The prediction of behavior from attitudinal and normative variables. In E. T. Higgins & A. W. Kruglanski (Eds.), *Motivational science: Social and personality perspectives* (pp. 177–190). New York: Psychology Press.

Aldwin, C. M., Sutton, K. J., & Lachman, M. (1996). The development of coping resources in adulthood. *Journal of Personality, 64*, 837–871.

Armfield, F. (1994). Preventing post-traumatic stress disorder resulting from military operations. *Military Medicine, 159*, 739–746.

Backer, R. A. (1987). *A stress inoculation training intervention for Marine Corps recruits.* Unpublished doctoral dissertation, California School of Professional Psychology.

Bartone, P. T. (2003). Hardiness as a resilience resource under high stress conditions. In D. Paton & J. M. Violanti (Eds.), *Promoting capabilities to manage posttraumatic stress: Perspectives on resilience* (pp. 59–73). Springfield, IL: Charles C. Thomas Publisher.

Bliese, P. D., & Castro, C. A. (2003). The soldier adaptation model (SAM): Applications to peacekeeping research. In T. W. Britt & A. B. Adler (Eds.), *The psychology of the peacekeeper: Lessons from the field* (pp. 185–204). Westport, CT: Praeger.

Bolton, E. E., Lambert, J. F., Wolf, E. J., Raja, S., Varra, A. A., & Fisher, L. M. (2004). Evaluating a cognitive-behavioral group treatment program for veterans with posttraumatic stress disorder. *Psychological Services, 1*, 140–146.

Boog, B. W. M. (2003). The empancipatory character of action research, its history and the present state of the art. *Journal of Community and Applied Social Psychology, 13*, 426–438.

Breed, H. (1998). Treating the new world disorder. In H. J. Langholtz (Ed.), *The psychology of peacekeeping* (pp. 239–254). Westport, CT: Praeger.

Britt, T. W. (1998). Psychological ambiguities in peacekeeping. In H. J. Langholtz (Ed.), *The psychology of peacekeeping* (pp. 11–128). Westport, CT: Praeger.

Britt, T. W. (2000). The stigma of psychological problems in a work environment: Evidence from the screening of service members returning from Bosnia. *Journal of Applied Social Psychology, 30*, 1599–1618.

Chemtob, C. M., Novaco, R. W., Hamada, R. S., & Gross, D. M. (1997). Cognitive-behavioral treatment for severe anger in posttraumatic stress disorder. *Journal of Consulting and Clinical Psychology, 65*, 184–189.

Chen, C. P. (2002). Integrating action theory and human agency in career development. *Canadian Journal of Counselling, 36*, 121–136.

Cigrang, J. A., Todd, S. L., & Carbone, E. G. (2000). Stress management training for military trainees returned to duty after a mental health evaluation: Effect on graduation rates. *Journal of Occupational Health Psychology, 5*, 48–55.

Cook, T. M., Novaco, R. W., & Sarason, I. G. (1982). Military recruit training as an environmental context affecting expectancies for control of reinforcement. *Cognitive Therapy and Behavior, 6*, 409–428.

Corrigan, P. (2004). How stigma interferes with mental health care. *American Psychologist, 59*, 614–625.

Crago, D. A. (1995). *The use of stress inoculation training with a military population.* Unpublished doctoral dissertation, California School of Professional Psychology.

Dallaire, R. (2002). *Shake hands with the devil: The failure of humanity in Rwanda.* New York: Carroll & Graf.

Datel W. E., & Lifrak, S. T. (1969). Expectations, affect change and military performance in the army recruit. *Psychological Reports, 24*, 855–879.

Deahl, M., Srinivasan, M., Jones, N., Neblett, C., & Jolly, A. (2000). Preventing psychological trauma in soldiers: The role of operational stress training and psychological debriefing. *British Journal of Medical Psychology, 73*, 77–85.

Dollard, J. (1944). *Fear in Battle.* Westport, CT: Greenwood.

Driskell, J. A., & Salas, E. (1991). Overcoming the effects of stress on military performance: Human factors, training, and selection strategies. In R. Gal & A. D. Mangelsdorff (Eds.), *Handbook of military psychology* (pp.183–193). New York: Wiley.

Dunning, C. (1990). Mental health sequelae in disaster workers: Prevention and intervention. *International Journal of Mental Health, 19*, 91–103.

Elder, G. H., & Clipp, E. C. (1989). Combat service and emotional health: Impairment and resilience in later life. *Journal of Personality, 57*, 311–341.

Epstein, S. (1962). The measurement of drive and conflict in humans: Theory and experiment. In M. R. Jones (Ed.), *Nebraska symposium on motivation* (pp. 127–206). Lincoln: University of Nebraska Press.

Epstein, S. (1983). Natural healing processes of the mind: Graded stress inoculation as an inherent coping mechanism. In D. Meichenbaum & M. E. Jaremko (Eds.), *Stress reduction and prevention* (pp. 39–66). New York: Plenum.

Epstein, S., & Fenz, W. D. (1965). Steepness of approach and avoidance gradients in humans as a function of experience. *Journal of Experimental Psychology, 70*, 1–12.

Everts, P. L. E. M. (2000). Command and control in stressful conditions. In C. McCann & R. Pigeau (Eds.), *The human in command: Exploring the modern military experience* (pp. 65–82). New York: Kluwer Academic/Plenum Publishers.

Fenz, W. D., & Epstein, S. (1967). Gradients of psychological arousal of experienced and novice parachutists as a function of an approaching jump. *Psychosomatic Medicine, 29*, 33–51.

Foa, E. B. (1997). Psychosocial treatments for posttraumatic stress disorder: A critical review. *Annual Review of Psychology, 48*, 449–480.

Folkman, S., & Lazarus, R. S. (1980). An analysis of coping in a middle-aged community sample. *Journal of Health and Social Behavior, 21*, 219–239.

Folkman, S., & Lazarus, R. S. (1985). If it changes it must be a process: Study of emotion and coping during three stages of a college examination. *Journal of Personality & Social Psychology, 48*, 150–170.

Forgas, J. P., Williams, K. D., & Laham, S. M. (2005). *Social motivation: Conscious and unconscious processes.* New York: Cambridge University Press.

Franke, V. C. (2003). The social identity of the peacekeeper. In T. W. Britt & A. B. Adler (Eds.), *The psychology of the peacekeeper* (pp. 31–51). Westport, CT: Praeger.

Gal, R. (1987). Combat stress as an opportunity: The case of heroism. In G. Belenky (Ed.), *Contemporary studies in combat psychiatry* (pp. 31–45). New York: Greenwood.

Gal, R., & Manning, F. J. (1987). Morale and its components: A cross-national comparison. *Journal of Applied Social Psychology, 17*, 369–391.

Hobfoll, S. E. (1988). *The ecology of stress.* New York: Hemisphere.

Hogan, J., & Lesser, P. (1996). Selection of personnel for hazardous performance. In J. E. Driskell & E. Salas (Eds.), *Stress and human performance* (pp. 195–222). Hillsdale, NJ: Erlbaum.

Hoge, C. W., Castro, C. A., Messer, S. C., McGurk, D., Cotting, D. I., & Koffman, R. L. (2004). Combat duty in Iraq and Afghanistan, mental health problems, and barriers to care. *New England Journal of Medicine, 351*, 13–22.

Holahan, C. J., & Moos, R. H. (1987). Personality and contextual determinants of coping strategies. *Journal of Personality and Social Psychology, 52*, 946–955.

Holahan, C. J., & Moos, R. H. (1990). Life stressors, resistance factors, and improved psychological functioning: An extension of the stress-resistance paradigm. *Journal of Personality and Social Psychology, 58*, 909–917.

Horne, B. (2004). The unspoken leadership challenge: Fear and courage. In B. Horne (Ed.), *In the Breach: Perspectives on leadership in the army today* (pp. 1–29). Kingston, Ontario: Director General Land Combat Development.

Hotopf, M., David, A. S., Hull, L., Palmer, I. I., Unwin, C., & Wessley, S. (2003). The health effects of peace-keeping in the UK armed forces: Bosnia 1992–1996. Predictors of psychological symptoms. *Psychological Medicine, 33*, 155–162.

Hytten, K., Jensen, A., & Skauli, G. (1990). Stress inoculation training for smoke divers and free fall lifeboat passengers. *Aviation, Space, and Environmental Medicine, 61*, 983–988.

Inzana, C. M., Driskell, J. E., Salas, E., & Johnston, J. H. (1996). Effects of preparatory information on enhancing performance under stress. *Journal of Applied Psychology, 81*, 429–435.

Israelashvili, M. (2002). Fostering adolescents' coping skills—An action approach. *Canadian Journal of Counselling, 36*, 211–220.

Israelashvili, M., & Taubman, O. (1997). Adolescents' preparation for military enlistment in Israel: A preliminary evaluation. *Megamot, 38*, 408–420.

Janis, I. L. (1949). Problems related to the control of fear in combat. In S. A. Stouffer, A. A. Lumsdaine, M. H. Lumsdaine, R. M. Williams, M. B. Smith, I. L. Janis et al. (Eds.), *The American soldier: Combat and its aftermath* (pp. 192–241). (Studies in social psychology in World War II, Vol. 2.). Princeton, NJ: Princeton University Press.

Jones, F. D., & Belenky, G. L. (1995). Summation. In F. D. Jones, L. Sparacino, V. L. Wilcox, J. M. Rothberg, & J. W. Stokes (Eds.), *War Psychiatry* (pp. 473–486). Washington, DC: Department of the Army, Office of the Surgeon General at TMM Publications, Borden Institute.

Kanfer, R. (1990). Motivation theory in industrial and organizational psychology. In M. D. Dunnette & L. M. Hough (Eds.), *Handbook of motivational and organizational psychology* (pp. 75–170). Palo Alto, CA: Consulting Psychologists Press.

Keinan, G., & Friedland, N. (1996). Training effective performance under stress: Queries, dilemmas, and possible solutions. In J. E. Driskell & E. Salas (Eds.), *Stress and human performance* (pp. 257–277). Mahwah, NJ:Erlbaum.

Kohn, P. M., O'Brien-Wood, C., Pickering, D. I., Decicco, T. (2004). The Personal Functioning Inventory: A reliable and valid measure of adaptiveness in coping. *Canadian Journal of Behavioural Science, 35*, 111–123.

Larsson, G. (1987). Routinization of mental training in organizations: Effects on performance and well-being. *Journal of Applied Psychology, 72*, 88–96.

Larsson, G., & Hayward, B. (1990). Appraisal and coping processes immediately before ejection: A study of Australian and Swedish pilots. *Military Psychology, 2*, 63–78.

Leach, J. (1994). *Survival psychology*. New York: New York University Press.

Litz, B. T., King, L. A., King, D. W., Orsillo, S. M., & Friedman, M. J. (1997). Warriors as peacekeepers: Features of the Somalia experience and PTSD. *Journal of Consulting and Clinical Psychology, 65*, 1001–1010.

Litz, B. T., Orsillo, S. M., Friedman, M., Ehlich, P., & Batres, A. (1997). Posttraumatic stress disorder associated with peacekeeping duty in Somalia for U.S. military personnel. *American Journal of Psychiatry, 154*, 178–184.

Manning, F. J., & Fullerton, T. D. (1988). Health and well-being in highly cohesive units of the U.S. Army. *Journal of Applied Social Psychology, 18*, 503–519.

Marshall, S. L. A. (1947). *Men against fire: The problem of battle command in future war.* Oxford, UK: The Infantry Journal Press.

Meichenbaum, D. H. (1985). *Stress inoculation training*. New York: Paradigm.

Meichenbaum, D., & Cameron, R. (1983). Stress Inoculation Training: Toward a general paradigm for training coping skills. In D. Meichenbaum & M. E. Jaremko (Eds.), *Stress reduction and prevention* (pp. 115–154). New York: Plenum.

Meichenbaum, D. H., & Deffenbacher, J. L. (1988). Stress inoculation training. *The Counseling Psychologist, 16*, 69–90.

Mischel, W. (2004). Toward an integrative model for CBT: Encompassing behavior, cognition, affect and process. *Behavior Therapy, 35*, 185–203.

Mischel, W., & DeSmet, A. L. (2000). Self-regulation in the service of conflict resolution. In M. Deutsch & P. T. Coleman (Eds.), *Handbook of conflict resolution: Theory and practice* (pp. 256-275). San Francisco, CA: Jossey-Bass.

Murphy, P. J., & Farley, K. M. J. (2000). Morale, cohesion, and confidence in leadership: Unit climate dimensions for Canadian soldiers on operations. In C. McCann & R. Pigeau (Eds.), *The human in command: Exploring the modern military experience* (pp. 311–331). New York: Kluwer Academic/Plenum.

Nair, E. (1989). *Stress inoculation in relation to war*. Unpublished doctoral dissertation, University of Nottingham.

Novaco, R. W. (1977). A stress inoculation approach to anger management in the training of law enforcement officers. *American Journal of Community Psychology, 5*, 327–345.

Novaco, R. W., Cook, T. M., & Sarason, I. G. (1983). Military recruit training: An arena for coping skills training. In D. Meichenbaum & M. E. Jaremko (Eds.), *Stress reduction and prevention* (pp. 377-418). New York: Plenum Press.

Noy, S. (1991). Combat stress reactions. In R. Gal & D. Mangelsdorff (Eds.), *The handbook of military psychology* (pp. 507–530). New York: Wiley.

Orasanu, J. M., & Backer, P. (1996). Stress and military performance. In J. E. Driskell & E. Salas (Eds.), *Stress and human performance* (pp. 89–125). Mahwah, NJ: Erlbaum.

Orsillo, S. M., Roemer, L., Litz, B. T., Ehlich, P., & Friedman, M. J. (1998). Psychiatric symptomatology associated with contemporary peacekeeping: An examination of post-mission functioning among peacekeepers in Somalia. *Journal of Traumatic Stress, 11*, 611–625.

Paton, D., Smith, L., Vionati, J. M., & Eranen, L. (2000). Work-related traumatic stress: Risk, vulnerability, and resilience. In J. M. Violanti, D. Paton, & C. Dunning (Eds.), *Posttraumatic stress intervention: Challenges, issues and perspectives* (pp. 187–204). Springfield, IL: Charles C. Thomas Publisher.

Pierce, T. W. (1995). Skills training in stress management. In W. O'Donohue & L. Krasner (Eds.), *Handbook of psychological skills training: Clinical techniques and applications* (pp. 306–319). Needham Heights, MA: Allyn & Bacon.

Ployhart, R. E., & Bliese, P. D. (in press). Individual ADAPTability (I-ADAPT) Theory: Conceptualizing the antecedents, consequences and measurement of individual differences in adaptability. In S. Burke, L. Pierce, & E. Salas (Eds.), *A prerequisite for effective performance within complex environments*. Oxford, UK: Elsevier Science.

Saunders, T., Driskell, J. E., Johnston, J., & Salas, E. (1996). The effect of stress inoculation training on anxiety and performance. *Journal of Occupational Health Psychology, 1*, 170–186.

Schurr, P. P., Rosenberg, S. D., & Friedman, M. J. (1993). Change in MMPI scores from college to adulthood as a function of military service. *Journal of Abnormal Psychology, 102*, 288–296.

Sherman, J. J. (1998). Effects of psychotherapeutic treatments for PTSD: A meta-analysis of controlled clinical trials. *Journal of Traumatic Stress, 11*, 413–435.

Shipley, P., & Baranski, J. V. (2002). Police officer performance under stress: A pilot study on the effects of visuo-motor behavior rehearsal. *International Journal of Stress Management, 9*, 71–80.

Solomon, Z., Margalit, C., Waysman, M., & Bleich, A. (1991). In the shadow of the Gulf War: Psychological distress, social support and coping among Israeli soldiers in a high-risk area. *Israeli Journal of Medical Science, 27*, 687–695.

Solomon, Z., Mikulincer, M., & Benbenishty, R. (1989). Locus of control and combat-related post-traumatic stress disorder: The intervening role of battle intensity, treat appraisal and coping. *British Journal of Clinical Psychology, 28*, 131–144.

Taylor, S. (1999). *Anxiety sensitivity: Theory, research, and treatment of the fear of anxiety*. Mahwah, NJ: Erlbaum.

Taylor, S. E. (1983). Adjustment to threatening events: A theory of cognitive adaptation. *American Psychologist, 38*, 1161–1173.

Taylor, S. E. (1991). *Health psychology* (2nd ed.). New York: McGraw-Hill.

Thompson, M. M., & Gignac, M. A. M. (2002). Adaptation to peace support operations: The experience of Canadian Forces augmentees. In P. Essens, A. Vogelaar, E. Tanercam, & D. Winslow (Eds.), *The human in command: Peace support operations* (pp. 235–263). Amsterdam, NL: Mets & Schildt.

Thompson, M. M., & Pastò, L. (2003). Psychological interventions in peace support operations: Current practices and future challenges. In B. T. Litz & A. B. Adler (Eds.), *The psychology of the peacekeeper* (pp. 223–242). Westport, CT: Praeger.

Updegraff, J. A, &. Taylor S. E. (2000). From vulnerability to growth: Positive and negative effects of stressful life events. In J. H. Harvey & E. D. Miller (Eds.), *Loss and trauma: General and close relationship perspectives* (pp. 3–28). Philadelphia: Brunner-Routledge.

Valach, L. (1990). A theory of goal-directed action in career analysis. In R. A. Young & W. A. Borgen (Eds.), *Methodological approaches to the study of career* (pp. 107–126). New York: Praeger Publishers.

Valach, L., & Young, R. A. (2002). Contextual action theory in career counselling: Some misunderstood issues. *Canadian Journal of Counselling, Special issue: Action Theory and Counselling, 36*, 97–112.

Weerts, J. M. P., White, W., Adler, A. B., Castro, C. A., Algra, G., Bramsen, H. M. et al. (2002). Studies on military peacekeepers. In Y. Danieli (Ed.), *Sharing the front line and the back hills* (pp. 31–48). Amityville, NY: Baywood.

Weisaeth, L. (2003). The psychological challenge of peacekeeping operations. In T. W. Britt & A. B. Adler (Eds.), *The psychology of the peacekeeper* (pp. 207–222). Westport CT: Praeger.

Wickens, C. D. (1987). Information processing, decision-making, and cognition. In G. Salvendy (Ed.), *Handbook of human factors* (pp. 72–107). Oxford, UK: John Wiley & Sons.

Wickens, C. D., & Flach, J. M. (1988). Information processing. In E. L. Wiener & D. C. Nagel (Eds.), *Human factors in aviation* (pp. 111–155). San Diego, CA: Academic Press.

Wyer, R. S. (1999). *Perspective on behavioral self-regulation: Advances in social cognition.* Mahwah, NJ: Erlbaum.

Yardley, M., & Newman, D. (1986). Stress in firearms training. *International Defense Review, 19*, 917–919.

Young, R. A., & Valach, L. (1994). Evaluation of career development programs from an action perspective. *Canadian Journal of Counselling, Special issue: Issues and solutions for evaluating career development programs and services, 28*, 299–307.

Zalazo, P. D., Astington, J. E., & Olson, D. R. (1999). *Developing theories of intention: Social understanding and self-control.* Mahwah, NJ: Erlbaum.

PART III

PSYCHOLOGICAL DEMANDS DURING AND AFTER DEPLOYMENT

CHAPTER 5

CODE OF CONDUCT AND THE PSYCHOLOGY OF CAPTIVITY: TRAINING, COPING, AND REINTEGRATION

*George Steffian, Brendon W. Bluestein, Jerry Ogrisseg,
Anthony P. Doran, and C. A. Morgan III*

Code of Conduct for Members of the U.S. Armed Forces

Article I
I am an American, fighting in the forces which guard my country and our way of life. I am prepared to give my life in their defense.

Article II
I will never surrender of my own free will. If in command, I will never surrender the members of my command while they still have the means to resist.

Article III
If I am captured I will continue to resist by all means available. I will make every effort to escape and aid others to escape. I will accept neither parole nor special favors from the enemy.

Article IV
If I become a prisoner of war, I will keep faith with my fellow prisoners. I will give no information or take part in any action which might be harmful to my comrades. If I am senior, I will take command. If not, I will obey the lawful orders of those appointed over me and will back them up in every way.

Article V
When questioned, should I become a prisoner of war, I am required to give name, rank, service number, and date of birth. I will evade answering further questions to the utmost of my

---

The views expressed in this chapter are those of the authors and do not reflect the official policy or position of the U.S. Department of Defense or the U.S. Government.

ability. I will make no oral or written statements disloyal to my country and its allies or harmful to their cause.

Article VI
I will never forget that I am an American, fighting for freedom, responsible for my actions, and dedicated to the principles which made my country free. I will trust in my God and in the United States of America. (Exec. Order No. 10631, 20 FR 6057, 1955)

"My mind worked hard to suppress the rising panic, but my thoughts weren't remotely clear or focused. I couldn't move, I couldn't hide, I couldn't make myself invisible....I no longer had any control of the situation" (Durant, 2003, p. 38).

Loss of control over one's immediate fate and sensations of helplessness and panic are only the first of many distressing psychological experiences that a captured service member is likely to face. These experiences will likely challenge a captive's capacity to cope and may have a profound long-term psychological impact. While detained, captives are likely to be cut off from all news of the outside world, receiving only the information their captors wish for them to hear. This isolation and selective exposure to information may increase their susceptibility to indoctrination efforts by the enemy and cause captives to question previously held convictions. A number of methods used by the enemy may erode or undermine a captive's morale and commitment to resistance: manipulation of the captive's environment, long periods of isolation, and physical debilitation. The use of physical coercion, threats, and selective, occasional reward creates a powerful system of reinforcement that increases the captive's dependence on his or her captors and, as a result, amplifies feelings of compliance in the captive. In stark contrast to the predictable, autonomous routine of normal life, the captive lives in a world of uncertainty, dependence, and humiliation. Autonomy, predictability, and self-esteem are key components that contribute to a person's psychological health. An environment that lacks these factors puts the captive at risk for psychological dysfunction (Engdahl, Thomas, Raina, & Blank, 1997) and for exploitation by the enemy.

Aware of the vulnerability of captive personnel to psychological dysfunction and exploitation, U.S. military leaders developed the Code of Conduct. The code is a covenant between the U.S. Government and its war fighters. Propagated as an executive order, the Code of Conduct has had a profound impact on military training, the experiences of U.S. service members while in captivity, and the country's approach to recovery, repatriation, and reintegration of military personnel. This chapter will outline the current state of research related to captivity, the captivity experience, and the reintegration of returned U.S. personnel, using the Code of Conduct as a central, organizing theme.[1]

Background

Throughout the history of warfare, captured enemy combatants have met a variety of fates. While the great powers of antiquity often killed or enslaved their captives, the trend toward the taking of prisoners for ransom and intelligence gathering increased throughout the medieval age. This practice evolved further with the greater emphasis on humanitarian principles during the Renaissance period and the growing conceptual separation of individual soldiers from the states for which they fought. During the American Civil War, General Order 100 issued under President Abraham Lincoln forbade "the use of any violence against prisoners, in order to extort the desired information or to punish them for having given false information" (Lieber, 1863). At the outset of the 20th century, the Hague Conventions of 1899 and 1907 resulted in international standards for the humanitarian treatment of prisoners of war (POWs), which were then extended under the Geneva Convention of 1929 to include the sick and wounded. While these agreements with the later Geneva Convention of 1949 have generally improved the treatment of captured combatants, a number of political, psychological, and sociological factors can coalesce to make the captive's experience a harrowing one.

Whether adhered to or not, the Hague and Geneva conventions provided military leaders with formalized principles and standards to guide their actions as *captors*. Before 1950, U.S. military leaders had given some thought to developing standards for guiding the conduct of U.S. POWs, yet had not issued any unified, consistent policy across services. Lessons learned during the Korean War were to change this. In 1951 Chinese communist forces assumed control over the majority of U.S. POWs held by the North Koreans and launched a systematic program of coercion and indoctrination designed to exploit them for propaganda purposes. Ill prepared for this, 192 of 4,460 surviving U.S. POWs were found chargeable with offenses against their country, and 21 refused to return to their homeland (FM 21-78, 1981; Cole, 1994). While instructed to provide only name, rank, and service number under the Geneva Conventions pertaining to the treatment of prisoners of war, no consistent guidance had been given on how to respond to the various forms of coercion and manipulation used by captors. American personnel were left without a paradigm for maintaining a posture of resistance to the enemy and loyalty to their country. In response to this situation, the Defense Advisory Committee on Prisoners of War drafted the Code of Conduct for Members of the United States Armed Forces (issued by President Dwight D. Eisenhower as Executive Order 10631 in August of 1955). By providing a set of principles to guide their actions as captives, the Code of Conduct has assisted military personnel in maintaining their identities as soldiers, sailors, and airmen by mandating that they continue the battle within the captive environment.

The Code of Conduct represents the cornerstone of U.S. policy toward potential captivity scenarios. It has formed the basis for preparatory training, military doctrine, and repatriation policy. Survival Evasion Resistance Escape (SERE) training is a formalized program of training designed around the articles of the Code of Conduct. Informed by the principles of stress inoculation training (Meichenbaum, 1985), SERE training involves didactic instruction and role-playing across increasingly stressful situations to improve confidence, stress tolerance, and performance with the ultimate goal of returning home with honor. Military psychologists who support SERE training (referred to as SERE psychologists) assume a number of roles as clinicians, consultants, and researchers. Their work serves to enhance the safety and effectiveness of these programs and has contributed to a greater understanding of how humans react physiologically, cognitively, and behaviorally to extreme stress.

The Code of Conduct provides not only an expectation for the captive's behavior but also an idea of what he or she can expect from the U.S. Government in return. For the captive, the code presents a moral standard rather than a legal one. Indeed, the code is not punitive in nature but relates to several articles of the Uniform Code of Military Justice (UCMJ) for which the captive is held accountable. As noted in the preamble, the Code of Conduct also makes three promises on behalf of the U.S. Government: (1) to care for the captive's dependents; (2) to never forget the captive; and (3) to use every practical means to contact, support, and gain release for the captive. In this sense, the code can be seen as a moral contract between the government and its war fighters. Substantial resources are allocated for the support of families of U.S. captives and for efforts to secure the captive's release. Once returned to U.S. control, a former captive can expect an extensive and highly orchestrated series of debriefings, medical and psychological interventions, as well as guidance on legal affairs, media relations, reunification with family members, and other concerns related to reintegration. SERE psychologists are called on to orchestrate this process of repatriation (DoD Instruction 2310.4, 2000).

In addition to these measures, servicemen and women who return home from captivity can expect lifetime support and monitoring of their physical and psychological health. This support may be delivered through Veterans Administration hospitals and/or through research centers that are devoted to the needs of former isolated personnel such as the Mitchell Center for Prisoner of War Studies. These established avenues for support are the primary source of scientific information about the long-term effects of captivity on physical and mental health. The challenge for military psychologists has been to integrate this epidemiological and clinical research with current knowledge of learning theory, neurobiology, and of stress inoculation theory in order to develop strategies that might enhance the future capabilities of war fighters to effectively cope psychologically within the captive environment and mitigate the impact of captivity experiences on subsequent psychological functioning.

A Comment on the Categories of Captivity Referred to in This Chapter

As previously indicated, military personnel face a range of captivity scenarios. What is common to all of these experiences is that the person experiences a loss of control whether it be over his or her environment, movement, nourishment, physical integrity, or eventual fate. While "prisoner of war," "detainee," and "hostage" are terms with legal connotations and have been used to denote specific categories or conditions of captivity, the term "captive" is a more generic term that is used in this chapter when referring to all captivity situations. In discussing research on captivity experiences, the terminology of the authors being reviewed will be used.

SERE Psychology—Consultation and Research

SERE psychologists take on a number of roles during Code of Conduct training for the military (Executive Order One 10631, 1955). The SERE psychologist provides services to SERE participants and training staff and also provides consultation about the training to military commanders. SERE training (specifically, the mock POW phase of training) exposes participants to a degree of stress that is not typically experienced in other forms of military training. Thus, to provide effective services and consultation, the SERE psychologist must be knowledgeable about the effects of acute stress on human cognition and behavior. In this section, we discuss some of the neurobiological research conducted within SERE training environments and underscore how these research findings serve to enhance our understanding and development of current training doctrine.

Fear is an important emotion that is elicited in nearly all animals (including humans) exposed to acute threat. From an evolutionary perspective, a fearful response to threat is adaptive in that an appropriate response (fight, flight, or freezing) can enhance the survival of the species. Nearly all species generate a measurable fear response as a reaction to threatening stimuli in the environment. Research of humans and animals has consistently demonstrated that specific regions of the brain (i.e., the amygdala) are critical for the fear response (LeDoux et al., 1990; LeDoux, 1992). Taken together, most research to date also indicates that the specific behaviors exhibited by nonhuman animals and humans when exposed to acute threat are "hard-wired," or "preprogrammed" responses.

This information is relevant to SERE psychologists in that nearly all participants in SERE training will experience and exhibit feelings and behaviors associated with flight/fight or freezing responses. For some students, the stress primarily induces a fight response and is associated with increased feelings of aggression. Such feelings can be distressing in that they must be inhibited in order for the student to continue to effectively train. Other students predominantly experience symptoms associated with the flight response that may increase wariness and cause students to avoid engaging in the training environment. Finally, a significant number of students at SERE experience and exhibit feelings and behaviors consistent with the mammalian freezing response. They struggle with feelings of being mentally disconnected from their environment and are unable to respond appropriately to their environment when a course of action is required. In sum, it is extremely common for SERE students to exhibit strong feelings during their time in the mock captivity setting. These strong feelings are the result of increased activation of fear and alarm centers in the brain as students struggle with the dilemma of coping with their stressful environment while adhering to the Code of Conduct. For many students, the mock POW experience of SERE is the first time they have been confronted with a highly unpredictable environment, and the stress they experience is often the result of uncertainty about the right course of action. They are highly competent individuals who typically have a strong sense of efficacy and rarely experience their actions as being "ineffective." The end result is that SERE students will exhibit behaviors and psychological reactions that may seem "unusual" or suggestive of clinical syndromes.

Over the past seven years, a team of research personnel has conducted a series of studies designed to evaluate the levels of stress experienced by participants in SERE training (Morgan, Hazlett, Doran, Steffian, & Southwick, 2004b; Morgan, Rasmusson, Wang, Hoyt, Hauger, & Hazlett, 2002; Morgan, Wang, Rasmusson, Hazlett, Anderson, & Charney, 2001).[2] The results of this research indicate that the stress level experienced by students is comparable to that experienced during actual combat-related military operations (Morgan, Wang, Rasmusson et al., 2001).

As is true of nonhuman mammals exposed to stress, students going through SERE training exhibit significant stress-induced alterations in epinephrine, norepinephrine, Adrenocorticotropic Hormone (ACTH), thyroid functioning, and cortisol. (See Figure 5.1.) In addition, students show a significant decrease in testosterone, estrogen, and weight. Finally, students exhibit stress-induced alterations in cognition and sensory perception that are also of a magnitude comparable to those seen in people exposed to real-world threat-to-life events—and that can interfere with performance (Morgan, Wang, Rasmusson et al., 2001; Morgan, et al., 2004).

This information is extremely valuable in that it demonstrates that SERE students are exposed to a level of stress that is of sufficient intensity to confer a "stress-protective" effect. Numerous animal studies have confirmed that to master the maladaptive effects of fear, animals must develop inhibitory memories or processes. To create inhibitory safety signaling in the brain, fear and alarm systems must also be activated while the animal is learning safety cues and signaling. This is relevant to SERE in

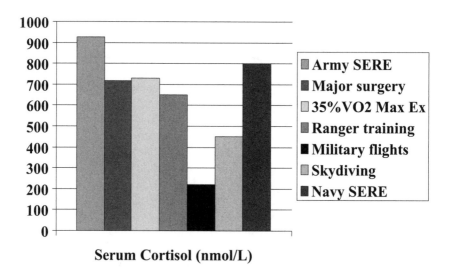

Figure 5.1
Comparison of Cortisol Levels

Source: Morgan, Wang, Mason et al., 2000.

that the training is based on the idea that the level of stress experienced by students is a key ingredient that promotes the learning and efficacy of the requisite skill sets. Indeed, SERE research has provided evidence that students who are not sufficiently challenged (as measured by robust stress-induced hormone changes while in the mock POW setting) do not exhibit a proficiency in the skills they have learned in the course. Thus, the research findings may be seen as a validation of the training doctrine.

In addition to providing information about the stressful nature of the course, SERE research has provided valuable insights about the impact of stress on human cognition and perception. Specifically, studies at SERE confirm that most people exposed to highly intense stress will exhibit symptoms of dissociation. The term dissociation refers to alterations in one's perception of the environment, one's body, and one's sense of the passage of time. It is thought to be the cognitive/perceptual aspect of the mammalian freezing response. The SERE research data about dissociation are relevant in that dissociation was previously believed by clinicians to be a pathological and abnormal response to stress. Recognition of dissociation as a normal part of the human response to stress has permitted SERE psychologists to provide more accurate assessments and consultation about the capacity of students who exhibit such experiences to continue in training.

SERE research has also shed light on what many professionals have long suspected —people differ in their capacities to cope with acute stress. We now know that differential abilities of students to cope with SERE stress results, in part, from the innate difference in the degree to which some individuals can release antiarousal hormones during exposure to stress. We also have learned that some people, because of their prior history of exposure to traumatic stress, are more vulnerable to stress-induced cognitive problem-solving difficulties. These data are also extremely relevant to SERE psychologists in that it is now possible to identify—prior to stress exposure —which students are more likely to exhibit difficulties during stress. Early identification of these students may permit the development of interventions designed to help them cope better with stress—and thereby enhance the students' abilities to be better equipped for real world operational activity. Alternatively, these data may enhance the ability of military assessment and selection programs to more effectively select people less vulnerable to the negative effects of stress.

Psychology of Captivity

In any circumstance of captivity, whether the captor follows or completely disregards international law, the captives will likely find themselves in an intolerable situation. The psychological processes within captivity provide insight into human behavior and response to extreme stress. This section begins with a discussion of the stages of captivity, discusses the determinants of resiliency within captivity, and attempts to define the psychological processes of captivity within the captive.[3]

Stages of Captivity

In general, captivity is comprised of a series of stages: *initial capture*, including the tactical interrogation; *movement*; and *long-term confinement* at a more permanent facility. The psychological consequences of these stages are a function of time, environment, situation, and level of previous training. More recent experiences of detained Americans have demonstrated that these stages are not quite as orthogonal and in succession as once believed.

The term "capture shock" has been used to describe the captive's experience during the initial moments of capture. As one author explained, this stage resembles the "Alice into the rabbit hole sensation" (Rochester & Kiley, 1998, p. 410). The captive typically experiences disorientation, confusion, unpredictability, disbelief and denial, terror, and overwhelming anxiety. Given the uncertainty of survival, most of Vietnam POWs and all Desert Storm POWs experienced capture shock (Anderson, 1996, p. 12). Capture shock has also been likened to an extreme culture shock (Anderson, 1996). Disorientation may relate to the transition from the culture of freedom to that of helplessness and fear. Anderson suggests that the convergence of the captor's culture, the POW's culture, and the culture of captivity yields capture shock.

Secondary to capture shock, interrogations performed at initial capture, often referred to as tactical interrogations, are typically positioned for gaining time-sensitive information. These interrogations have the least amount of oversight and supervision and can be the most dangerous. Without prior governmental guidance, the captors may not see any value in maintaining the welfare of the prisoner. Tactical questioning is typically led by untrained interrogators and is often highly mismanaged.

While the detainee is the most vulnerable at initial capture, he or she is also typically the most valuable to the captor during what as been termed the "golden hour." This golden hour can actually last a number of hours following capture and has the potential for yielding time-sensitive and high-value information to the captor. The initial unpredictability of capture, fear of the unknown, and capture shock result in a desire of the captive to more readily engage the captor. Resistance is likely minimal, and the captive may initially be cooperative. Even the trained captive will likely provide some sensitive information. Often, captives will associate cooperation with security, predictability, and beneficial treatment. Most captives overcome initial capture shock within a matter of hours or days. Subsequently, they may engage in resistance strategies, withdraw, mislead, or protect information.

In the *movement* phase, the captive is moved either to an interim facility, where the detainee may undergo additional questioning, or to a permanent facility. The movement typically provides the greatest chances of successful escape, but it can also be quite chaotic and dangerous. The permanent facility is the site of the *long-term* phase of captivity and may be in-theater or in an associated country. Depending on the environment, the captive's circumstances may improve. Former British POW, SAS Sgt. Andy McNab, commenting on the permanent facility he finally was moved to, said that "compared with the interrogation center, this was Buckingham Palace" (Anderson, 1996, p.12). Nevertheless, the possibility of death is always present, even if the captive attempts to ignore it. Burney (1952) states in reference to repatriation and death,

> I assured myself that there was still time, that anything was possible except the one event which I had excluded. But my assurances only served to convince me that I was wrong and that probably I had made it necessary for me to be wrong by setting the limit in the first place. I recalled the old injunction to beware of tempting Providence and assumed that I had broken the rule. (p. 114)

In the long-term captivity scenarios of the Korean war, the first two to three months following capture were noted to have often been the most problematic (Hunter, 1996). Following this period, the captive is likely to adjust to some of the ambiguity as well as the stress of physical and psychological exploitation. The environmental aspects and their psychological consequences on the trained and untrained captive across the phases of captivity are described in the following Table 5.1. The psychological responses of captives can vary widely. Training may serve to enhance the individual's confidence and hope in surviving and returning with honor.

Just as clinical thinking can be misapplied to student behavior during Code of Conduct training, it can also be misapplied to the captivity experience. For instance, when Vietnam POWs were repatriated, some were questioned about prisoner-to-prisoner sexual assault. Some physicians insisted that, based on knowledge of civilian prison environments, the POWs were simply not admitting to sexual assault. This assumption proved to be incorrect. Indeed, while POWs have experienced extraordinary stress in captivity, typical assumptions about behavior generated from civilian incarceration experiences, as well as psychiatric diagnoses are generally not applicable in the POW experience (Ursano, Wheatley, Carlson, & Rahe, 1987).

Motivations of the Captor and Captive

Typically, the captor's goal is to yield useful information and propaganda. The captor may first create an environment of unpredictability and then dependency. Control of the captive is subsequently established through the modulation of food, sleep, and hygiene. A sense of dependency within the captive's environment can then result. Dependency feeds into the logic that survival needs are contingent upon compliance by the captive. Compliance is then rationalized by the captive as a means of survival. The principle of cognitive dissonance theory, discussed later, would suggest that we often change our beliefs so they become consistent with our actions. This theory suggests that compliance with a captor's request can promote beliefs more sympathetic to the captor's cause. Thus, combined with behavioral conditioning, compliance can lead to cooperation and develop further into full indoctrination and collaboration. This progression may be disrupted by a number of factors. For example, the social influence of a fellow captive held in high positive regard may enhance a group/individual resistance posture.

Table 5.1
Characteristics of Captivity Environments

	Typical Captivity Environment		
	Initial capture	Movement	Long-term confinement
Level of intensity	Volatile. High risk of physical harm and death.	Escape opportunities at their highest.	Minimal chance of escape. Decreased chance of harm.
Interrogation quality	Low level of sophistication.	Varied level of sophistication.	Sophisticated interrogation and exploitation techniques are likely.
Exploitation motivation and quality	Exploitation is likely for personal or group gain.	Exploitation is likely for personal or group gain.	Exploitation is typically for organizational gain.
Dislocated expectations	Predictability is very poor. Health care is likely nonexistent.	Predictability is poor. Health care and quarters are variable.	Environment likely to become very predictable.
Untrained captive's response	Capture shock. Can initially be cooperative. Anxiety and disorientation.	Physical and mental deterioration.	Moments of despair, learned helplessness, hope, faith.
Trained captive's response	Capture shock. Resistance. Anxiety and disorientation.	Maintains situational awareness. Looks for means to escape.	Hope, faith, moments of despair, avoids learned helplessness.

The basic motives promoted by the Code of Conduct for the American service member are to survive and return with honor. In general, the captive is motivated to survive, protect information, avoid exploitation, attempt escape, and/or be repatriated. Of course, this is overly simplistic, because cultural, social, and religious factors may change the assessment of motivation. The will to survive varies by individual and group. Col. Bill Richardson, held by the North Koreans for 34 months, with his legs severely injured, fell into a deep slit trench latrine. Out of the will to survive, he managed to work his way out of the latrine only to be placed in a crowded room where other injured were housed to die. Col. Richardson was able heal his wounds and eventually be repatriated. While many have persevered through almost intolerable circumstances, a great number of POWs who have had the means to survive lost the will to survive and subsequently perished.

Psychological Principles of Captivity

Every method of exploitation is based on principles of human behavior and associated vulnerabilities within the individual's social and cultural context. The captor may take advantage of the psychological consequences beginning in the initial capture stage and throughout internment at a permanent facility. However, "Each man [has] his own priorities and compulsions, and therefore vulnerabilities" (Rochester & Kiley, 1998, p. 443). Physical exploitation and torture often yield psychological effects that are even more difficult to cope with. The term "brainwashing" was developed in the 1950s following the experiences of POWs held by North Korean and Chinese captors. The term is misleading in that the brain is not altered in any way, but rather the individual is often persuaded through the use of indoctrination, conditioning, and the following psychological factors:

Abstinence-Violation Effect (AVE)

AVE concerns the cognitive and emotional attributions of failure to global and uncontrollable factors (Rawson, Obert, McCann, & Marinelli-Casey, 1993; Walton, Castro, & Barrington, 1994). Rules are strictly applied, and when presented with even a minor violation of the rule, subsequent violations are likely to result. Unrealistic expectations about one's behavior, low self-efficacy, guilt, and discouragement over past behavior lead to a decreased ability to succeed in other high-risk situations (Shiffman et al., 1997). For the U.S. captive, the alteration of the Code of Conduct in 1977 instructing service members to "resist to their utmost" may help to diffuse the AVE. When an individual violates expectations of behavior in captivity, he or she can hopefully set aside emotions of guilt, shame, and despair in favor of hope and commitment. The result may be an improved ability to re-engage in resistance behavior. One of the results of SERE training can be that students establish more realistic expectations of how they will cope with captivity stress and thus become more able to recover from setbacks.

Learned Helplessness

Learned helplessness is a concept developed by Maier and Seligman (1976), who found that when tasked with an unsolvable problem, less effort is placed on future tasks. When the captive is unable to affect his/her environment, he/she may become overwhelmed by anxiety. Anxiety-laden cognitions, specifically inward-focused thoughts, interfere with performance (Mikulincer, 1986). Learned helplessness can lead to panic, despair, hopelessness, and even death. As it relates to the captive's experience, the object of the captor is typically not to induce complete helplessness, but to behaviorally shape the captive toward both a specifically desired outcome and a general state of dependency on the captor. The tendency toward helplessness is determined by the captive's attribution of outcomes to either "self-determination" or "luck or fate" (Hunter, 1996).

Mindlessness

The ability to put an individual off center is central in the success of the "Mutt and Jeff," or "good cop/bad cop" interrogation technique (Dolinski, 2001). Surprisingly, the transition from fear to relief is not necessarily the primary influence of behavior. Rather, "mindless" compliance is just as likely to be obtained by transitioning the captive's emotions from relief to fear. This change in emotional conditions, or "see-saw," promotes unpredictability and a subsequent disruption of cognitive operations. The result is what the author labels mindlessness, providing for a propensity to follow the "path of least resistance." Using the tools of exploitation, the captor attempts to dislocate the captive's expectations. In other words, the captor may induce unpredictability through sensory manipulation, random scheduling, sleep deprivation, torture, and numerous and often illogical trivial demands. Consequently, captives may find themselves temporarily disorganized and at a point of increased suggestibility (Sargant, 1957).

Emotions

The trained captor will often effectively use the emotions of the captive to further exploitation. Guilt, despair, hopelessness, false hope, and even anger are vulnerable to exploitation. For example, it is not uncommon for guilt to develop out of failing to meet one's personal expectations of resistance. Indeed, in a study of captivity experiences by Hunter (1996), POWs reported usually lasting 30 minutes to 3 hours before exhibiting behavior that could be viewed as capitulation and even collaboration. The captor may use the subsequent feelings of guilt to encourage the captive to give up continued attempts to resist. Lee (1953), in his seminal work on the lie detector, explained that while it is an unreliable instrument, it can "scare" the individual into confessing, guilty or not. He explains that individuals susceptible to the technique of appealing to emotions may more easily yield a confession.

Bypassing Resistance

Bypassing resistance is one of the most effective vulnerabilities to exploitation. A common presupposition is that pressures exerted are linearly related to compliance. However, as seen in historical and recent POW accounts, the opposite is usually true. The indirect approaches, specifically the friendly approach, are typically most successful in yielding accurate information. Engaging captives in a battle against their resistance posture is likely to only cue them to resist rather than comply. Gudjonsson (2003) proposes that most effective methods of interrogation enhance the ability to convince an individual that it is in his or her best interests to disclose information.

Social Reciprocity Demands

Social reciprocity refers to the social desire to reciprocate or "return the favor." Social reciprocity exploits the dependency on basic necessities the captive experiences toward the captor. Social reciprocity is only one of many *social expectations* that are habitually followed.

Anticipatory Anxiety

Anticipatory anxiety is created by the tendency for an individual to catastrophize, or expect the worst, in a captivity environment. The Kubark Manual, the CIA's declassified manual on interrogation, indicates that it is the anticipatory fear of punishment, even if just implied, that may yield the greatest amount of information. As the manual states, "The threat to inflict pain, for example, can trigger fears more damaging than the immediate sensation of pain." The manual continues to explain, "Sustained long enough, a strong fear of anything vague or unknown induces regression, whereas the materialization of the fear, the infliction of some form of punishment, is likely to come as a relief" (pp. 90–91).

In actuality, one of a captive's most important tools in captivity is his or her psychological composure. A captor can manipulate and control the external environment almost at will, but only the detainee has control of his/her internal process.

"Barbed-Wire Psychosis" or "Barbed-Wire Disease"

While misnomers, the "barbed-wire psychosis" and "barbed-wire disease" terms refer to the tendency for a POW to experience a decreased tendency to resist or escape (Vischer, 1919). Often the reluctance to escape is based on a rational evaluation of the captivity environment. Nevertheless, Rochester and Kiley (1998, p. 444) suggest that "some men 'shut down' and became passive or numb in captivity." A vicious cycle develops beginning with a "passive surrender to fate, apathy, not thinking, letting things go—a surrender to a complete zombie-like existence of mechanical dependency on the circumstances" (Rochester & Kiley, 1998, p. 444). This cycle is enhanced in environments like those experienced by POWs of the Korean conflict and Vietnam War who "endured extreme stress, prolonged fear of death, malnutrition, diseases, symptomatic attacks on the prisoner's mind and lack of all humanity" (Meerloo, 1955, p. 56). This explained why uprisings similar to those noted by the American POWs in the WWII European theater were generally not observed in the Japanese prison camps (Meerloo, 1955). Similar to the colloquial "institutionalization" experienced in civilian prisons, this psychological phenomenon can also result in contention between POWs who desire to attempt escape and those who do not. Nevertheless, "barbed-wire psychosis" should not be mistaken for the rational reluctance to escape without a developed plan.

Stockholm Syndrome

Stockholm Syndrome is a term coined following an unsuccessful bank robbery in Stockholm, Switzerland, where the robber barricaded himself and hostages in a bank vault. While in the vault, many hostages developed an irrational affinity toward the robber, and some later continued to correspond with the robber while he was in prison. The misplaced empathy and resultant behavior has been labeled the Stockholm Syndrome. Three elements should be present for the syndrome to occur (Fuselier, 1988):

1. Negative feelings on the part of the captive toward authorities, or a situation where the captor and captive are isolated together.
2. Positive feelings on the part of the captive toward the captor.
3. Positive feelings reciprocated by the captor.

Positive feelings are typically secondary to the dependency experienced as the captive understands that his/her life is in the hand of the captor. The captive can feel grateful that conditions are not worse or that his or her life was spared. The Stockholm Syndrome can ultimately result in collaboration. Variables that contribute to this effect include intensity, dependency, positive interactions between captive and captor, and greater situational intensity. This syndrome, however, is rarely observed and often is mistaken for rational empathy. For instance, one POW, in captivity for little over a month, left a message to his Serbian guards:

> *Thank you (Hvala),*
> *To all the Serbian guards of this prison. Thank you for your kindness and respect. I have much liking for Serbian people after this and I will continue to pray to God for (peace sign) and an end to this war.*
> *Thank you mostly for the cigarettes you have gave me!*
> *God with you.* ("POW Left 'Thank You,'" 1999)

This POW's treatment by the guards who provided humane treatment contrasted sharply with the treatment by his initial captors and initial guards. The empathy felt and appreciation expressed was not altogether irrational. Nevertheless, the desire to express affinity for guards who provide better treatment is a danger many captives encounter when maintaining a resistance posture.

Cognitive Dissonance

Cognitive dissonance was identified by Leon Festinger and James M. Carlsmith in 1959 to explain the dissonance that results when an individual holds two contradictory opinions or behaviors. The individual will attempt to eliminate or reduce the dissonance by removing or diminishing the importance of one or developing a new schema that incorporates both. The magnitude of opinion change is related to the strength of the perceived pressures applied, to include rewards, punishment, and social expectations. The degree of true opinion change is inversely related to the degree of felt pressures. To clarify with a captivity-related example, indoctrination backed by strong punishments or rewards will likely be less effective than when these rewards or punishments are just sufficient to affect behavior or express attitudes.

Interpersonal Contention

While isolation is difficult to manage, interpersonal contention is sometimes more productive for the enemy. As Vietnam-era POW Howard Dunn suggested, disagreements "created greater schisms among the prisoners...than their captors ever could have hoped to achieve" (Rochester & Kiley, 1998, p. 439). Conflict can be created when captives are housed together or when two separate groups of captives, previously with their own hierarchical structure, are combined.

False Confessions

It is not uncommon for a captor to desire a confession from captives. Written or verbal confessions can significantly generate negative world opinion for the captive's government. The psychology behind obtaining these confessions is similar to that observed in civilian police departments. The captor can either maximize or minimize the consequences for resisting. Maximization can suggest severe and even life-threatening consequences. Minimization can imply insignificant or reduced consequences secondary to compliance. The following discussion attempts to glean lessons from research on the psychological vulnerabilities of false confessions within the civilian sector.

Kassin (1997) describes three types of false confessions: voluntary, coerced-compliant, and coerced-internalized false confessions. Voluntary false confessions, motivated by the desire to protect another or for fame or recognition, are rarely observed in captivity. These confessions can be related to social psychological principles of obedience to authority (Milgram, 1994). Intense interrogative pressures can yield a coerced-compliant false confession. The pressure to escape or avoid punishment of either oneself or another captive, to avoid further averse interrogations, or to gain a special favor often yields this type of false confession. Essentially, the captive determines that the "short term benefits of confessing outweigh the long-term costs" (Kassin, 1997). Coerced-compliant false confessions are also related to the captive's perception of evidence against him or her and heightened suggestibility (Kassin, 1997).

As a result of environmental and historical factors, some individuals may be more susceptible to coerced-internalized false confessions. Typical stresses of captivity, sleep deprivation, semi-starvation, and poor environmental conditions can promote heightened suggestibility, a general shift in memory, and an agreement to false logic and misleading questions. Contributing historical/personal factors may include childhood history, naiveté, and lower intelligence. While rarely observed, the captive can arrive at a true belief in his or her culpability (Kassin, 1997). Coerced-internalized confessions can set the potential stage for collaboration and even defection.

The propensity toward false confessions is associated with suggestibility. What psychological factors lead to a heightened interrogative suggestibility and compliance? Gudjonsson (1997) stated that suggestibility is the most important vulnerability. The tendency toward suggestibility has been related to a number of variables, including low intelligence, poor memory recall (Clare & Gudjonsson, 1993), state and evaluative anxiety, neuroticism, and social desirability (Gudjonsson, 2003). Sleep deprivation significantly heightens suggestibility. However, confidence in the suggested statement (and possibly confession) under sleep deprivation increases reluctance to revise it (Blagrove & Akehurst, 2000).

Psychological Principles of Exploitation

The tools used by captors have historically been ineffective in eliciting time-limited, sensitive, or useful information. Their success in obtaining useful propaganda and inducing collaboration has likewise been limited. Nevertheless, the methods of exploitation used by (foreign) captors worldwide have been quite effective in creating psychological torment in the detainee.

Torture

While the long-term psychological effects of torture will be described elsewhere, this section will cover the impact of torture while the service member is in captivity. The use of physical torture has historically yielded poor information and paradoxically serves to enhance resistance. Furthermore, the practice serves to decrease the legitimacy of the offending organization or country. Physical torture, in most instances, has produced false confessions or inaccurate or unreliable information. Ron Jones, peacetime detainee in Saudi Arabia, provided a false confession as a result of torture. He was brought to the police station for questioning, where he experienced falanga (the beating of the soles of the feet so as not to leave visible signs of torture). Jones responded to the torture, "I'll tell you anything you want, just don't hit me again" and subsequently signed a false confession (Sweeny, 2002).

Social Isolation and Sensory Deprivation

Social isolation and sensory deprivation are two common pressures that can also be the most psychologically severe. Social isolation may have one of the most destructive effects on psychological resilience and the will to survive (Hunter, 1996). Long-term isolation can lead to extreme loneliness, boredom, depression, and anxiety. Christopher Burney provides an autobiographical account of his 18 months spent in isolation with interrogators and guards as his only contact with others. Through his captivity and isolation, he recounts the journey from loneliness to despair and on to liberty. While routine is initially lost in captivity, isolation creates a wish in the POW for a break in that routine. Only when the routine is violently disrupted does the POW desire the stability once again (Burney, 1952). The despair encountered in isolation can often be overwhelming and may undermine the will to survive.

POWs develop a number of tools to cope with isolation. Former POWs have reported watching shadows, insects, lizards, and other creatures move across their cell, reconstructing their lives from "pieces of a puzzle, with precision, and engaging in detailed activities of their imagination" (Rochester & Kiley, 1998, p. 415). Cdr. Howie Rutlege, a POW in Vietnam for seven and a half years states that while in captivity, he built five houses in his imagination. Similarly, Lt. Cdr. Bob Shumaker, a POW in Vietnam for eight years, spent around 12 hours a day creating and designing his dream house (Rochester & Kiley, 1998). Rutlege vividly describes his triumph over the experience of long-term isolation, "Being alone is another kind of war, but slowly I learned that it, too, can be won…a man in solitary confinement must quit regretting what he cannot do and build a new life around what he can do" (Rochester & Kiley, 1998, p. 414). Card games using the tap code, hidden chessboards, and other communication games would sometimes last over several weeks (Rochester & Kiley, 1998) and were instrumental in defeating isolation.

Sensory deprivation is not only isolation from interpersonal contact, but it also typically results in the complete reduction of sensory stimuli. Sensory deprivation has been conducted in specially constructed tanks of water and Epsom salts, or may be established through the combined use of earmuffs, white noise, blackout goggles, masks, and/or heavy mitts. Effects of sensory deprivation are mixed. Sensory deprivation has often been used for meditation. Following about 40 minutes, alpha and beta waves give way to hypnogogic theta waves, which typically occur in short duration prior to sleep. Extended theta waves may be relaxing and create enlightening experiences. However, as the time in deprivation is extended, the result becomes increasingly intense. Hallucinations and dissociative phenomena eventually result.

Sleep Deprivation

Sleep deprivation has often been used by captors to enhance dependency and malleability of behavior. Lack of sleep for prolonged periods may result in anxiety, irritability, blurred vision, memory problems, confusion, slurred speech, hallucinations, paranoia, disorientation, and ultimately death. However, sleep deprivation even for one night has recently been revealed in brain scans to affect the areas of the brain used for language, attention, and working memory function (Drummond et al., 2000), suggesting that even minor disruptions in sleep can degrade the captive's ability to cope effectively with challenges faced in captivity.

A West Berlin journalist captured and incarcerated in an East German prison was kept awake for 10 days, at which time he experienced weakness, uncontrolled shivering, and hallucinations (Sargant, 1957). John Schlapobersky, exploited with sleep deprivation in 1960s apartheid South Africa stated,

> I was kept without sleep for a week in all. I can remember the details of the experience, although it took place 35 years ago. After two nights without sleep, the hallucinations start, and after three nights, people are having dreams while fairly awake, which is a form of psychosis….By the week's end, people lose their orientation in place and time—the people you're speaking to become people from your past; a window might become a view of the sea seen in your younger days. To deprive someone of sleep is to tamper with their equilibrium and their sanity. (Lane & Wheeler, 2004, p. 1)

With minor deprivation of sleep, under 35 hours, the parietal and prefrontal areas of the brain can flexibly compensate for some of the decline in functioning (Horne, 2000; Drummond et al., 2000). One can negate some sleep deprivation effects by engaging in active tasks. Eventually, however, the effects of prolonged sleep deprivation can no longer be postponed (Drummond et al., 2000).

Unpredictability, Loss of Routine, and Denial of Privacy

While the unpredictability of captivity can be disengaging and disorienting, the boredom induced by predictability can have a similarly deleterious effect. POWs often coped with boredom by studying languages, poetry, mathematics, and philosophy. Storytelling became an art and was often based on television shows and movies seen before captivity. Games and humor became a survival tool to pass the time. Adm. (Ret.) Robert Shumaker (personal communication, 2004) reminisced that cabbage had become an almost intolerable staple, so much so that in the midst of an American bombing, another POW ran out into the middle of the yard, yelling at the planes, "bomb the cabbage fields." Admiral Shumaker recounts that "they laughed about that one for a long time."

Psychological Factors of Survival and Resiliency

In the most stressful of circumstances, it becomes clear that the captive's level of resiliency may determine the ability for the captive to resist physical and psychological coercion. As Article III states, "I will continue to resist by all means available." However, individual resiliency determines the degree of "ability" referred to in Article V, "I will evade answering further questions to the utmost of my ability." Research has examined personality factors that may predispose POWs to developing posttraumatic stress disorder following captivity (Sperr, Sperr, Craft & Boudewyns, 1990). However, there has been little research that describes the factors contributing to resiliency. Many surviving POWs have historically demonstrated a dramatic ability to cope and persevere amid the extreme stress and adversity of captivity (Singer, 1981). BG (Ret.) Jon A. Reynolds, who served as a fighter pilot during the Vietnam War, was shot down and held as a POW for seven years. He believes that his ability to survive captivity was

Figure 5.2
Personality Resiliency Factors that Contribute to the Ability to Cope with Captivity Stress

made out of personal and professional standards; integrity, positive attitude, and keeping the spirit to go on. [The] professional part refers to discipline even when the going gets tough, keeping the mind active, a daily regimen, and faith in God, country and your fellow comrades. (personal communication, 2005)

As CW2 Dave Williams stated regarding using hope and faith in his country to maintain cohesion of his fellow POWs, "I never thought the Americans weren't looking for us. I dreamed every night they were storming the building" (Cummings, 2004).

The ability for one to cope with captivity "is influenced by: (1) culture of the captor, (2) duration of captivity, (3) harshness of captivity, (4) support received from others, if held with other captives, (5) innate predispositions, (6) commitment to the ideology or task that placed them in jeopardy initially, (7) maturity, (8) personal value systems, and (9) satisfaction with family relations during the precapture period" (Jessen, 1995, p. 1). In addition, certain elements determine an individual's will to survive. *Talent* is the individual's innate abilities, including intelligence and creativity. *Desire* is the will to persist and survive in the most extreme circumstances, and *optimism* is the positive appraisal of the individual's ability to cope in the environment. These elements promote three factors that encourage personal hardiness. First, *commitment* to a greater cause, *control over* external events, and finally, conceptualizing the event as a *challenge* rather than a defeat (Jessen, 1995). Figure 5.2 diagrams these relationships.

The American Psychological Association posits ten ways to optimize resiliency. The following nine factors from this list may be relevant to enhancing resiliency in the POW environment: (1) making connections with others and/or a higher power provides social support and strengthens resilience (most POWs found a new faith in each other and God) (Rochester & Kiley, 1998); (2) assisting others; (3) maintaining a daily routine; (4) making time to eat properly, exercise, and rest; (5) having a plan; (6) nurturing a positive view of yourself; (7) recalling the ways you have successfully handled hardships in the past, and drawing on these skills to meet current challenges; (7) trusting yourself to solve problems and make appropriate decisions; (8) considering the broader context of the stressful situation and keeping a long-term perspective; and (9) maintaining hope (American Psychological Association, 2005).

Training in a Survival, Evasion, Resistance and Escape (SERE) course may also assist in enhancing resiliency, confidence, and hope. From the "1956 working group on survival training," Torrance (Melton, Biderman, & Torrance, 1955) wrote that both the will to survive and the ability to learn in the survival course are enhanced by reducing the tendency to exhibit reckless behavior, impulsiveness, blaming of others, inflexibility, frustration, complacency, and denial. Based on the experience of POWs in North Korea, the "1956 working group" identified the following factors of survival: decisiveness, ingenuity, personal resourcefulness, flexibility, ability to maintain calmness, realistic optimism, patience, tolerance of the unpleasant, sensitivity to others, appropriate release of aggression, unobtrusiveness, and control of childhood anxieties (Melton, Biderman, & Torrance, 1956).

Apart from education in survival techniques, SERE training prepares the students to feel confident that they are able to overcome and survive in a severely stressful and potentially dangerous environment (Melton, Biderman, & Torrance, 1955). One POW from a recent conflict emphasized how SERE training enhanced his confidence that he could survive and return with honor. Torrance termed this process "Survival Inoculation Training." Skillful instruction is transitioned to exposure to fears in a systematic process. Today, SERE training models are based primarily on Stress Inoculation Training (SIT; Meichenbaum, 1985). Much like Torrance's Survival Inoculation Training model, SIT is comprised of three phases: conceptualization/education, skills acquisition and rehearsal, and application and follow-through (Meichenbaum, 1985).

Rather than a cookbook approach, SIT fosters flexibility. The goal is to assist students in managing their cognitive and emotional appraisals of both captivity stressors and available coping resources and in practicing responses across graded exposure to a set of increasingly stressful situations. The military's SERE training programs make use of this general protocol within the context of a mock POW camp in order to prepare service members for possible internment. Of the U.S. POWs held captive during Desert Storm, all who had attended SERE training believed it to be useful, and 8 out of 10 believed their training to be "very useful." One of the POWs felt his SERE training was not as useful as it could have been, primarily because he did not experience the mock POW camp (Anderson, 1996). SERE training was also reported to be helpful to Vietnam War POWs.

> While most POWs had attended some form of SERE training, and while no course can ever prepare an individual completely for becoming a prisoner of war, SERE training aided the prisoners in recognizing the importance of discipline, leadership, and cohesiveness. (Rochester & Kiley, 1998, p. 442)

Nevertheless, many Vietnam POWs expressed that their training was of limited use, given longer-term confinement (Rochester & Kiley, 1998). Typically, the captors do not set specific rules for being a POW, and the rules that are set are often arbitrary, trivial or based on a culture unfamiliar to the captive. The captor rarely describes the rules to the POW before they have been violated.

Therefore, predeployment cultural training, or the exposure to concepts and customs specific to a culture, can assist POWs in understanding and adapting to the rules of the facility and culture. As one POW from Desert Storm stated, cultural study helped him to "understand how they had treated prisoners in the past and gave…awareness of how they might act [and] gave me a basis for giving them credible responses during interrogations." Another POW from this study stated that understanding the captor's culture "is still very beneficial" and psychologically prepares one for what to expect in captivity (Anderson, 1996, p. 29).

Repatriation

Up to this point, we've reviewed some of the major psychological issues confronted by captives and how current research findings support the idea that captivity-type "stress" can induce biological and psychological alterations that may, if prolonged, significantly debilitate a person's ability to adhere to the Code of Conduct and cause significant postcaptivity psychological dysfunction. Given the complexity, stressful nature, and potential gravity of captivity, returned captives might be expected to face extensive debriefing and other interventions upon their return to friendly control. There is some degree of truth in that assumption. All returned U.S. personnel undergo a process called repatriation. It is important to understand what repatriation is and is not, and that will be covered in the next section.

Although the repatriation process has been established for some time, no controlled studies on the efficacy and impact of repatriation have been conducted. Nevertheless, the procedures used by professionals who conduct repatriations are highly consistent with recent publications of evidence-based guidelines for interventions for Combat and Ongoing Operation Stress Responses (COSR) and Acute Stress Reaction (ASR) (National Institute of Mental Health, 2002; Department of Veterans Affairs/Department of Defense, 2004).

The Repatriation Mission

The repatriation of a returned service member is considered by the military to be an operational mission. Although physicians and other medical personnel, including psychologists, are involved in the process, it is neither a medical mission nor a mental health mission. The primary purpose of the repatriation mission is to gather as much critical information about the returned captive's experiences as possible so as to save the lives of allied personnel, assist in the defeat of the enemy, improve survival and personnel recovery training, and return members to their units and families in an efficient and effective fashion. It is self-evident that these goals cannot be accomplished unless the health and emotional well-being of the returned captive are included among the top priorities.

In spite of the intense interest exhibited by politicians or the media about the repatriation of people who are returned from captivity experiences,[4] repatriation is straightforward. One returned POW seemed to capture the essence of this by talking about his sudden "rock star" status. Almost as quickly, the spotlight is turned off and the returnee is back to anonymity. Managing this "roller coaster" requires an understanding of the procedures and principles that affect both the retrieval of accurate information and adjustment to stressful situations.

Procedures and Principles of Repatriation

Once the goals of repatriation are understood, the procedures become transparent. For example, if health and welfare are the first priority, it naturally follows that the returned captives will receive a medical assessment. To gather information, the service member needs to be interviewed or debriefed about the experience. Because the media takes such an interest in these events, the returned captive will need assistance by experts in public affairs. Some of the other procedures are not as apparent but nonetheless are crucial to achieving the overall mission.

For the returnee, repatriation starts the moment he or she is returned to friendly forces. After being evacuated to a safe area, the first priority is to ensure that the returned captive is medically stable and able to answer questions. Because of the likelihood a returned captive has sustained injury from battle, capture, ejection from an airplane, or from punishment inflicted by the captor, the safe area is usually a field medical facility. This does not necessarily mean that the returnee will receive definitive medical care at this time. There may be good reasons to delay definitive medical care for a medically stable returned captive. For example, the service member may have time-sensitive information that could save the lives of others. Thus, the next priority is a brief individual operational debrief. Depending on a number of factors, such as complicated medical circumstances, length of captivity, media or political interests, the returned captive may be evacuated to a relatively fixed facility for more extensive debriefings or definitive medical care, including possible evacuation back to the United States. Ideally, as advocated with protocols for managing combat stress, the returned service member is kept as close to the fight and returned to regular duties as soon as possible. However, in practice, this rarely happens. Also central to these decisions is the concept of decompression, which will be discussed later.

The coordination for repatriation activities often starts before the recovery of the repatriated POW. There is greater appreciation today on the part of military leaders for the need to interact with family members in a meaningful way after a service member becomes isolated or is taken captive. This not only prevents the impersonal "telegram" notifications, but it also provides an opportunity to prepare service members for their normal reactions to these circumstances as well as the reactions they might expect of their loved ones upon their return. The information provided to family members helps to promote the idea that, until compelling evidence is provided to the contrary, the assumption should be that the family and the returnee are experiencing normal reactions to an abnormal event. The families are also given information on the purposes and procedures of the repatriation process, and recommendations on how they can best support their loved one during this time. Such family assistance is handled by military Casualty Affairs Officers, often in conjunction with psychologists oriented to SERE psychology. Ideally, the Casualty Affairs Officer is able to contact the family to inform them and answer questions as soon as possible. However, given the ubiquitous media, it is difficult to prevent families getting bad news first from other sources. After it is confirmed that the service member has been recovered alive, this connection with the family is used to try to educate and encourage them to reunite with their loved one at a stateside location. While this may seem like an obstruction to some, past returned personnel have consistently indicated a preference for more time to "decompress" before returning home.

What Is Decompression?

Decompression, though often poorly understood, is a critical concept to successful recall of information from captivity, personal readjustment, and family readjustment. Essentially, decompression involves several factors. First, if more than one service member was returned from the same event, "team integrity" should be maintained, and the personnel should not be dispersed to different locations at least until the formal debriefing process has concluded. Second, the group of returned captives needs to have unstructured time together to tell their "war stories" to "normalize" their experiences. While their operational debriefings should occur individually to maximize uncontaminated recall of information, these personnel frequently express the need for an opportunity to talk to each other. The SERE psychologist is present or available throughout the process but usually adopts a nonintrusive stance with the returnees unless direct interaction is requested or there is a concern or question asked by the returned captives about their postcaptivity reactions. The initial assumption on the part of a SERE psychologist is that the returned captive is healthy and resilient. Because these service members may be experiencing symptoms of stress related to their experience, they may be worried that the presence of such symptoms means they are "crazy" or "sick." Psychoeducation about the normal responses to traumatic events such as captivity can significantly reduce a returned captive's worry and anxiety that he or she is "ill."

In addition to providing education about stress reactions, the SERE psychologist may also work with the returned service member to help that individual develop a plan of action that will promote a healthy readjustment to life at home. In these meetings, returned service members are encouraged by the SERE psychologist to think not only about how they will successfully reunite with their families and units, but also how they will cope with the increased interest in their lives and requests for their time from various sources. The final purpose for the presence of the SERE psychologist is to monitor the repatriation process itself to advise the repatriation team leader as to whether the process of repatriation is overwhelming the service member.

Having returned from captivity, the former captive is likely to be particularly sensitive to feeling a loss of control over his or her environment or the events surrounding the repatriation. These feelings can be particularly intense when returned captives are being rushed from one location to the next because of "pressure" to get them home quickly, or from overly lengthy debriefing sessions or excessive visits from "well-wishers." The SERE psychologist is the key adviser to the team leader on these issues. In sum, the overriding goal is to help returned service members reestablish a sense of control and predictability that has been absent during their period of captivity.

Other Team Members

In addition to the debriefers, the medical staff, casualty affairs personnel, public affairs representatives, and the SERE psychologist, there are other essential members to the repatriation team. The team leader is the person in charge of the process who balances all competing factors and manages the event. A Judge Advocate General (JAG) officer is available for general legal guidance, especially related to questions about behavior in captivity; to answer questions about what the service member can say to others about the captivity (in addition to the public affairs guidance); and to address issues of information classification.

There is also a chaplain available for returned captives who request spiritual guidance. The chaplain's role is to assist in confirming that the service member's basic life assumptions are intact. Time for prayers and other rites is made for the returnee, though all involvement with the chaplain is at the service member's discretion. While it is common for returned captives to feel more religious after returning, the well-used cliché, "there are no atheists in foxholes or captivity" has not always proven to be true. A member of the returned service member's unit typically accompanies the returnee throughout the repatriation process as well. This person can help reinforce the expectation of a return to normal activities and serves as a useful conduit to obtain such logistical items as fresh uniforms, civilian clothes, and so forth, or just as "a regular person" to talk to.

Questions and Myths

People who are unfamiliar with repatriation often ask whether U.S. officials and psychologists place too much emphasis on it. Such individuals may point out that the traditional formula for treating combat stress ("three hots and a cot") is adequate and that an overemphasis on repatriation detracts from the returned captive's resumption of a normal life.

This is a fair question and one that may not be ultimately answered until adequate longitudinal studies are conducted. However, the current emphasis by U.S. officials on repatriation is based on clinical observations within the past three decades: A number of instances have occurred where returning POWs were "overwhelmed" by sudden and intense exposure to officials and the media. These instances have led to the current view that such exposure does not promote resumption of normal life.

Another frequently raised question about repatriation procedures is the controlled, titrated exposure of the returned captive to his/her family members. Although it may seem counterintuitive to claim that former captives adapt better if delayed in their return to family and friends, experience has suggested that this is often the case. Most returned captives realize the value of the repatriation process and are motivated to "complete their mission." When former captives are returned with a group from the same captivity situation, they tend to be extremely motivated to decompress together, and family involvement can interfere with this. There is also a natural tendency on the part of repatriated service members' commands, families, and communities to have big fanfare such as ceremonies and the awarding of medals immediately upon return. Such attention can be problematic for many returnees. First and foremost, until some passage of time has occurred, the service member may not have an adequate appreciation of his or her own actions during captivity. For a period of time, the returnee may struggle with negative self-appraisal of his or her actions while in captivity or may experience survivor guilt if not everyone returned. Second, there may not be enough information available to military leaders at the time of return to warrant the award of medals. There are formal processes in place to determine the appropriateness and award of medals for various actions. These processes should be followed to prevent embarrassing corrections at later dates or the improper awarding of medals that could alienate the returnee from a primary source of social support—the unit.

Finally, a common question that is asked when the issue of repatriation arises, is whether repatriation is similar to a psychological debriefing technique known as Critical Incident Stress Management. Although both CISM and repatriation are designed to take care of the health and welfare of operational personnel, they serve different purposes (Mitchell & Everly, 1995; Everly & Mitchell, 1999). The differences between these processes are such that CISM is not allowed to be a component of repatriation. Repatriation does not lend itself to or assume that returnees are in need of psychological intervention. Rather, repatriation is a semistructured process by which information is gathered to save the lives of others, inform training processes, and keep returned personnel in a protected environment to allow them to "decompress" before dealing with the inevitable stressors they will face upon returning to their normal lives. There are different assumptions about the types and purposes of debriefing activities. When repatriated, it is not mandatory that returnees have some type of psychological intervention or "debriefing." However, because many returnees may request consultation with a mental health professional, SERE psychologists are available throughout the process.

Long-Term Psychological Consequences of Captivity

The long-term adjustment of returned captives is a topic of interest to many. While the research in this area is fraught with inconsistencies, certain clinical patterns have emerged. This section offers a brief overview of the research on epidemiology and predictors of psychological sequelae among repatriated captives and their families.

Epidemiology

A range of postcaptivity difficulties have been documented, including posttraumatic stress disorder (PTSD) and other anxiety disorders, depression, adjustment disorders, and various cognitive problems. Several authors have shown psychiatric illness to be more prevalent among former POWs than among veterans exposed to combat alone (Dent, 1999; Sutker, Allain, & Winstead, 1993; Sutker, Winstead, Galina, & Allain, 1990), while fewer studies have found no differences between these groups (e.g., Hunt & Robbins, 2001). Thus, the general consensus in the literature is that captivity represents a unique stressor with substantial clinical implications above and beyond the impact of combat experiences alone.

Perhaps the most widely studied diagnosis among repatriated POWs is PTSD. As a result of different diagnostic criteria and sampling time frames, prevalence rates of PTSD have ranged from 20 percent (Speed, Engdahl, Schwartz, & Eberly, 1989) to 90 percent (Sutker, Winstead, Galina, & Allain, 1991) among former POWs. While onset varies (Ursano & Rundell, 1990) and some research has documented recovery one to two years after repatriation (Hall & Malone, 1976), reports on the persistence of PTSD across the life span of repatriated POWs are mixed. Many reports have found PTSD to persist in both severity across the life span (Hunt & Robbins, 2001; Sutker, et al., 1991), while some have found otherwise. Dent (1999) observed marked declines in the prevalence of depression and anxiety disorders between 1982 and 1991 in a sample of Australian Army personnel captured and held prisoner of war by the Japanese in 1942, suggesting that the "impact of the POWs' tragic wartime experience had at last begun to fade" (p. 111).

As is the case with PTSD in the general population, comorbidity is not uncommon. Among former POWs interned in Japan, Germany, and North Korea, Engdahl, Dikel, Eberly, and Blank (1998) found that those with a lifetime diagnosis of PTSD were almost twice as likely to have at least one comorbid lifetime psychiatric disorder than those without PTSD (66 percent versus 34 percent). In this study, comorbid diagnoses with the highest frequencies were panic disorder, major depressive disorder, alcohol abuse/dependence, and social phobia. Kluznik, Speed, Van Valkenberg and Magraw (1986) observed that 67 percent of former WWII POWs from the Pacific theater with a diagnosis of alcoholism also had a history of PTSD. Regardless of comorbid diagnoses, depressive symptoms have repeatedly been shown to be greater in former POWs than non-POW controls (e.g., Tennant, Goulston, & Dent, 1986). Sutker and colleagues (1991) reported that POWs from the Korean conflict scored significantly higher on the Minnesota Multiphasic Personality Inventory (MMPI) Depression, Psychasthenia, Schizophrenia and Social Introversion scales than did their combat veteran controls from this conflict. A similar pattern was also observed with former POWs and combat veterans from the Pacific theater of World War II (Sutker et al., 1993). These former POWs also showed deficits on standardized memory and problem-solving tests and were more likely to complain of difficulty concentrating than did combat veteran controls. Indeed, Ursano and Rundell (1990) noted widely cited organic mental syndromes with a number of possible etiological factors, including "head trauma, food and water deprivation or untreated physical illness" (p. 177). This finding is not without contradiction, however, as Williams, Hilton and Moore (2002) found that Vietnam veteran POWs performed better than controls on standard neuropsychological and intelligence testing. Although the research findings may vary in the details, they are in agreement that many returnees will experience significant psychological and medical problems that warrant treatment.

Predictors of Distress

As is true in other arenas of life, people differ in their vulnerability to physical and psychological illness as a result of captivity. Most research addressing why and how people may differ in their vulnerability to stress has identified a number of key variables. Broadly speaking these are: personal variables, factors related to captivity, and factors related to life after release from captivity, such as support from friends or family members.

Personal Variables

Numerous studies have investigated the contribution of both personal variables and those related to the captivity environment to subsequent psychological dysfunction. Of the personal variables cited as predictive of negative psychological outcomes, age at capture has received substantial attention and appears to be negatively correlated with degree of later distress. In a study by Page and colleagues (1991), lower age at capture was the demographic variable that was most predictive of reported postcaptivity depressive symptoms in Pacific theater World War II POWs (beta = −3.26) and Korean conflict POWs (beta = −2.25). Engdahl and colleagues (1997) also found lower age at capture to be moderately predictive of subsequent PTSD, generalized anxiety disorder, and social phobia among these groups.

Saab, Chaaya, Doumit, and Farhood (2003) conducted a cross-sectional study on Lebanese captives from an Israeli detention center during the war in Lebanon. In addition to reported food and water deprivation and increased religiosity after release, the authors found lower education to be predictive of postcaptivity distress. Similarly, Page and colleagues (1991) found years of education to be negatively correlated to subsequent depressive symptoms for World War II and Korean conflict POWs.

The results of these studies may be viewed as implying only negative outcomes for former POWs. On the contrary, Ursano and Rundell (1990) refer to the ability of some POWs to not only cope effectively with the stress of captivity but also to benefit psychologically from their captivity experiences. Solomon, Waysman, Neria, Ohry, Schwarzwald, and Weiner (1999) found that active coping and resistance to giving up during captivity correlated positively with number of subsequent positive life changes among Israeli former POWs.

Captivity Variables

Although there is evidence that individual differences may play the greatest role in determining a person's response to a traumatic stressor (Bowman, 1997), the extant information about the effects of captivity on humans provides an adequate argument for a "dose effect" (i.e., the severity and duration of exposure to trauma) in the development of PTSD. Unlike most trauma experienced by civilians or military personnel, captivity stress is typically long-standing and debilitating in nature. At present, the best scientific evidence suggests that it is the severity of traumatic experiences while in captivity that best predicts subsequent psychological symptoms.

The most general comparisons of captivity experiences have been made between those of European and Pacific theater POWs during World War II. Based on accounts from the International Red Cross, the treatment of U.S. POWs in German POW camps was considered essentially humane (Nelson, 1989). In comparison, the deprivation and maltreatment experienced in the Pacific theater were far more severe. These differences are highlighted by the disparity in death rates between European and Pacific theater POWs. In Europe, 1 percent of POWs died in captivity; in the Pacific, 37 percent died in captivity. Also far more prevalent in the Pacific was physical torture, with approximately 90 percent of returned POWs from the Pacific reporting having experienced some form of physical punishment (Miller, 1993). As might be imagined, Pacific theater veterans of WW II have consistently reported more numerous medical and psychiatric symptoms and greater levels of disability than have European theater POWs (e.g., Beebe, 1975).

Several studies have employed more direct measures of severity of captivity to predict subsequent dysfunction. Weight loss during captivity has been used by many as an index of captivity severity. Engdahl, Dikel, Eberly, and Blank (1997) found that weight loss during captivity contributed to a regression equation that accounted for 33 percent of the variance in PTSD diagnoses among former World War II and Korean conflict POWs. These same authors (Engdahl et al., 1998) subsequently found greater captivity weight loss among those who were later diagnosed with PTSD than those who were not. In perhaps the largest study of former POWs, Page, Engdahl, and Eberly (1991) surveyed 1,320 from World War II and the Korean Conflict, finding similar results for World War II Pacific theater POWs only.

Crocq, Hein, Duval, and Macher (1991) surveyed 817 Alsatian World War II veterans who had been imprisoned in the USSR and found both length and severity of captivity to be greater in those later diagnosed with PTSD. The author's severity of captivity index included solitary confinement, physical punishment, death threats, severe interrogations, witnessing another POW's death, and health variables such as loss of teeth, protein deficiency edemas, and night blindness. Chi square analyses demonstrated significantly higher endorsement of each of these variables among those with a diagnosis of PTSD than among those without.

Engdahl and colleagues (1998) found torture to be more prevalent in the experiences of those World War II POWs who were diagnosed with PTSD than those who were not. Vietnam War POWs who endured longer periods of isolation have demonstrated higher rates of psychiatric disorders than those who endured shorter periods (Van der Kolk, 1984). Thus, irrespective of preexisting pathology, certain POW captivity experiences alone demonstrate consistent relationships with subsequent psychological sequelae and thus appear sufficient to create clinically significant dysfunction after repatriation.

Social Support

Just as social support has been shown to play an important role in the postwar adjustment of Vietnam War veterans (Boscarino, 1996; King, King, Fairbank, Keane, & Adams, 1998), it has also been cited as a mediator of posttraumatic response among former POWs. In Engdahl and colleagues' 1997 study, postcaptivity social support contributed to the prediction of PTSD in World War II and Korean conflict POWs. Ursano and Rundell (1990) also cited the importance of supportive social relationships in mitigating the impact of traumatic stress. Solomon and colleagues (1999) found a lack of positive social experiences to be predictive of negative life changes among Israeli former POWs. The authors suggested that the responses of the social environment:

> may enable a corrective emotional experience after prolonged coercion, abuse and deliberate brutality at the hands of other human beings. The social environment may encourage and promote gradual readjustment by supporting the ex-POW's resumption of his previous roles in society, by bolstering his self-esteem, and injured sense of belonging and by giving him a chance to abreact and share his experience. (p. 423)

Thus, a healthy, responsive social network can provide the returned captive with an opportunity to "work through" traumatic experiences, whereas a rejecting one can amplify feelings of isolation, betrayal, and victimization related to the mistreatment experienced in captivity. Perhaps the most important social network, the captive's family, is the topic of the next section.

Impact on the Family

Hall and Simmons (1973) discussed the common psychiatric difficulties reported by wives of service members held POW or missing in action during the Vietnam War. The sample was restricted to those seeking psychiatric treatment and assigned to group psychotherapy. Their study not only demonstrated the importance of assessment and intervention for family members of those missing or held captive, but also specifically described the target symptoms reported. These included but were not limited to psychophysiological symptoms, sleep disturbances, exaggerated fears, and anxiety states. Children of these wives were reported to have role confusion, separation anxiety, and sleep disturbances.

Hunter (1988) proposed that the effects of captivity on the captive's children were multidetermined by "social support, parental coping and child personality vulnerabilities" (p. 316). In a retrospective study of family hardiness, Campbell and Demi

(2000) interviewed adult children of fathers missing in action since the Vietnam War. The authors conceptualized family adjustment from a family resiliency perspective, correlating measures of family hardiness with grief symptoms, intrusive thoughts, and avoidance. Intrusive thoughts and preoccupation with thoughts of the missing parent were not correlated with hardiness, and the researchers concluded that hardiness did not protect against these. Conversely, measures of hardiness, including commitment, challenge, and sense of control, were negatively correlated to reported symptoms of avoidance and existential loss. Qualitative data collected from telephone interviews seemed to corroborate the importance of maternal coping observed by Hunter (1988). As noted by Campbell and Demi (2000), the loss experienced by a family that learns a parent is missing in action is an ambiguous one. In fact, the ambiguity itself is a significant source of stress.

The return of a parent from captivity poses a unique set of challenges to a family. Coping with the returned captive's psychological reactions has perhaps been the most-frequently-cited difficulty faced by families. However, several factors pertaining to the family's adaptation during the captivity period must also be considered. Roles are likely to have shifted in the parent's absence, with family members having taken on responsibilities once shouldered by the service member. Shifts in sources of spousal social support may also create stress on the marital relationship upon reunification. The returned parent may have missed significant developmental changes in his or her children, and this may, in turn, complicate the parenting challenges presented by child behavioral disturbances. Given that both captive and family have undergone significant changes in response to their experiences, it is not surprising that reunification is fraught with difficulty. Indeed, Nice, McDonald, and MacMillian (1981) reported the divorce rate of returned POWs from the Vietnam War to be three times higher than the rate for matched controls five years after their return. In summary, the research to date suggests that parental captivity has a negative impact on family functioning and that the adjustment of children is often affected. Further investigation is needed, however, to better understand the myriad of possible effects of captivity on the family.

Future Directions

Captivity presents a unique and highly stressful set of challenges that military personnel must face. If managed effectively, these challenges are met in a way that minimizes the negative impact on both captive and his or her country. Among the U.S. Armed Forces, the Code of Conduct and its associated training programs serve to improve the captive's ability to meet these challenges by establishing a set of principles that guide the captive's behavior in the captive environment. SERE training is designed to instill the Code of Conduct principles and accompanying behaviors under realistic and increasingly stressful conditions in order to increase the combatant's confidence and sense of agency in potential future captivity scenarios. While no controlled research has addressed the effectiveness of SERE training in accomplishing these goals, preliminary neurohormonal studies and anecdotal reports reviewed in this chapter suggest that it is both conceptually valid and valuable in the eyes of former captives.

Recent changes in the nature of armed conflict, developments in technology, military strategy, and the growing threat of terrorism have necessitated a consequent evolution in SERE training. Increased capability for rapid penetration deep into enemy territory has resulted in major shifts in both logistical considerations and the increased exposure of a wider range of military personnel to hostile action. As guerilla fighters, insurgents, and terrorists have become the primary target of military operations, soldiers are now deployed to combat environments with no clear front line of engagement. Complicating matters is the military's increased reliance on civilian contractors who are required to operate in harm's way. As such, a growing number of civilians are encountering levels of risk comparable to that faced by military personnel. That the Code of Conduct does not apply to civilians raises questions. What, if anything, should be expected of civilian personnel (especially nongovernmental employees) if captured? How should those who survive be repatriated, and how will they fare psychologically?

Recent large-scale military operations in the Balkans, Afghanistan, and Iraq have resulted in the deployment of large numbers of military personnel worldwide. For example, as of September 2004, 170,647 U.S. military personnel were deployed in and around Iraq in support of Operation Iraqi Freedom (Washington Headquarters Services, Directorate for Information Operations and Reports [WHS/DIOR], 2005). When combined with the numbers of relief workers, civilian contractors, members of the media, and other U.S. nationals living abroad, the result has been a dramatic increase in hostage-taking opportunities. Moreover, developments in information technology and access to media coverage have heightened the impact of hostage exploitation, making this a more attractive strategy for terrorists. Among certain terrorist groups, there appears to have been a shift from using live hostages for bargaining power to publicizing their murder in order to achieve political objectives. In this context, a survival-of-a-hostage scenario may be less likely, and greater importance must be placed on prevention.

As the Chinese government's detention of U.S. EP-3 crew members in 2001 demonstrated, the "detaining" of foreign military personnel by nonwarring countries has offered a viable means of publicizing such incidents for national and international political gain. International laws that govern actions of captor and captive as well as opportunities for diplomatic solutions differ significantly in these situations, compared to wartime captivity. Detained military personnel require the same degree of guidance offered to POWs in order to set the standard for honorable behavior within the captive environment.

In the face of such developments, it has become evident that traditional Code of Conduct training, predicated on a Cold War-era POW scenario no longer adequately addresses the range of captivity scenarios with which military personnel must contend. SERE training and research must evolve to prepare a broader range of personnel to avoid or survive a diverse spectrum of captivity scenarios. Continued assessment of returned captives will improve our understanding of the effects of these scenarios on military personnel and their families.

Notes

1. A word on the generalizability of statements made in this chapter to non-U.S. personnel: As the experience and research focus of the authors is limited primarily to U.S. personnel, this chapter is written with the U.S. service member in mind. Research about captivity experiences of members of other nations has been included where appropriate; however, the majority of works cited involve only U.S. captives. As such, the reader is cautioned about making generalizations to other populations that may be invalid because of cultural and/or doctrinal differences in the training, assessment, and handling of potential and former captives.
2. The research team includes members from Yale University and the U.S. Army and Navy.
3. This section is not a discussion of interrogation techniques, a guide for conducting interrogations, or recommendations for exploitation. Furthermore, the coercive techniques described are not necessarily in accordance with the Uniform Code of Military Justice, Land of Law Warfare, Geneva Conventions Relating to the Treatment of Prisoners of War or Secretary of Defense guidance. When techniques are mentioned, they are only in service of the discussion on the possible psychological consequences of captivity or to document historic accounts of POWs in captivity.
4. Past experience suggests that even the medical community can become voyeuristic with these new-found celebrities if not monitored.

References

American Psychological Association. (2005). Retrieved October 11, 2005, from http://www.helping.apa.org/dl/the_road_to_resilience.pdf

Anderson, M. A. (1996). *Captivity and culture: Insights from the Desert Storm prisoners of war experience.* [Master's Thesis] Newport, RI: Naval War College.

Bebee, G. W. (1975). Follow-up studies of World War II and Korean War prisoners, II: Morbidity, disability and maladjustments. *American Journal of Epidemiology, 101,* 400–422.

Blagrove, M., & Akehurst L. J. (2000). Effects of sleep loss on confidence-accuracy relationships for reasoning and eyewitness memory. *Experimental and psychological application, 6,* 59–73.

Blumberg, H., Kaufman, J., Martin, A., Whiteman, R. Zhang, J., Gore, J., Charney, D., et al. (2003). Amygdala and hippocampal volumes in adolescents and adults with bipolar disorder. *Archives of General Psychiatry, 60,* 1201–1208.

Boscarino, J. A. (1995). Post-traumatic stress and associated disorders among Vietnam veterans: The significance of combat exposure and social support. *Journal of Traumatic Stress, 8* (2), 317–336.

Bowman, M. (1997). Individual differences in posttraumatic response: Problems with the adversity-distress connection. Mahwah, NJ: Lawrence Erlbaum Associates.

Bracha, H. (2004). Can premorbid episodes of diminished vagal tone be detected via histological markers in patients with PTSD? *International Journal of Psychophysiology, 51,* 127–133.

Burney, C. (1952). *Solitary Confinement.* Welwyn Garden City, Herts, U.K.: Alcuin.

Campbell, C. L., & Demi, A. S. (2000). Adult children of fathers missing in action (MIA): An examination of emotional distress, grief and family hardiness. *Family Relations, 49*(3), 267–276.

Campbell, S., Marriott, M., Nahmias, C., & MacQueen, G. (2004). Lower hippocampal volume in patients suffering from depression: A meta analysis. *American Journal of Psychiatry, 161,* 598–607.

Carlsson, K., Petersson, K., Lundqvist, D., Karlsson, A., Ingvar, M., & Ohman, A. (2004). Fear and the amygdala: Manipulation of awareness generates differential cerebral responses to phobic and fear-relevant (but nonfeared) stimuli. *Emotion, 4,* 340–353.

Clare, I. C., & Gudjonsson, G. H. (1993). Interrogative suggestibility, confabulation, and acquiescence in people with mild learning disabilities (mental handicap): Implications for reliability during police interrogations. *British Journal of Clinical Psychology,* 295–301.

Cole, P. M. (1994). *POW/MIA issues, volume 1, the Korean War.* Santa Monica, CA: Rand.

Croq, M. A., Hein, K. D., Duval, F., & Macher, J. P (1991). Severity of the prisoner of war experience and post-traumatic stress disorder. *European Psychiatry, 6,* 39–45.

Crowe, W. J. (1993). *The line of fire, from Washington to the Gulf, the politics and battles of the new military.* New York: Simon & Schuster.

Cummings, T. (2004, April). *Cavalry pilot recounts days as POW.* Guidon. Retrieved November 3, 2005, from http://www.flw-guidon.com/news/Calvary0415.dwt

Davis, M. (1992). The role of the amygdala in fear potentiated startle: Implications for animal models of anxiety. *Trends in Pharmacological Science, 10,* 2818–2824.

Dent, O. F. (1999). Long-term consequences of wartime imprisonment: A review of the Concord Hospital POW project. *Australian Journal of Aging, 18*(3), 109–113.

Department of the Army Field Manual No. 21-78. (1981).

Department of Defense Instruction 2310.4 (2000). Repatriation of prisoners of war (POW), hostages, peacetime government detainees and other missing or isolated personnel. VA/DoD Clinical Practice Guidelines for the Management of Post-traumatic Stress. Washington, DC: Department of Veterans Affairs/Department of Defense

Dolinski, D. (2001). Emotional seesaw, compliance, and mindlessness. *European Psychologist, 6,* 194–203.

Drummond, S. P., Brown, G., Gillin, B., Stricker, J., & Buxton, R. B. (2000). Altered brain response to verbal learning following sleep deprivation. *Nature, 403,* 655–657.

Durant, M. J., & Hartov, S. (2003). *In the company of heroes.* New York: G. P. Putnam's Sons.

Engdahl, B., Dikel, T. N., Eberly, R., & Blank, A. (1997). Posttraumatic Stress Disorder in a community group of former prisoners of war: A normative response to severe trauma. *The American Journal of Psychiatry, 154*(11), 1576–1581.

Engdahl, B., Dikel, T. N., Eberly, R., & Blank, A. (1998). Comorbidity and course of psychiatric disorders in a community sample of former prisoners of war. *The American Journal of Psychiatry, 155*(12), 1740–1745.

Everly, G. S., Jr., & Mitchell, R. J. (1999). *Critical Incident Stress Management (CISM): A new era and standard of care in crisis intervention* (2nd ed.). Ellicott City, MD: Chevron.

Executive Order No. 10631, 20 FR 6057 (1955), reprinted as amended in Executive Order No. 12017 (1977) and Executive Order No. 12633 (1988).

Festinger, L., & Carlsmith, J. M. (1959). Cognitive consequences of forced compliance. *Journal of Abnormal and Social Psychology, 58,* 203–210.

Fuselier, G. D. (1988). Hostage negotiation consultant: Emerging role for the clinical psychologist. *Professional Psychology: Research and Practice, 19*(2), 175–179.

Gianaros, P., Van der Veen, F., & Jennings, J. (2004). Regional cerebral blood flow correlates with heart period and high-frequency heart period variability during working-memory tasks: Implications for the cortical and subcortical regulation of cardiac autonomic activity. *Psychophysiology, 41*, 521–530.

Goosens, K., & Maren, S. (2004). NMDA receptors are essential for the acquisition, but not expression, of conditional fear and associative spike firing in lateral amygdala. *European Journal of Neuroscience, 20*, 537–548.

Goulston, K. J., & Dent, O.F. (1986). The psychological effect of being a prisoner of war: Forty years after release. *American Journal of Psychiatry, 143*, 618–621.

Gudjonsson, G. (1997). Disputed confessions and the criminal justice system. Maudsley Discussion Paper #2, Institute of Psychiatry, London.

Gudjonsson, G. H. (2003). Psychology brings justice: the science of forensic psychology. *Criminal Behavior and Mental Health, 13*, 159–167.

Gudjonsson, G. H. (1983). Suggestibility, intelligence, memory recall and personality: An experimental study. *The British Journal of Psychiatry, 142*, 35–37.

Hall, R. C. W., & Malone, P. T. (1976). Psychiatric effects of prolonged captivity: A two-year follow-up. *American Journal of Psychiatry, 133*, 786–790.

Hall, R. C. W., & Simmons, W. C. (1973). The POW wife, a psychiatric appraisal. *Archives of General Psychiatry, 29*, 690–694.

Haney, C., Banks, C., & Zimbardo, P. (1973). Interpersonal dynamics in a simulated prison. *International Journal of Criminology and Penology, 1*, 69–97.

Horne, J. (2000). Neuroscience: Images of lost sleep. *Nature, 403*, 605–606.

Hunt, N., & Robbins, I. (2001). The long-term consequences of war: The experience of World War II. *Aging and Mental Health, 5*(2), 183–190.

Hunter, E. J. (1998). Long-term effects of parental wartime captivity on children: Children of POW and MIA servicemen. *Journal of Contemporary Psychotherapy, 18*(4), 312–328.

Jessen, J. B. (1995). Resilience: Can the will to survive be learned? Paper Presented at the Survival 1995 Symposium, Portsmouth, U.K.

Joint Personnel Recovery Agency. (2004). Requirements for qualification and use of DoD Survival, Evasion, Resistance, and Escape (SERE) psychologists in support of the Code of Conduct training. JPRA instruction manual.

Kassin, S. M. (1997). The psychology of confession evidence. *American Psychologist, 52*(3), 224–233.

King, L. A., King, D. W., Fairbank, J. A., Keane, T. M., & Adams, G. A. (1998). Resilience-recovery factors in post-traumatic stress disorder among female and male Vietnam veterans: Hardiness, postwar social support, and additional stressful life events. *Journal of Personality and Social Psychology, 74*(2), 420–434.

Kluznik, J. C., Speed, N., Van Valkenberg, C., & Magraw, R. (1986). Forty-year follow-up of United States prisoners of war. *American Journal of Psychiatry, 143*, 1443–1446.

Knapp, B., Wilson, A., Pascoe, J., Supple, W., & Whalen, P. (1990). A neuroanatomical systems analysis of conditioned bradycardia in the rabbit. In M. Gabriel & J. Moore (Eds.), *Learning and computational neuroscience: Foundations of adaptive networks* (pp. 53–90). Cambridge, MA: MIT Press.

Lane, M., & Wheeler, B. (2004). The real victims of sleep deprivation. *BBC News Online Magazine.* Retrieved October 11, 2005, from http://news.bbc.co.uk/1/hi/magazine/3376951.stm

LeDoux, J. (1992). Brain mechanisms of emotion and emotional learning. *Current Opinions of Neurobiology, 2*, 191–198.

LeDoux, J., Cicchetti, P., Xagoraris, A., & Romanski, L. (1990). The lateral amygdaloid nucleus: Sensory interface of the amygdala in fear conditioning. *Journal of Neuroscience, 10*, 1062–1069.

LeDoux, J., Farb, C., & Ruggiero, D. (1990). Topographic organization of neurons in the acoustic thalamus that project to the amygdala. *Journal of Neuroscience, 10*, 1043–1054.

Lee, C. D. (1953). *The instrumental detection of deception: The lie text.* Springfield, IL: Charles C. Thomas.

Lieber, Francis (1863). *Instructions for the government of armies of the United States in the field; General Orders no. 100.* Washington, DC: War Department, Adjt. General's Office.

MacMillan, S., Szeszko, P., Moore, G., Madden, R., Lorch, E., Ivey, J., Benerjee, S., & Rosenberg, D. (2003). Increased amygdala: hippocampal volume rations associated with severity of anxiety in pediatric major depression. *Journal of Child and Adolescent Psychopharmacology, 13*, 65–73.

Maier, S.F., & Seligman, M. E. P. (1976). Learned helplessness: Theory and evidence. *Journal of Experimental Psychology: General, 105*, 3–46.

Meerloo, J. (1956). *The rape of the mind: The psychology of thought control, menticide and brainwashing.* Cleveland: The World Publishing.

Meichenbaum, D. (1985). *Stress inoculation training.* New York: Pergamon Press.

Melton, A. W., Biderman, A. D., & Torrance, E. P. (1954). *Report of the working group on survival.* Lackland AFB, TX: Headquarters Air Force Personnel and Training Research Center.

Melton, A. W., Biderman, A. D., & Torrance, E. P. (1955). *Report of the working group on survival training: Yearly update.* Lackland AFB, TX: Headquarters Air Force Personnel and Training Research Center.

Melton, A. W., Biderman, A. D., & Torrance, E. P. (1956). *Report of the working group on survival training: Yearly update.* Lackland AFB, TX: Headquarters Air Force Personnel and Training Research Center.

Mikulincer, M. (1986). Motivational involvement and learned helplessness: The behavioral effects of the importance of uncontrollable events. *Journal of Social and Clinical Psychology, 4*, 402–422.

Milgram, S. (1974). *Obedience to authority; An experimental view.* New York: Harper & Row.

Miller, T. W. (1993). Long-term effects of torture in former prisoners of war. In M. Basoglu (Ed.), *Torture and its consequences: Current treatment approaches* (pp. 107–135). New York: Cambridge University Press.

Mitchell, J. T., and Everly, G. S., Jr. (1995). *Critical incident stress debriefing: An operations manual for the prevention of traumatic stress among emergency services and disaster workers* (2nd ed.). Elliot City, MD: Chevron.

Molinari, V., & Williams, W. (1995). An analysis of aging World War II POWs with PTSD: Implications for practice and research. *Journal of Geriatric Psychiatry, 28*(1), 99–114.

Morgan, C. A., III, Akins, D., Steffian, G., Doran, A., Hazlett, G., & Southwick, S. (2005). Heart rate variability under stress: Preliminary results at military survival and dive schools. Unpublished manuscript.

Morgan, C. A., III, Hazlett, G., Doran, A., Garrett, S., Hoyt, G., Thomas, P. et al. (2004). Accuracy of eyewitness memory for persons encountered during exposure to highly intense stress. *International Journal of the Law and Psychiatry, 27*(3), 265–279.

Morgan, C. A., III, Hazlett, G., Doran, A., Garrett, S., Hoyt, G., Thomas, P. et al. (2005). Performance on the Rey Osterrieth Complex Figure Task under severe stress. Manuscript submitted for publication.

Morgan, C. A., III, Hazlett, G., Doran, A., Steffian, G., & Southwick, S. (2004a). New uses for the polygraph in detecting concealed information. Unpublished manuscript.

Morgan, C. A,. III, Hazlett, G., Doran, A., Steffian, G., & Southwick, S. (2004b). Stress induced symptoms of dissociation and physical health complaints in female US Navy personnel enrolled in survival school training. Unpublished manuscript.

Morgan, C. A., III, Loftus, E., Hazlett, G., Doran, A., Garrett, S., Hoyt, G. et al. (in press). Accuracy of the Wechsler Face Test in predicting identification of an attacker. *International Journal of Law and Psychiatry.*

Morgan, C. A., III, Rasmusson, A., Wang, S., Hoyt, G., Hauger, R., & Hazlett, G. (2002). Neuropeptide-Y, cortisol, and subjective distress in humans exposed to acute stress: Replication and extension of previous report. *Biological Psychiatry, 52*(2), 136–142.

Morgan, C. A., III, Southwick, S., Hazlett, G., Rasmusson, A., Hoyt, G., Zimolo, Z. et al. (2004). Relationships among plasma dehydroepiandrosterone in humans exposed to acute stress. *Archives of General Psychiatry, 61*(8), 819–825.

Morgan, C. A., III, Wang, S., Mason, J., Hazlett, G., Fox, P., Southwick, S. M., et al. (2000). Hormone profiles in humans experiencing military survival training. *Biological Psychiatry, 47*, 891–901.

Morgan, C. A., III, Wang, S., Rasmusson, A., Hazlett, G., Anderson, G., & Charney, D. (2001). Relationship among plasma cortisol, catecholamines, neuropeptide-Y, and human performance during exposure to uncontrollable stress. *Psychosomatic Medicine, 63*(3), 412–422.

Morgan, C. A., III, Wang, S., Richardson, E., Hazlett, G., Schnurr, P., & Southwick, S. (2001). Symptoms of dissociation in humans experiencing acute uncontrollable stress: A prospective investigation. *American Psychiatric Association, 158*, 1239–1247.

National Institute of Mental Health. (2002). *Mental health and mass violence: Evidence-based early psychological intervention for victims/survivors of mass violence. A workshop to reach consensus on best practices.* NIH Publication No. 02-5138. Washington, DC: U.S. Government Printing Office.

Nelson, L. F. (1989). When the war doesn't end. *Journal of Psychosocial Nursing, 27*(7), 26–30.

Nice, D., McDonald, B., & McMillian, T. (1981). The families of U.S. Navy prisoners of war five years after reunion. *Journal of Marriage and the Family, 43*(2), 431–437.

Page, W. F., Engdahl, B. E., & Raina, E. E. (1991). Prevalence and correlates of depressive symptoms among former prisoners of war. *The Journal of Nervous and Mental Disease, 179*(11), 670–677.

POW left "thank you" note for Serb guards. (1999, May 4). Retrieved October 11, 2005, from http://www.cnn.com/US/9905/04/prisoners.note/

Rawson, R. A., Obert, J. L., McCann, M. J., & Ling, W. (1993). Neurobehavioral Treatment for Cocaine Dependency: A Preliminary Evaluation. *NIDA Research Monograph, 135*, 92–115.

Rochester, S. I., & Kiley, F. (1999). *Honor bound: American prisoners of war in Southeast Asia, 1961–1973.* Annapolis, MD: Naval Institute Press.

Rojas, D. C., Smith, J. A., Benkers, T. L., Camou, S. L., Reite, M. L., & Rogers, S. J. (2004). Hippocampus and amygdala volumes in parents of children with autistic disorder. *American Journal of Psychiatry, 161*, 2038–2044.

Saab, B. R., Chaaya, M., Doumit, M., & Farhood, L. (2003). Predictors of psychological distress in Lebanese hostages of war. *Social Science and Medicine, 57*, 1249–1257.

Salm, A., Pavelko, M., Krouse, E., Webster, W., Kraszpulski, M., & Birkle, D. (2004). Lateral amygdaloid nucleus expansion in adult rats is associated with exposure to prenatal stress. *Brain Research and Development, 148*, 159–167.

Sargant, W. (1957). *Battle for the mind: A physiology of conversion of brain washing.* London: William Heinemann.

Schumann, C., Hamstra, J., Goodlin-Jones, B., Lotspeich, L., Kwon, H., Buonocore, M. et al. (2004). The amygdala is enlarged in children but not adolescents with autism; the hippocampus is enlarged at all ages. *Journal of Neuroscience, 24*, 6392–6401.

Shiffman, S., Engberg, J., Paty, J. A., Perz, W., Gnys, M., Kassel, J. D. et al. (1997). A day at a time: Predicting smoking lapse from daily urge. *Journal of Abnormal Psychology, 106*, 104–116.

Singer, M. T. (1981). Vietnam prisoners of war, stress, and personality resiliency. *American Journal of Psychiatry, 138*, 345–346.

Solomon, Z., Waysman, M. A., & Neria, Y., Ohry, A., Schwarzwald, J., & Wiener, M. (1999). Positive and negative changes in the lives of Israeli former prisoners of war. *Journal of Social and Clinical Psychology, 18*(4), 419–435.

Sotres-Bayon, F., Bush, D., & LeDoux, J. (2004). Emotional perseveration: An update on prefrontal-amygdala interactions in fear extinction. *Learning and Memory, 11*, 525–535.

Southwick, S., Morgan, C., III, Vythilingam, M., Krystal, J., & Charney, D. (2003, Fall). Emerging neurobiological factors in stress resilience. *PTSD Research Quarterly, 14*(4), 1–3.

Speed, N., Engdahl, B., Schwartz, J., & Eberly, R. (1989). Posttraumatic Stress Disorder as a consequence of the POW experience. *Journal of Nervous and Mental Disorders, 177*, 147–153.

Sperr, E. V., Sperr, S. J., Craft, R. B., & Boudewyns, P. A. (1990). MMPI profiles and posttraumatic symptomatology in former prisoners of war. *Journal of Traumatic Stress, 3*, 369–378.

Sullivan, G., Apergis, J., Bush, D., Johnson, L., Hou, M., & LeDoux, J. (2004). Lesions in the bed nucleus of the stria terminalis disrupt corticosterone and freezing response elicited by contextual not a specific cue-conditioned fear stimulus. *Neuroscience, 128*, 7–14.

Sutker, P. B., Allain, A. N., & Winstead, D. K. (1993). Psychopathology and psychiatric diagnoses of World War II Pacific theater prisoner of war survivors and combat veterans. *The American Journal of Psychiatry, 150*(2), 240–245.

Sutker, P. B., Bugg, F., & Allain, A. N. (1990). Person and situation correlates of posttraumatic stress disorder among POW survivors. *Psychological Reports, 66*, 912–914.

Sutker, P. B., Galina, Z. H., West, J., & Allain, A. N. (1990). Trauma-induced weight loss and cognitive deficits in former prisoners of war. *Journal of Consulting and Clinical Psychology, 58*, 323–328.

Sutker, P. B., Winstead, D. K., Galina, Z. H., & Allain, A. N. (1991). Cognitive deficits and psychopathology, among former prisoners of war and combat veterans of the Korean conflict. *The American Journal of Psychiatry, 148*(1), 67–72.

Sweeny, J. (2002). Saudi Arabia: State of denial, BBC web article. Retrieved October 11, 2005, from http://news.bbc.co.uk/1/hi/programmes/correspondent/2480379.stm

Tennant, C. C., Goulston, K. J., & Dent, O. F. (1986). The psychological effect of being a prisoner of war: Forty years after release. *American Journal of Psychiatry, 143*, 618–621.

Ursano, R. L., & Rundell, J. R. (1990). The prisoner of war. *Military Medicine, 155*(4), 176–180.

Ursano, R. L., Rundell, J. R., Fragala, M. R., Larson, S. G., Jaccard, J. T., Wain, H. J. et al. (1996). The prisoner of war. In A. E. Norwood & R. J. Ursano (Eds.), *Emotional aftermath of the Persian Gulf War: Veterans, families, communities, and nations* (pp. 443–476). Washington, DC: American Psychiatric Association Press.

Van der Kolk, B. A. (1984). *Posttraumatic stress disorder: Psychological and biological sequelae.* Washington, DC: American Psychiatric Press.

Vischer, A. L. (1919). *Barbed Wire Disease: A Psychological Study of the Prisoners of War.* London: Oxford Press.

Walton, M. A., Castro, F.G., & Barrington, E. H. (1994). The role of attributions in abstinence, lapse, and relapse following substance abuse treatment. *Addictive Behaviors, 2,* 319–331.

Washington Headquarters Services, Directorate for Information Operations and Reports (WHS/DIOR) (2005). Selected Manpower Statistics, Fiscal Year 2005.

Williams, D., Hilton, S. M., & Moore, J. (2002). Cognitive measures of the Vietnam-era prisoners of war. *Journal of the American Medical Association, 288*(5), 574–575.

CHAPTER 6

COMBAT STRESS CONTROL: PUTTING PRINCIPLE INTO PRACTICE

Steve J. Lewis

The major heading the [combat stress control] team said, "I'm feeling a lot of anger in this room"…I'm thinking: yeah we're angry. There are people out there who killed our friends and who are still trying to kill us. Of course he sensed anger. We're all pissed off. Who wouldn't be? I think the combat stress team approach is better suited for a single incident, something like an accident to help you get over that bump and move on…this is not just one event; it's every day…we're not just recovering from April 4; we're worried about dying tonight. (Steele, 2004, p. 24)

This quote was relayed to a reporter by a U.S. soldier in Iraq after a week of heavy fighting. After the fighting, a combat stress control team was sent to meet with the soldiers. This quote is a telling description of the challenges combat stress control faces to maintain itself as a credible force multiplier, a military asset that supports the efficiency and efficacy of the war fighter. Over ten years ago, the U.S. Army published its field manual describing the practices and procedures used to provide combat stress control on the battlefield. Since its publication, and following the end of the Cold War, the U.S. military has witnessed a period of almost constant overseas presence, ranging from intense ground combat to peacekeeping and humanitarian assistance operations. In fact, it's been recognized that since the end of the war and prior to the global war on terrorism in Afghanistan and Iraq, the United States witnessed a threefold increase in the number of overseas deployments (Levy, Thie, Sollinger, & Kawata, 2000). This increase comes at a cost with more soldiers participating in multiple deployments and, more recently, a greater reliance on "part-time" or

The views expressed in this chapter are those of the author and do not reflect the official policy or position of the U.S. Department of Defense or the U.S. Government.

citizen-soldiers of the National Guard and reserve components. Mental health providers and military leaders alike are concerned with the costs of these deployments on individual soldier well-being (Adler, Dolan, & Castro, 2000; Bolton, Litz, Britt, Adler, & Roemer, 2001; Britt & Adler, 1999; Hall & Jansen, 1995; MacDonald, Chamberlain, Long, Pereira-Laird, & Mirfin, 1998; Wong et al., 2001) and family functioning (McCarroll et al., 2000; Zeff, Lewis, & Hirsch, 1997). At the center of enhancing and protecting soldier and family well-being are combat stress control activities.

Although treatment of combat stress casualties occurred throughout the history of warfare, it wasn't until the Korean War that the U.S. Army established mobile psychiatric detachments that reinforced existing mental health teams and provided mobile consultation throughout a defined broad area. (For a comprehensive review of the history of Army psychiatry see Rock et al., 1995.) These teams evolved into today's combat stress control (CSC) units and the various mental health sections organic to combat divisions (e.g., the U.S. Army's 82nd Airborne Division has its own 10-person section of mental health providers and paraprofessional counselors) and field medical organizations. My own experience has been as a commander of a 24-person combat stress control team in Europe that deployed in support of a peacekeeping force in Bosnia in 1996 and as a mental health provider assigned to a combat division in Iraq in 2003. The aim of this chapter is to present my own observations on the provision of combat stress control during both combat and peacekeeping operations. I'll examine the historical developments that led to today's combat stress control principles, the elements of a combat stress control program, the challenges associated with providing CSC support, and future directions. To ensure common understanding, I'll use current doctrinal terms recognized throughout the U.S. Department of Defense. Combat stress control, for the purpose of this chapter, describes both actions by leaders and mental health activities provided to soldiers throughout the deployment cycle, from predeployment activities in garrison environments, to deployment activities in the field, and then postdeployment activities upon return from combat or peacekeeping operations. These actions are intended to reduce or prevent the development of combat and operational stress reactions (COSRs) and ultimately reduce the development of posttraumatic stress disorder (PTSD).

Combat Stress Control: An Overview

It has long been recognized that participation in combat leaves an indelible mark on the psyche of the combatant. In the history of modern warfare, soldiers who broke down in combat were originally described as suffering from "shell shock," the putative cause of their breakdown a result of the concussion received from the constant artillery barrages endured during trench warfare (Jones, 1995a). By World War II, the term evolved from psychoneurosis to combat exhaustion, highlighting the recognition that emotional breakdown was not necessarily a form of malingering or "psycho" behavior to avoid combat but rather physical and psychological exhaustion from the physically and emotionally demanding challenges of combat (Jones,

1995b, p. 38). By the end of World War II, the lessons learned in managing psychiatric casualties during war became indoctrinated. Today, combat and operational stress reactions are "the expected, predictable, emotional, intellectual, physical, and/ or behavioral reactions of service members who have been exposed to stressful events in combat or military operations other than war" (Department of Defense, 1999). This definition implies that these are normal, although extreme, reactions to the demands of peacekeeping or combat. In addition, such reactions are assumed to exceed the resources available to the individual soldier. The range of symptoms associated with COSRs are depicted in Table 6.1.

Historically, COSR casualty rates differed based on the type of warfare (i.e., peacekeeping, high-intensity combat, low-intensity combat) and intensity of combat operations (as measured by the number of wounded/killed in action). In Korea, for example, the psychiatric casualty rates for U.S. servicemen was 37 per 1,000 (Jones & Wessely, 2001). In contrast, data provided by Pincus and Benedek (1998), indicated that approximately 6.75 per 1,000 soldiers serving in the Former Yugoslavia during Operation Joint Endeavor required brief treatment in a forward-based mental health facility; fewer than 2 per 1,000 required evacuation. Finally, the rate of psychiatric evacuations per 1,000 service members during Operation Iraqi Freedom was estimated to be approximately 3.5 (U.S. Army Office of the Surgeon General, 2003). To understand these differences, a conceptual model of combat and operational stress is proposed that provides insight into the various aspects of the person and the environment that put individuals at risk for developing a COSR along with understanding protective factors that enhance individual and group reactions to combat.

Gal and Jones (1995), building on a transactional model of stressor appraisal, conceptualized a model of combat stress reactions that not only focused on the appraisal a soldier makes of the differing stressors inherent in combat operations but also included a social informational influence component. Specifically, Gal and Jones proposed that unit commanders served to mediate the soldier's appraisal of the combat environment. Research suggests that the broader social environment, such as coworkers, can also affect an individual's appraisal of the work or deployed environment (Fenlason & Beehr, 1994; Heaney, House, Israel, & Mero, 1995; Lamerson, 1996). This form of social informational influence is considered especially salient when the mission or environment becomes vague or ambiguous. The nature of this appraisal process is graphically depicted in Figure 6.1. As the conceptual model depicts, combat and operational stressor appraisal is moderated by both individual and unit factors. This appraisal process affects the coping mechanisms employed by the soldier and ultimately the soldier's stress reaction (both positive and negative). Today's combat and peacekeeping environment provides a number of stressors that individually or cumulatively may contribute to negative appraisals and the development of COSRs. While each deployment environment is unique, recent research has identified a number of potential and nearly universal stressors.

Table 6.1
Combat and Operational Stress Reactions

Physical	Behavioral	Cognitive	Emotional
Somatic complaints	Inattention, carelessness	Hypervigilance	Fear, anxiety
Headaches	Sleep disturbance	Loss of confidence	Anger, rage
Exhaustion	Social isolation, withdrawal	Loss of hope and faith	Grief
Nausea	Impaired duty performance	Memory impairment	Guilt, self-doubt
Impaired speech	Erratic behavior, outbursts	Suicidal ideation	Terror
Impaired vision, touch, hearing	Recklessness, indiscipline	Homicidal ideation	Depression
Weakness and paralysis	Going absent without leave, desertion	Apathy	
Excessive sick call	Combat refusal	Delusions, hallucinations	
	Criminal behavior		
	Torture		
	Alcohol or drug abuse		
	Panic		
	Negligent injury, self-inflicted wounds		

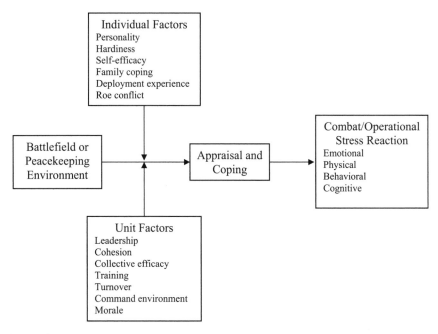

Figure 6.1
Graphical Depiction of a Cognitive Model of Combat Stress Reactions

Combat Stressors

Combat is an obvious stressor associated with combat stress reactions. As described by Martin and colleagues (1992), combat stressors include exposure to death and wounding of combatants and noncombatants and personal threat. Research shows a great deal of variability in exposure to death or wounding of friendly combatants in recent conflicts. For example, 75 percent of soldiers who fought during Operation Iraqi Freedom observed wounded or dead American soldiers (Hoge et al., 2004). In contrast, only 9 percent of soldiers who participated in Operation Desert Storm in 1990 witnessed dead or wounded American soldiers (Martin et al., 1992). However, not all soldiers in combat experience combat stress reactions of such severity that makes them incapable of performing their duties. Thus, it is important for mental health providers to understand what factors both individually and combined might predict combat stress reactions so that interventions are appropriately targeted. For example, in their research of Israeli soldiers who developed combat stress reactions during the 1982 Lebanon War, Solomon, Mikulincer, and Hobfoll (1986) observed that the lack of both instrumental and emotional support from leaders along with battle intensity served as predictive factors for those who broke down in combat. Additionally, they observed that loneliness, as predicted by battle intensity and the lack of officer support, was the strongest predictor of combat breakdown. Their research supports the notion that individual factors, unit factors, and battlefield factors contribute to the soldier's appraisal of the combat environment. Other battlefield factors worth mentioning include type of battle (e.g., offense, defense, day/night operations, guerilla warfare), length and intensity of combat, battle uncertainty, and environmental conditions.

Peacekeeping Stressors

The antecedent variables depicted in the conceptual model are also pertinent in understanding stressors associated with peacekeeping and operations other than war. In addition to individual and unit factors, the peacekeeping environment may contribute to the extent to which soldiers develop operational stress reactions. Given the rise of the number of peacekeeping operations, recent research has focused on stressors and outcomes for these missions (Hall, 1996; Hall & Jansen, 1995; Lamerson, 1996; Lamerson & Kelloway, 1996; Lewis, 2004; Litz, 1996; Litz, Orsillo, Friedman, Ehlich, & Batres, 1997; Wong et al., 2001; Young et al., 1999). In their survey of medical personnel deployed to support a peacekeeping mission, Bartone, Adler, and Vaitkus (1998) observed that multiple stressors affected soldier well-being. These include separation from family, exposure to potentially traumatic events, mission ambiguity, role conflict, and poor leadership. In fact, Britt (1998) argues that psychological ambiguity is a critical factor associated with poor psychological well-being during and after peacekeeping operations. A number of researchers support Britt's contention. Miller and Moskos (1995) observed that soldiers experienced a significant degree of ambiguity associated with the role of humanitarian during Operation Restore Hope in Somalia. Such ambiguity led to adoption of either a warrior role or humanitarian role. Their findings indicated that both roles contributed to psychological distress when encountering aspects of the environment that conflicted with the role the soldier adopted (e.g., the "humanitarian" who continues to receive direct and indirect fire while trying to deliver humanitarian aid). Litz and colleagues (1997), seeking to identify predictive factors of PTSD associated with peacekeeping operations, observed that negative aspects of peacekeeping (à la mission ambiguity), and low-magnitude stressors such as separation from family members significantly contributed to the development of PTSD. These studies and others recognize that various stressors, not just trauma exposure, are common in deployed environments and should be considered targets of intervention by CSC personnel and leaders.

Combat Stress Control Principles

The model of combat stress reactions presented earlier in this chapter and depicted in Figure 6.1 identifies targets of intervention that are directed at both the individual appraisal of the combat environment and those activities that enhance the social environment. It's important to remember that combat stress control is not just the sole responsibility of mental health providers but also encompasses the various actions leaders may take to enhance the social environment. Mental health providers

Table 6.2
BICEPS Principles of Combat Stress Control Treatment Activities

---

B—Brevity; treatment services provided are brief in nature, with an emphasis on rapid recovery to stable level of functioning.

I—Immediacy; treatment services are provided as soon as the soldier begins to exhibit maladaptive combat stress reactions.

C—Centrality; treatment services are coordinated across the joint services with a unity of effort providing.

E—Expectancy; treatment services emphasize the transient nature of combat stress reactions, with the expectation of rapid return to full duty.

P—Proximity; treatment services are provided as close to the point of injury (or as close to the soldiers unit of assignment) as possible.

S—Simplicity; treatment services are relatively simple, with an emphasis on meeting basic needs of safety, sleep, sanitation, etc.

---

must be knowledgeable about these activities and traits of healthy organizations to be able to provide information and assistance to unit leaders in order to promote organizational well-being. From a mental health intervention perspective, through years of lessons learned on the battlefield and working with people in crisis, six key principles have been promulgated (Hicklin, 2003; True & Benway, 1992). Understood easily as BICEPS (Table 6.2) these principles provide the basis of mental health-related combat stress control activities.

The BICEPS principles grew from the principles of proximity to battle, immediacy, and expectation of recovery (PIE) promulgated by French, British, and American psychiatrists in World War I and later employed in subsequent conflicts to include World War II, Korea, and Vietnam, and by the Israeli Army in the Lebanon conflict (Jones & Wessely, 2003). The BICEPS principles support the primary goals of primary prevention and early intervention activities performed by mental health providers in combat; serve as the guiding framework in developing treatment interventions for COSR casualties; and conform with the theoretical conceptualization of COSRs as temporary responses to the rigors of combat and noncombat operations. Finally, these principles serve to help military planners determine how to best deploy and utilize mental health personnel.

Combat Stress Control Activities

The language of health prevention and wellness defines CSC activities. More specifically, CSC support activities fall under either primary or secondary prevention (Baker & Armfield, 1996; Department of Defense, 1999). Primary prevention interventions are designed to prevent the development of an illness before actual exposure. Examples include the provision of condoms to prevent the spread of sexually transmitted disease and immunization programs. Secondary prevention seeks to reduce the development of long-term disability by providing services at the earliest sign of illness. For example, screening tests in health care settings ensure prompt and early delivery of services.

CSC Primary Prevention

The key to primary prevention is to prepare soldiers before the onset of the stressor to develop resiliency and prevent the development of COSRs and has the ultimate aim of reducing the number of combat veterans who later develop PTSD. One of the key elements of U.S. Army doctrine is to encourage leaders, both officers and noncommissioned officers, to take measures to prevent the development of COSRs. To promote leadership involvement, field manuals were developed specifically outlining the various strategies to enhance combat stress control. Examples include (Department of the Army, 1994b),

1. Conduct realistic and demanding training.
2. Promote unit cohesion and esprit de corps.
3. Keep information flowing.
4. Stabilize the home front.
5. Prepare the unit to endure battle losses.
6. Prepare for nuclear, biological, or chemical weapons threat.
7. Practice sleep discipline.
8. Protect the physical well-being of the troops.
9. Assure physical fitness.

Each of these is intended to promote individual readiness and collective efficacy, develop hardy soldiers, prepare soldiers and families for the rigors of extended separation, build cohesive units with strong social support from peers and leaders, enhance leader effectiveness, and reduce the potential for mission ambiguity and role conflict. While many of these strategies seem intuitive, I've found it is vitally important to back these principles up with empirical data whenever available.

A recent study of soldiers deployed to Iraq observed that over 70 percent of the respondents were not psychologically prepared for the rigors of combat and exposure to traumatic events (U.S. Army Office of the Surgeon General, 2003). This finding points to the need for tough and realistic training that enhances both self- and collective efficacy (i.e., the belief in one's unit to successfully perform combat and peacekeeping operations) both of which can enhance personal resiliency. Jex and Bliese (1999) observed that collective efficacy moderated the relationship between work overload and job satisfaction. Their findings empirically demonstrated that individuals who were in units with high levels of collective efficacy experienced greater job satisfaction under conditions of high workload than counterparts in units with low collective efficacy. Such job satisfaction can also contribute to lower levels of psychological distress. Similarly, collective efficacy has been observed to enhance group performance in both novel and routine environments (Marks, 1999).

Cohesion and leadership have also been demonstrated to promote enhanced psychological well-being in deployed environments. An early study of soldiers assigned to special operations, airborne, and mechanized infantry units, for example, demonstrated that soldiers in units with the highest ratings of cohesion experienced significantly higher levels of psychological and physical well-being (Manning & Fullerton, 1988). Other, more recent studies, have also documented the positive relationship between group cohesion and psychological well-being (Arincorayan, 2000; Bliese & Britt, 2001; Bliese & Halverson, 1998). The behaviors of leaders not only foster a social environment that builds cohesion, but independently contribute to improved coping and psychological well-being. For example, research has demonstrated that when leaders exhibited more directive and supportive leadership styles in a vague or ambiguous peacekeeping environment, soldiers experienced less psychological distress postdeployment than in units where leaders were rated as less effective (Lewis, 2004). These findings provide preliminary evidence for the moderating relationship depicted in the conceptual model.

Combat stress control personnel are responsible for getting out and about once deployed. Pincus and Benedek (1998) suggest that their aggressive command consultation program initiated early in the deployment cycle promoted enhanced access to mental health services and may have even contributed to a substantial reduction in the number of suicides during their one-year deployment to Bosnia. Likewise, in their study of British peacekeepers deployed to Bosnia, Deahl and colleagues (2000) contend that the low rates of PTSD observed in their sample could be attributed to a robust operational stress training package delivered to soldiers before their deployment. Primary preventive efforts promote credibility with the supported command and provide leaders with specific guidance to prevent and reduce the number of COSRs (Martin & Campbell, 1999). While not inclusive, examples of primary prevention CSC activities include:

1. Command consultation—activities designed to inform noncommissioned officers, commanders, and others on the potential stressors in the deployed environment.

2. Unit surveys—information collection with small groups of soldiers or individuals designed to identify unit-specific problems, identify stressors, and provide psychoeducational information on combat stress control. (Examples of questions to ask during a unit survey are outlined in Table 6.3.) These can also be conducted in the form of questionnaires as described by Pincus and Benedek (1998).

3. Psychoeducational classes and briefings—examples of classes and briefings that CSC personnel should be prepared to provide include identification and treatment of COSRs, briefings to medical providers on COSRs, suicide-prevention awareness, leadership counseling, effective leadership with an emphasis on countering mission ambiguity, and preparation of families for soldier absence/return.

4. Handouts and public service announcements—CSC personnel need to be able to provide brief information to soldiers and leaders on a number of topics to include depression, suicide, combat stress control, rapid anxiety management strategies (e.g., breathing retraining, cognitive reframing, etc.), managing conflict, sexual assault prevention, and redeployment. Throughout my own deployments, I was asked to provide information to be used in camp newsletters, redeployment activities, and public service announcements broadcast over theater-available radio produced by the Armed Forces Network.

These activities serve multiple purposes. First, they're intended to prepare soldiers and leaders for the rigors of combat. Second, as discussed earlier, these activities are intended to enhance the credibility of CSC and mental health personnel to leaders

Table 6.3
Unit Survey/Morale Survey Sample

These are a sample of questions to measure morale, cohesion, leadership, loyalty to the unit, and command climate. Interview questions should be structured from observations from previous encounters and leader concerns.

1. What is the unit's general mission?
2. How does your job affect the success of that mission?
3. What is the reputation of this unit among other units?
4. Are disciplinary actions on the rise or higher than sister units?
5. What training activities has the unit participated in lately?
6. How does recent or coming training support the unit's mission?
7. What operations have you conducted recently?
8. Do you feel you were adequately prepared to conduct these operations?
9. How is training and personal time managed?
10. What are the leader's values and priorities?
11. Does the group believe its leaders are competent, trustworthy, and concerned for soldier well-being?
12. Are leaders available when problems arise?
13. Does information about changes, coming events, and so forth, get all the way down to the lowest level through the chain of command or via informal channels?
14. How are family problems/concerns resolved?
15. Do you have confidence in your peers?
16. Are people in this unit close to each other?
17. Do subordinates receive credit for their accomplishments?
18. What helps morale in this unit?
19. What improvements would you recommend to your leaders?
20. If you could change one thing what would it be?
21. Do you feel you were psychologically prepared for the rigors of combat/peacekeeping?

and soldiers. One aspect of credibility is to have concrete and at times quantifiable information for leaders about the current stress threat (obtained during predeployment and deployment unit surveys), trends, and strategies to enhance soldier and unit performance. Third, routine and regular contact with mental health providers in differing contexts along with credible information on the nature of COSRs may help to reduce the stigma commonly associated with seeking mental health services (Britt, 2000; Hoge et al., 2004).

Secondary Prevention

Often considered the bread and butter of combat stress control activities, secondary prevention efforts in CSC are intended to minimize the impact of COSRs and other emotional problems on individual and unit performance (see Table 6.4 for an overview of CSC implementation strategies). Ultimately, secondary preventive strategies seek to reduce or eliminate long-term psychological problems to include PTSD. Examples of secondary prevention activities include:

1. Neuropsychiatric triage—the rapid evaluation of COSR casualties and disposition of the casualty to the appropriate level of care.
2. Management and treatment of COSRs and other emotional problems—use of simple and brief treatment methods and crisis intervention strategies (to include psychological debriefings).
3. Psychoeducational programs intent on normalizing combat stress reactions and providing practical advice on anxiety management and stressor appraisal.
4. Screening programs before and after deployment to identify those experiencing psychological distress to ensure they have access to care throughout all phases of deployment (Department of the Army, 1994a).

Research on early intervention with victims of motor vehicle accidents, for example, demonstrates that specific interventions provided shortly after the trauma helped reduce acute stress reactions and reduced the development of PTSD (Bryant, Harvey, Dang, Sackville, & Basten, 1998). In the deployed environment, such early intervention can be facilitated by providing services as close to the soldiers' unit as possible by separating the mental health assets into smaller teams. Pincus and Benedek (1998) reported using an approach in which such smaller mental health teams traveled to all the base camps within their area of responsibility providing outpatient treatment and consultation. Those who displayed more acute stress reactions were held at facilities close to their unit and offered respite, coping skills, and stress management training. Similarly, a study of suicides during Operation Iraqi Freedom in 2003 observed that proximity and access to mental health teams may have contributed to improved psychological well-being. In contrast, those who experienced trouble accessing mental health teams because of either a remote assignment or lack of awareness of available CSC providers expressed increased stress and arousal symptoms (U.S. Army Office of the Surgeon General, 2003).

Table 6.4
Keys to Successful CSC Program Implementation

Combat stress control is the commander's responsibility. He or she is aided in this responsibility by mental health and CSC personnel who work in concert with other support personnel (i.e., chaplains, NCOs, medical personnel, and principal staff). Early involvement with commanders promotes access to care and credibility among soldiers and NCOs. From my own experience, the following strategies have been successful in providing combat stress control:

Conduct an initial stress threat assessment and continually update it. Upon arrival in any theater, I immediately begin to conduct a stress threat assessment. For me, this involves gathering information on stressors affecting soldiers, using both observation and informal interviews with soldiers, leaders, and other support personnel listed above. The stress threat assessment is a continuing process and requires periodic review as the deployment environment changes. Once sufficient information has been gathered, I begin to disseminate my findings. Whenever possible, I quantify those observations that are quantifiable. Lastly, this assessment is not credible without promoting realistic strategies that leaders can use to minimize the impact of these stressors. This is where empirical research on unit dynamics and intervention strategies can prove beneficial.

Emphasize the mission of combat stress control. Most commanders are concerned about psychiatric evacuations and loss of combat power resulting from these evacuations. Reminding commanders that a rapid return to duty is a primary goal of CSC interventions will alleviate many of these concerns. Education about the interventions used, the rationale, and likely response will also promote credibility.

Understand the mission and composition of the unit. Having a thorough understanding of the units you're supporting, their mission, composition of personnel (i.e., jobs, ranks, etc), and any other unique information (i.e., National Guard versus active-duty unit) ensures that interventions are tailored to the unit. Similarly, commanders recognize that you're interested in how to best help him or her accomplish their mission.

Table 6.4 continued

Plan unit interventions and obtain unit support. One time I was on a routine visit to an outlying encampment when I was approached by a chaplain requesting that I perform a psychological debriefing with a platoon of infantrymen after they had been involved in a hectic firefight. I met with the commander, and he also believed it would be helpful. I was scheduled to leave the camp later that day, so time was critical. I gathered the soldiers and soon realized that not only were the soldiers upset about being called together during "down time," but they also believed that their leaders viewed them as too aggressive and that I was being asked to address this with them. Despite my best efforts to keep the discussion moving through the recent action, the lack of preparation and limited prior involvement with these young men only seemed to detract from the interaction. In hindsight, I would have preferred to meet with the command group and the primary leaders of the unit longer and gain a better understanding of what the unit desired prior to agreeing to "do something."

Keep information flowing. Whenever possible, keep the leadership well informed about CSC successes, stress threat information, trends, and areas of concern. Be ready to discuss redeployment strategies early in the deployment cycle. Short sound bites or "drive-bys" of critical information on such topics as enhancing unit cohesion, social support, fighting boredom, anxiety management, suicide awareness, sexual assault awareness, command referral guidelines, or depression are invaluable in promoting CSC prevention. Keep accurate data on utilization and be ready to address general trends. Lastly, whenever a soldier is evacuated out of your area for psychiatric care, continue to monitor progress and prepare the command for the soldier's return.

Of the secondary preventive strategies most often cited in the literature, psychological debriefings (sometimes referred to as critical incident stress debriefings, critical event debriefings, and historical group debriefings) remain one of the most controversial, albeit most widely used, interventions. Psychological debriefing research with military personnel in combat and peacekeeping operations has demonstrated mixed results (Deahl et al., 2000; Lewis, 2003; Solomon, Mikulincer, & Hobfoll, 1986). Inherent in the debate surrounding psychological debriefings is the ability of this intervention, alone or as part of a more comprehensive organizationally bound stress management program, to alleviate acute stress reactions and prevent the development of PTSD. While the evidence remains inconclusive, practitioners are cautioned in embracing the putative long-term efficacy of psychological debriefing. Conservatively speaking, debriefings enhance unit cohesion and social support, allow the group to reach a consensus as to what happened (Shalev, Peri, Rogel-Fuchs, Ursano, & Marlowe, 1998), provide concrete anxiety management strategies, educate recipients about stress reactions, and promote future use of mental health resources. The quote at the beginning of this chapter highlights one of the major challenges still to be overcome by mental health personnel when debriefing is mandated following combat operations. The soldiers appeared to perceive the debriefing as simply a one-shot intervention and not part of a regular combat stress control program. This shortcoming points to the importance of combat stress personnel developing routine relationships with leaders and soldiers before implementing any intervention strategy to reinforce the credibility and relevance of CSC programs.

In addition to psychological debriefings, doctrinal treatment strategies for acute combat stress casualties are best described using the acronym "four Rs" (Department of the Army, 1994a). These include (a) reassure the soldier that his or her reaction is a nonpathological response to the demands of combat, (b) rest, (c) replenish (e.g., eat, shower, rehydrate), and (d) restore confidence. The four Rs encompass three of the BICEPS principles (brevity, expectancy, and simplicity) described earlier in this chapter. Simplistically understood as "three hots, a cot, and a shower," case studies reveal that these strategies were able to return soldiers to their units shortly after they were given brief respite from the rigors of combat (Jones, 1995b; Solomon & Benbenishty, 1986). While historically the return to duty rate in modern combat and peacekeeping operations is high, Shalev (1997) contends that, overall, combat stress strategies are ineffective in the later development of PTSD. Ultimately, despite a large contention of mental health providers in Iraq, CSC interventions did little to actually prevent the development of PTSD beyond those rates observed with Vietnam era veterans (Hoge et al., 2004).

Postdeployment secondary-prevention activities take the shape of screening and psychoeducational programs. As early as 1997, legislation mandated that service members be screened for psychological problems upon being redeployed from overseas duty (Department of Defense, 1997). The *VA/DoD Clinical Practice Guideline for the Management of Post-Traumatic Stress Disorder* (2004) recommends regular screening for PTSD in primary care settings. In addition to required screening, CSC personnel are able to help the unit command identify potential high-risk soldiers by evaluating individuals who experienced significant relationship turmoil, severe illness or death of a family member, financial problems, or had a history of emotional problems before deployment. Finally, the deployment cycle should not be complete until soldiers and families are educated about potential problems that may arise following an extended operational absence. Briefings and classes on the emotional cycle of deployment should be offered to both soldiers and their family members within 60 days of redeployment to highlight potential areas of conflict and to acknowledge the changes that have occurred since deployment.

Future Directions

Combat stress control activities have been part of the doctrinal template within the U.S. Army for over ten years. Only recently, the Department of Defense required the other services to develop a combat stress control doctrine (Department of Defense, 1999). The extent to which the doctrine is well established both within the services and across the services remains poor. In the most comprehensive study of mental health services in Iraq, broad differences in interventions, application of doctrine, and primary and secondary prevention strategies were observed.

> More than half of the behavioral health providers interviewed reported that they did not know what COSC doctrine was, or did not support it.…Providers were divided between the medical and preventive models as a means of delivering behavioral health.…Without instruments to assess Soldier/unit needs, behavioral health providers made assumptions about needs of the community and relied upon familiar intervention models. Providers with COSC training favored preventive strategies to promote wellness in the population—sometimes to the exclusion of needed clinical interventions. Providers with medical or clinical backgrounds resorted to the "medical model" to evaluate and treat behavioral health disorders to the population—to the exclusion of doing preventive outreach and interventions. (U.S. Army Office of the Surgeon General, 2003, pp. 16–17)

These differences point to some of the major challenges facing combat stress control. The greatest priority facing combat stress control support is to demonstrate effectiveness. At the root of this issue is relevance and credibility. As mentioned previously, in spite of the "sufficient" numbers of mental health providers in recent combat operations in Iraq (U.S. Army Office of the Surgeon General, 2003, p. 15), subsequent postdeployment studies identify rates of PTSD symptomatology similar to Vietnam-era veterans (Hoge et al., 2004). If the ultimate strategy of CSC operations is prevention, then the rate of psychiatric illness, specifically PTSD, is the hallmark of successful prevention. Therefore, it can be concluded that current CSC programs were not effective in preventing or reducing the prevalence of psychological problems from the Iraq conflict because the rates of psychological problems are not lower than those found in previous conflicts (Jones & Wessely, 2003).

In addition to monitoring return-to-duty rates and rates of psychiatric illness occurrence, researchers and CSC personnel need to continue to examine organizational dynamics. Not only should researchers and CSC personnel examine the extent to which these characteristics buffer soldiers from developing stress reactions but also what programs, if any, enhance organizational and leader effectiveness. Personnel providing CSC support should be prepared to measure dynamics like cohesion, collective efficacy, self-efficacy, leadership effectiveness, and morale and be prepared to report these findings to units as well as examine across-group differences. Whenever possible, standardized measures should be used, although there have been examples of self-developed measures distributed widely to soldiers in deployed operations. Similarly, more in-depth information on these organizational characteristics may be achieved through qualitative inquiry, using small focus groups in the manner of a unit survey.

Inherent in the issue of effectiveness is the use of empirically validated intervention strategies. For example, as discussed earlier, psychological debriefings are widely used by CSC personnel and were in fact cited by the latest analysis of behavioral health services in the War in Iraq as a primary intervention strategy that should be regularly employed (U.S. Army Office of the Surgeon General, 2003). While intuitively appealing, there remain many questions and doubts about the effectiveness of psychological debriefings (Bisson, McFarlane, & Rose, 2000; Lewis, 2003). As mentioned previously, debriefings offer leaders an additional tool to enhance organizational effectiveness. A controlled study of group debriefings at the end of a peacekeeping tour in Kosovo suggested that perception of organizational support was greater in groups that received a debriefing in comparison to groups that received no intervention or a psychoeducational briefing (Adler et al., 2004). This study was unique and promising in that it was prospective and used intact naturally occurring groups that were exposed to similar traumatic events. Current efforts are under way to replicate this study with those returning from extended combat operations. More recently, and similarly promising, the Veterans Administration and Department of Defense collaboratively published practice guidelines for the treatment of combat stress reactions, acute stress disorders, and PTSD (Department of Veterans Affairs & Department of Defense, 2004). These guidelines should serve as a starting point for all practitioners who serve in peacekeeping and combat operations, because they develop specific treatment interventions for individuals suffering from COSRs. Not only should CSC personnel use empirically-based interventions, but they also are uniquely situated to be both the developers and researchers of new technologies aimed at both primary and secondary preventive efforts. Whenever possible, CSC leaders should seek to collaborate with researchers to validate and test various technologies. In my own experience, I've found military research psychologists are very interested in the topic of combat stress control and invaluable in developing potential outcome measures to evaluate program effectiveness.

A continual challenge for all mental health activities in the military is the perceived stigma that individuals experience when they seek help for emotional problems (Britt, 2000; Hoge et al., 2004). Research on stigma shows that knowledge about emotional problems along with firsthand experience/knowledge of someone who suffers from a mental illness is most effective in reducing the stigma associated with seeking help (Alexander & Link, 2003; Couture & Penn, 2003). However, there remains little understanding of how to breach this stigma with a male-dominant organization and within an organizational culture that considers emotional problems as indicative of character weakness and defect. Illustrative of this phenomenon, a senior NCO in an infantry unit I provided support to, once rebuked his soldiers who were seeking mental health services by asking them, "What's the matter with you, you got sand in your vagina?"

One possibility is to promote CSC programs using the language and strategies in sports psychology. Sports psychologists have embraced cognitive–behavioral strategies to promote performance and anxiety management in pressure-filled situations. Combat stress control would do well by simply changing the language from "stress management" to "performance enhancement," for example. While some may view this suggestion as simply relabeling the same interventions, I argue that this strategy involves a completely new Zeitgeist. The stigma issue presents a great opportunity for practitioners and researchers to collaborate on the effectiveness of a program with an emphasis on performance enhancement, anxiety reduction, cognitive restructuring, guided imagery, and improvement of self- and collective efficacy.

Inarguably, combat stress control has made substantial gains in military circles and continues to influence delivery of emergency mental health services and crisis intervention both inside and outside the armed forces. Recent evidence of these gains include the Department of Defense requirement to establish programs across the services and standardize these programs whenever possible, the joint Department of Defense and Veterans Administration practice guidelines, and the interest in soldier well-being observed almost regularly in the popular media. The current focus of CSC activities on primary and secondary prevention appears to be effective in determining intervention strategies and is pivotal in reducing the emphasis on pathology. The psychiatric principles, identified nearly a century ago, remain pertinent in understanding the underlying philosophy of combat stress control. However, challenges still remain that should only serve to enhance the credibility and relevancy of combat stress control in modern warfare and peacekeeping operations. Overcoming these challenges requires an emphasis on connecting researchers and practitioners to test conceptual models and intervention strategies and to improve measures that can determine the effectiveness of prevention programs.

References

Adler, A. B., Dolan, C. A., & Castro, C. A. (2000, September). *US soldier peacekeeping experiences and wellbeing after returning from deployment to Kosovo.* Paper presented at the International Applied Military Psychology Symposium, Split, Croatia.

Adler, A., Suvak, M. K., Litz, B. T., Castro, C. A., Wright, K. M., Thomas, J., & Williams, L. (2004). *A controlled trial of group debriefing in the military: Preliminary findings.* Poster presented at the 38th annual meeting of the Association for Advancement of Behavior Therapy, New Orleans, LA.

Alexander, L. A., & Link, B. G. (2003). The impact of contact on stigmatizing attitudes toward people with mental illness. *Journal of Mental Health, 12*(3), 271–289.

Arincorayan, D. F. K. (2000). *Leadership, group cohesion and coping in relationship to soldiers' stress levels.* Unpublished doctoral dissertation, The Catholic University of America, Washington, DC.

Baker, M. S., & Armfield, F. (1996). Preventing post-traumatic stress disorders in military medical personnel. *Military Medicine, 161*(5), 262–264.

Bartone, P. T., Adler, A. B., & Vaitkus, M. A. (1998). Dimensions in psychological stress in peacekeeping operations. *Military Medicine, 163,* 587-593.

Bisson, J. I., McFarlane, A. C., & Rose, S. (2000). Psychological debriefing. In E. B. Foa, T. Keane & M. J. Friedman (Eds.), *Effective treatments for PTSD* (pp. 39–59). New York: Guilford.

Bliese, P. D., & Britt, T. W. (2001). Social support, group consensus and stressor-strain relationships: Social context matters. *Journal of Organizational Behavior, 22,* 425–436.

Bliese, P. D., & Halverson, R. R. (1998). Group consensus and psychological well-being: A large field study. *Journal of Applied Social Psychology, 28,* 563–580.

Bolton, E. E., Litz, B. T., Britt, T. W., Adler, A., & Roemer, L. (2001). Reports of prior exposure to potentially traumatic events and PTSD in troops poised for deployment. *Journal of Traumatic Stress, 14,* 249–256.

Britt, T. W. (1998). Psychological ambiguities in peacekeeping. In H. J. Langholtz (Ed.), *The psychology of peacekeeping* (pp. 111–128). Westport, CT: Praeger.

Britt, T. W. (2000). The stigma of psychological problems in a work environment: Evidence from the screening of service members returning from Bosnia. *Journal of Applied Social Psychology, 30,* 1599–1618.

Britt, T. W., & Adler, A. B. (1999). Stress and health during medical humanitarian assistance missions. *Military Medicine, 164,* 275–279.

Bryant, R. A., Harvey, A. G., Dang, S. T., Sackville, T., & Basten, C. (1998). Treatment of acute stress disorder: A comparison of cognitive-behavioral therapy and supportive counseling. *Journal of Consulting and Clinical Psychology, 66*(5), 862–866.

Couture, S. M., & Penn, D. L. (2003). Interpersonal contact and the stigma of mental illness: A review of the literature. *Journal of Mental Health, 12*(3), 291–305.

Deahl, M. P., Srinivasan, M., Jones, N., Thomas, J., Neblett, C., & Jolly, A. (2000). Preventing psychological trauma in soldiers: The role of operational stress training and psychological debriefing. *British Journal of Medical Psychology, 73,* 77–85.

Department of Defense. (1997). *Joint medical surveillance* (Department of Defense Directive No. 6490.2). Washington, DC: Author.

Department of Defense. (1999). *Combat stress control (CSC) programs* (Department of Defense Directive No. 6490.5). Washington, DC: Author.

Department of the Army. (1994a). *FM 8-51, combat stress control in a theater of operations.* Washington, DC: Author.

Department of the Army. (1994b). *FM 22-100, leaders' manual for combat stress control.* Washington, DC: Author.

Department of Veterans Affairs & Department of Defense. (2004). *VA/DoD clinical practice guideline for the management of post-traumatic stress disorder* (Report). Washington, DC: Author.

Fenlason, K., & Beehr, T. A. (1994). Social support and occupational stress: Effects of talking to others. *Journal of Organizational Behavior, 15,* 157–176.

Gal, R., & Jones, F. D. (1995). A psychological model of combat stress. In F. D. Jones, L. R. Sparacino, V. L. Wilcox, J. M. Rothberg, & J. W. Stokes (Eds.), *War psychiatry* (pp. 133–148). Falls Church, VA: U.S. Army Office of the Surgeon General.

Hall, D. P. (1996). Stress, suicide, and military service during Operation Uphold Democracy. *Military Medicine, 161*, 159–162.

Hall, D. P., & Jansen, J. A. (1995). Stress and arousal in deployment of a combat support hospital. *Military Medicine, 160*, 581–583.

Heaney, C. A., House, J. S., Israel, B. A., & Mero, R. P. (1995). The relationship of organizational and social coping resources to employee coping behaviour: A longitudinal analysis. *Work and Stress, 9*, 416–431.

Hicklin, T. A. (2003). Methods for controlling combat stress: Evolving over time. *Psychiatric Annals, 33*, 720–724.

Hoge, C. W., Castro, C. A., Messer, S. C., McGurk, D., Cotting, D. I., & Koffman, R. L. (2004). Combat duty in Iraq and Afghanistan, mental health problems, and barriers to care. *The New England Journal of Medicine, 351*(1), 13–22.

Jex, S. M., & Bliese, P. D. (1999). Efficacy beliefs as a moderator of the impact of work-related stressors: A multilevel study. *Journal of Applied Psychology, 84*, 349–361.

Jones, E., & Wessely, S. (2001). Psychiatric battle casualties: An intra- and interwar comparison. *British Journal of Psychiatry, 178*, 242–247.

Jones, E., & Wessely, S. (2003). "Forward psychiatry" in the military: Its origin and effectiveness. *Journal of Traumatic Stress, 16*, 411–419.

Jones, F. D. (1995a). Psychiatric lessons of war. In F. D. Jones, L. R. Sparacino, V. L. Wilcox, J. M. Rothberg, & J. W. Stokes (Eds.), *War psychiatry* (pp. 1–33). Falls Church, VA: U.S. Army Office of the Surgeon General.

Jones, F. D. (1995b). Traditional warfare combat stress casualties. In F. D. Jones, L. R. Sparacino, V. L. Wilcox, J. M. Rothberg, & J. W. Stokes (Eds.), *War psychiatry* (pp. 35–61). Falls Church, VA: U.S. Army Office of the Surgeon General.

Lamerson, C. D. (1996). *Peacekeeping stress: Testing a model of organizational and personal outcomes.* Unpublished doctoral dissertation, University of Guelph, Ontario, Canada.

Lamerson, C. D., & Kelloway, E. K. (1996). Towards a model of peacekeeping stress: Traumatic and contextual influences. *Canadian Psychology, 37*, 195–204.

Levy, C. M., Thie, H., Sollinger, J. M., & Kawata, J. H. (2000). *Army PERSTEMPO in the post cold war era.* Santa Monica, CA: RAND.

Lewis, S. J. (2003). Do one-shot preventive interventions for PTSD work? A systematic research synthesis of psychological debriefings. *Aggression and Violent Behavior, 8*, 329–343.

Lewis, S. J. (2004). A multi-level, longitudinal study of the strain reducing effects of group efficacy, group cohesion, and leader behaviors on military personnel performing peacekeeping operations. *Dissertation Abstracts International, 64*(10), 3846A (UMI No. AAT 3109514).

Litz, B. T. (1996). The psychological demands of peacekeeping for military personnel. *NCP Clinical Quarterly, 6*(1), 3–8.

Litz, B. T., Orsillo, S. M., Friedman, M. J., Ehlich, P., & Batres, A. (1997). An investigation of posttraumatic stress disorder associated with peacekeeping duty in Somalia for United States military personnel. *American Journal of Psychiatry, 154*, 178–184.

MacDonald, C., Chamberlain, K., Long, N., Pereira-Laird, J., & Mirfin, K. (1998). Mental health, physical health and stressors reported by New Zealand defense force peacekeepers: A longitudinal study. *Military Medicine, 163*, 477–481.

Manning, F. J., & Fullerton, T. D. (1988). Health and well-being in highly cohesive units of the U.S. Army. *Journal of Applied Psychology, 18*, 503–519.

Marks, M. (1999). A test of the impact of collective efficacy in routine and novel performance environments. *Human Performance, 12*(3–4), 295–309.

Martin, J. A., & Campbell, S. J. (1999). The role of the social work officer in support of combat and noncombat operations. In J. G. Daley (Ed.), *Social work practice in the military* (pp. 137–164). New York: Haworth.

Martin, J. A., Vaitkus, M. A., Marlowe, D., Bartone, P. T., Gifford, R. K., & Wright, K. M. (1992, September/October). Psychological well-being among US soldiers deployed from Germany to the Gulf War. *Journal of the U.S. Army Medical Department*, 29–34.

McCarroll, J. E., Ursano, R. J., Liu, X., Thayer, L. E., Newby, J. H., Norwood, A. E., & Fullerton, C. S. (2000). Deployment and the probability of spousal aggression by U.S. Army soldiers. *Military Medicine, 165*, 41–44.

Miller, L. L., & Moskos, C. (1995). Humanitarians or warriors? Race, gender, and combat status in Operation Restore Hope. *Armed Forces & Society, 21*, 615–637.

Pincus, S. H., & Benedek, D. M. (1998). Operational stress control in the former Yugoslavia: A joint endeavor. *Military Medicine, 163*, 358–362.

Rock, N. L., Stokes, J. W., Koshes, R. J., Fagan, J., Cline, W. R., & Jones, F. D. (1995). U.S. Army combat psychiatry. In F. D. Jones, L. R. Sparacino, V. L. Wilcox, J. M. Rothberg, & J. W. Stokes (Eds.), *War psychiatry* (pp. 149–175). Falls Church, VA: U.S. Army Office of the Surgeon General.

Shalev, A. Y. (1997). Treatment failure in acute PTSD: Lessons learned about the complexity of the disorder. *Annals New York Academy of Sciences, 621*, 372–387.

Shalev, A. Y., Peri, T., Rogel-Fuchs, Y., Ursano, R. J., & Marlowe, D. (1998). Historical group debriefing after combat exposure. *Military Medicine, 163*, 494–498.

Solomon, Z., & Benbenishty, R. (1986). The role of proximity, immediacy, and expectancy in frontline treatment of combat stress reaction among Israelis in the Lebanon War. *American Journal of Psychiatry, 143*(5), 613–617.

Solomon, Z., Mikulincer, M., & Hobfoll, S. E. (1986). Effects of social support and battle intensity on loneliness and breakdown during combat. *Journal of Personality and Social Psychology, 51*, 1269–1276.

Steele, D. (2004). Stress and pain in Iraq: "My guys…all shot up." *Army, 54*, 20–28.

True, P. K., & Benway, M. W. (1992). Treatment of stress reaction prior to combat using the "BICEPS" model. *Military Medicine, 157*, 380–381.

U.S. Army Office of the Surgeon General. (2003). *Operation Iraqi Freedom mental health advisory team report* (Report). Washington, DC: Author.

Wong, A., Escobar, M., Lesage, A., Loyer, M., Vanier, C., & Sakinofsky, I. (2001). Are UN peacekeepers at risk for suicide? *Suicide and Life-Threatening Behavior, 31*, 103–112.

Young, B. H., Litz, B. T., Ruzek, J. L., Watson, P. J., Friedman, M. F., Gusman, F. D., & Ford, J. D. (1999). *Peacekeepers: A military mental health practitioner's guidebook*. Menlo Park, CA: National Center for Post-Traumatic Stress Disorder.

Zeff, K. N., Lewis, S. J., & Hirsch, K. A. (1997). Military family adaptation to United Nations operations in Somalia. *Military Medicine, 162*, 384–387.

CHAPTER 7

PREDICTORS AND PREVALENCE OF POSTTRAUMATIC STRESS DISORDER AMONG MILITARY VETERANS

Shira Maguen, Michael Suvak, and Brett T. Litz

Military service is arguably among the most dangerous occupations. Historically, direct combat has been viewed as the exclusive source of danger, conflict, and trauma and as the necessary and sufficient cause of postservice mental health problems, such as posttraumatic stress disorder (PTSD). However, a wealth of research on military stress in the last 25 years has revealed that direct combat is only one of many sources of severe stress and trauma. A very complex set of interrelated individual, cultural, economic, and social factors affect risk for postservice mental health problems, some of which pre- and post-date service-related experiences (e.g., Weathers, Litz, & Keane, 1995).

Recent research has also shown that in the face of severe military service demands, including horrific combat, most men and women do exceptionally well across the life span. While it is true that a large majority of soldiers become productive and effective veterans, maturing and growing from their service experiences, it is also true that chronic postservice mental health problems such as PTSD represent a significant public health concern. Veterans with PTSD are heavy service utilizers, have a variety of comorbid mental health and medical conditions, and are not likely to get the care they need. Even when available, PTSD treatment is not effective for everyone. By definition, veterans with PTSD also have significant occupational, relational, and/or intrapersonal disturbances that cause clinically significant distress (APA, 1994). Thus, the identification of reliable risk and resilience factors, generically referred to as "predictors," is critical to informing efforts to inoculate soldiers via training and preparation and to identifying those most at risk for chronic service and postservice mental health problems (Litz, Gray, Bryant, & Adler, 2002).

In this chapter, we describe the epidemiology of military-related PTSD. We also review the various preservice, service, and postservice factors that have been shown to predict PTSD in veterans of war and peacekeeping missions.

Elements of Military Stress and Trauma

In the span of a person's military service, he or she may be exposed to a number of highly stressful and challenging circumstances, life-threatening deployments, and accidental exposure to violence and injury. Deployment to war zones is the duty that poses the highest risk for trauma exposure and posttrauma mental health problems. In Figure 7.1, we describe an abridged set of potentially traumatizing events, severely stressful experiences, and contextual features of the war-zone milieu. Figure 7.1 also presents two global resilience categories that have a salutogenic influence on postservice adjustment: military cohesion and personal resilience (e.g., coping styles, personality traits, and demographic variables), which are represented with minus signs signifying risk reduction (cohesion and support is reciprocally related to war-zone stress). Additionally, the figure depicts a general background risk category that serves to magnify the possibility of mental health problems, namely adversity and stress back home (e.g., relationship and financial problems), reciprocally associated with

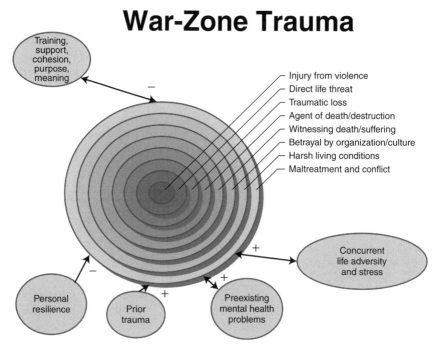

Figure 7.1
Schematic Diagram of a Model of War-Zone Trauma

war-zone stress, as well as prior trauma, and preexisting mental health problems (which is also reciprocally related to war-zone stress and demands), each represented with a plus sign signifying potentiation of risk.

The concentric circles in the middle of Figure 7.1 represent several important features of the hazards of war-zone duty. The size of the circle roughly corresponds to the risk of exposure. Physical injury and direct life threat are the least likely during major combat missions, because most soldiers deployed to missions do not have combat duty. However, events represented by smaller circles are more acutely destabilizing, horrific, and draining of coping resources. The larger circles represent extremely high magnitude and potentially traumatizing events, which pose the greatest risk for enduring postevent mental health disturbances and functional impairments (e.g., King, King, Foy, Keane, & Fairbank, 1999). To appreciate the long-term psychological impact of military trauma, it is critical to assess severe high-impact experiences as well as general contextual features (e.g., harsh living conditions or perceived maltreatment by command). Together these stressors pose a cumulative burden on coping, well-being, and psychological health. All the categories of experiences represented by concentric circles in Figure 7.1 have been shown to influence recovery and adaptation to war-zone service.

Finally, it should be emphasized that the lasting psychological legacy of the sacrifices and traumas of war also need to be appreciated in their cultural, political, and social context. The best example of this would be the Vietnam War. Had the Vietnam War been a popular and resounding success during a time of national consensus and unity, many Vietnam veterans would have construed their sacrifices and their behavior in the war zone differently than they did, which, arguably, would have lessened the associated mental health impact across the life span.

Posttraumatic Stress Disorder

Posttraumatic stress disorder consists of a constellation of symptoms that develop in response to a traumatic event. The current (fourth) edition of the *Diagnostic and Statistical Manual of Mental Disorders* (APA, 1994) includes two necessary criteria for an event to be considered traumatic: Criterion A1, an event during which a person experiences, witnesses, or is confronted with actual or threatened death or serious injury or is faced with a threat to the physical integrity of self or other, and Criterion A2, when the person reacts to the stressors with a feeling of fear, helplessness, and/or horror. PTSD is composed of 17 different symptoms, clustered into heterogeneous categories. More specifically, as defined by the DSM-IV, PTSD consists of three symptom clusters: (1) reexperiencing of the event (e.g., intrusive thoughts), (2) avoidance of reminders of the event and emotional numbing (e.g., restricted range of affect), and (3) hyperarousal (e.g., exaggerated startle response). Although the DSM-IV places the three emotional numbing symptoms (disinterest, detachment, and restricted range of affect) into the avoidance symptom cluster, factor analytic studies have provided evidence that emotional numbing is a distinct, fourth orthogonal cluster (e.g., King, Leskin, King, & Weathers, 1998). To receive a diagnosis of

PTSD, a person must have experienced a traumatic event that meets both conditions of Criterion A and endorse one or more reexperiencing symptoms (Criterion B), three or more avoidance and numbing symptoms (Criterion C), and two or more hyperarousal symptoms (Criterion D). In addition, the symptoms must persist for at least one month (Criterion E) and cause clinically significant distress or impairment (Criterion F).

Current conceptualizations of PTSD have been greatly influenced by research examining the mental health of soldiers who have been exposed to combat stressors. Well before PTSD was introduced as a formal diagnostic category in the DSM-III (APA, 1980), Abram Kardiner, a psychiatrist at the VA Medical Center in Bronx, New York, developed the first formulation of traumatic war neurosis based on his experiences working with veterans of World War I (see Flora, 2002). The introduction of PTSD into the DSM-III marked a significant shift in the care of veterans who developed psychological problems stemming from traumatic combat experiences. Before then, psychological problems occurring in combat veterans were largely viewed as character flaws or dismissed as "combat fatigue." Most contemporary accounts recognize that a variety of factors are related to the development of PTSD, including characteristics of the individual (e.g., pretrauma demographic and psychosocial characteristics and posttrauma resources and experiences) and characteristics of the traumatic event (e.g., King et al., 1999).

In this chapter, we focus primarily on research conducted on U.S. veterans after the inclusion of PTSD into DSM-III in 1980 (Vietnam War, the first Gulf War, and humanitarian and peacekeeping missions, e.g., Somalia, Bosnia, and Kosovo). We start by describing the epidemiology of PTSD, which is followed by reviews of risk and resilience research. We appreciate that this review is necessarily narrow and provincial, but it is this way by necessity: the majority of large-scale studies have been conducted on veterans in the United States.

The Epidemiology of PTSD in Veterans

Vietnam Veterans

In 1983, the U.S. Congress mandated the National Vietnam Veterans Readjustment Study (NVVRS) to establish "the prevalence and incidence of post-traumatic stress disorder (PTSD) and other psychological problems in readjusting to civilian life" among Vietnam veterans (as cited by Kulka et al., 1990b, p. xxiii). This study was, and perhaps remains, the largest and most thorough investigation of the nature and etiology of PTSD. The study began in September of 1984 and was completed in November of 1988 (Kulka et al., 1990a, 1990b). Therefore, veterans were assessed 15–20 years after their service in Vietnam. The study used a national probability sample of 1,632 Vietnam-theater veterans (veterans who served in Vietnam or surrounding regions sometime between August 1964 and May 1975; 432 women and 1,200 men), 716 Vietnam-era veterans (veterans who served in the military during the same period but were stationed in the United States or other non-Southeast Asian countries; 304 women and 412 men), and 668 civilian counterparts (218 women and 450 men).

A representative subset of participants was given a formal structured psychiatric interview (the Structured Clinical Interview for DSM-III-R; SCID; Spitzer, William, & Gibbon, 1987), which was used to calibrate the utility of the self-report instruments designed to evaluate the prevalence of PTSD. The balance of the participants were administered questionnaires and surveys measuring prewar, war-zone, and postwar variables (the National Survey of the Vietnam Generation). The method of PTSD assessment was a strength of the NVVRS. Because PTSD was a new diagnostic category in 1983, PTSD-related measures were in the process of being developed and validated when the NVVRS began. As a result, multiple measures of PTSD were used to establish prevalence rates, and PTSD diagnoses were made based on the convergence of information across multiple indicators (Schlenger et al., 1992).

The prevalence rates for *current* PTSD were 15 percent for male and 9 percent for female Vietnam veterans. This was significantly higher than the prevalence rates for Vietnam-era veterans (3 percent for males and 1 percent for females) and civilian counterparts (1 percent for males and <1 percent for females). The NVVRS estimated *lifetime* prevalence rates of PTSD to be 31 percent for male and 27 percent for female Vietnam veterans. In addition, 11 percent of males and 8 percent of females had current partial PTSD (i.e., had a significant number of PTSD symptoms but did not meet full diagnostic criteria). Thus, the NVVRS estimated that more than a quarter of male Vietnam theatre veterans met criteria for a PTSD diagnosis at some point since discharge from the service.

Since the NVVRS was the most thorough, representative, and methodologically sound study of PTSD in Vietnam veterans, the prevalence rates reported are arguably the most accurate estimates (see Weathers et al., 1995 for a review of other studies that have estimated the rates of PTSD among Vietnam veterans). However, there were a few important limitations to the NVVRS, the most notable being that veterans were assessed cross-sectionally, 15–20 years post-Vietnam. Therefore, little can be ascertained about the course of PTSD or generally the psychosocial burden of Vietnam combat veterans across the life span. Another limitation of the NVVRS was that there was no attempt to verify or validate reports of service characteristics and events. The latter concern pervades all epidemiological studies of military trauma. This is an especially important problem, given that retrospective reports of war-zone experiences have been shown to be inconsistent across time; they also covary with degree of reported distress and self-reported PTSD symptoms (e.g., Roemer, Orsillo, Borkovec, & Litz, 1998).

Gulf War Veterans

In the first few months of 1991, the United States led a very large coalition of forces to remove Iraqi forces from Kuwait. Formal combat operations, backed by heavy armor, ostensibly lasted three to four days as a result of the devastating impact of sustained air operations. Consequently, soldiers deployed to the Gulf War were relatively infrequently exposed to the severe traumas displayed in the middle of Figure 7.1. However, the Gulf War was associated with considerable sustained arousal and anxiety in anticipation and preparation for chemical and biological warfare and SCUD attack (e.g., Perconte, Wilson, Pontius, Dietrick, & Spiro, 1993). In addition, the Gulf War entailed harsh weather conditions and possible exposure to environmental toxins, such as diesel fuel and smoke.

As a consequence of toxic exposure, some Persian Gulf War veterans have complained of medically unexplained symptoms, such as fatigue, joint pain, skin rash, memory loss, and/or diarrhea, commonly referred to as "Gulf War Syndrome." A variety of expert evaluations of the alleged Gulf War Syndrome have determined that veterans are not suffering from a single, common ailment, but rather from a variety of illnesses with overlapping symptoms, some of which appear to be psychosomatic and associated with exposure to psychological stressors (and responses) during and after deployment. After over ten years of formal medical examinations of Persian Gulf veterans, investigators have not found evidence of infectious diseases beyond the range of illnesses common in the population at large. Nevertheless, epidemiological and intervention studies of Persian Gulf War veterans has, and continues to be, a high priority for the Department of Defense and the Department of Veterans Affairs.

The first published studies that examined PTSD symptomatology among Gulf War veterans employed samples of convenience. For example, Perconte and colleagues (1993) examined PTSD symptomatology in a sample of 591 Gulf War reservists, 439 of whom were deployed to Southwest Asia, 26 of whom were deployed to Europe, and 126 of whom were activated and not deployed. Using a cutoff score of 89 on the Mississippi Scale for Combat Related PTSD (Keane, Caddell, & Taylor, 1988), they found that 16 percent of the Gulf War reservists met criteria for PTSD, which was significantly higher than reservists deployed to Europe (4 percent) and reservists called up but not deployed.

The Iowa Persian Gulf Study Group (1997) examined PTSD symptomatology in a random sample of four types of veterans (Gulf War active-duty soldiers, Gulf War National Guard Reserve, non-Gulf War active-duty soldiers, and non-Gulf War National Guard Reserve) stratified by age, sex, race, rank, and branch of service. The sample was limited in that only military personnel who listed Iowa as their place of residence were included. Telephone interviews were conducted with 1,896 Gulf War veterans (985 active duty and 911 National Guard/reservist) and 1,799 non-Gulf War military personnel (968 active duty and 831 National Guard/reservist) from September 1995 through May 1996, approximately five years after the Gulf War. The Study Group used the PTSD checklist (PCL; Weathers, Litz, Herman, Huska, & Keane, 1993), a well-validated self-report measure of DSM-IV PTSD symptoms, to assess symptoms, employing a cutoff score of 50 or higher. Prevalence rates of PTSD were estimated to be 2 percent for active-duty and National Guard/Reserve Gulf War veterans. This was statistically greater than the corresponding 1 percent estimates for non-Gulf War military personnel.

Also examining PTSD symptoms approximately five years post-Gulf War, Kang, Natelson, Mahan, Lee, and Murphy (2003) estimated the prevalence rates of PTSD in a large, nationally representative, population-based sample of 20,917 veterans (11,441 Gulf War and 9,476 non-Gulf War). Kang and colleagues also used a PCL cutoff score of 50 or higher to identify PTSD cases. The estimate of the prevalence rates of PTSD in the Gulf War veterans' sample was 10 percent, which was significantly higher than the 4 percent estimate for non-Gulf war veterans.

Given the many similarities between the studies conducted by the Iowa Persian Gulf Study Group and Kang and colleagues (e.g., same measure of PTSD with same cutoff score, participants surveyed approximately five years after the Gulf War, carefully designed sampling plans, similar overall response rates), the disparity of the prevalence rates for PTSD among Gulf War veterans reported in the two studies is surprising (2 percent versus 10 percent). There were a few minor methodological differences between the two studies. For instance, the Iowa Study conducted phone interviews with all participants, while approximately two-thirds of the participants in the study by Kang and colleagues completed paper-and-pencil questionnaire packets administered via the mail. Only participants (approximately one-third of the sample) who did not initially respond to the mailing completed phone interviews in this study. However, statistical analyses revealed no differences between those participants who completed self-report measures and those who completed phone interviews. Another difference is that the study by Kang and colleagues sampled a higher proportion of National Guard/reservists (approximately 65 percent) than the Iowa Study (46 percent) did. However, the Iowa Study reported no differences in rates of PTSD between active-duty and National Guard/reserve Gulf War veterans, and Kang and colleagues adjusted for a slight difference in rates of PTSD between these groups when deriving the overall estimate of PTSD rates. Finally, the Iowa Persian Gulf Study Group sampled military personnel who listed Iowa as their residence, while the study by Kang and colleagues employed a nationally representative sample. While these methodological differences may account for some of the discrepancy between rates of PTSD reported in these two studies, these differences were accounted for statistically, and the two studies are more similar than they are different. Therefore, it is unclear why the discrepancy in PTSD rates between the two studies is so large.

The Gulf War studies reviewed thus far employed cross-sectional designs. Wolfe, Erickson, Sharkansky, King, and King (1999) assessed PTSD symptoms using the Mississippi Scale for Combat-Related PTSD in 2,949 Army personnel within five days of returning to the United States. They reassessed 78 percent of the original sample 18 to 24 months later. Using a cutoff score of 94, results demonstrated that upon returning to the United States, 3 percent of Gulf War veterans met criteria for PTSD, while after about two years this rate increased to 8 percent.

Military Operations in Iraq and Afghanistan Post 9/11/01

To date, there has only been one large-scale study examining the consequences of combat duty in Iraq and Afghanistan since the events of September 11, 2001. Hoge and colleagues (2004) surveyed four combat infantry units, including 2,530 soldiers from an Army infantry brigade that was surveyed one week predeployment to Iraq;

1,962 and 894 soldiers from two other Army infantry brigades, who were surveyed three to four months after deployment to Afghanistan and Iraq, respectively; and 1,850 Marines surveyed three to four months postdeployment to Iraq. Findings indicate that the rate of PTSD before deployment was 9 percent among soldiers deployed to Iraq. The rate of PTSD among Army soldiers deployed to Afghanistan was 12 percent, while rates among Army and Marine soldiers returning from Iraq were 18 percent and 20 percent, respectively. As expected, rates of PTSD were significantly higher postdeployment than at predeployment. Furthermore, soldiers deployed to Iraq had significantly higher rates of PTSD than those deployed to Afghanistan, perhaps because of higher rates of combat exposure reported by soldiers returning from Iraq. Thus far, it appears that rates of PTSD reported among veterans returning from Iraq are higher than those of veterans returning from the Gulf War (i.e., in 1991), although future studies are needed to verify this finding and elucidate the course of PTSD over time in this cohort.

Peacekeeping Operations

Since the end of the Cold War, the U.S. military has been called on to conduct a variety of peacekeeping operations around the world. Peacekeeping missions involve a unique combination of stressors that are an amalgam of war-zone-like activity and challenges uniquely associated with humanitarian missions under dangerous conditions (e.g., witnessing human suffering). Litz, Gray, and Bolton (2003) recently reviewed the literature on the prevalence of PTSD in peacekeepers. In this section, we summarize this review and discuss findings from a few studies that have been completed since the review was published.

Litz and colleagues reported that estimates of the prevalence of PTSD following peacekeeping missions have varied from about 3 percent to 15 percent. The upper end of this spectrum (15 percent) was reported in a study examining PTSD in a sample of Norwegian peacekeepers who served in southern Lebanon (Mehlum, 1994), and the lower end (3 percent) was reported in a study conducted on Dutch peacekeepers in the former Yugoslavia (Bramsen, Dirkzwager, & Van der Ploeg, 2000). Given the diverse demands of different peacekeeping missions, the variability in these rates is not surprising. Some peacekeeping operations have involved benign observer operations (e.g., Sinai), while others have involved highly dangerous peace-enforcement missions (e.g., Somalia). For example, in one of the largest studies to date, Litz, King, King, Orsillo, and Friedman (1997) examined PTSD symptomatology in 3,310 active-duty U.S. military personnel deployed to Somalia as part of Operation Restore Hope and Operation Continue Hope. U.S. soldiers deployed to Somalia were exposed to well-armed civilian populations that were actively engaged in interclan war. Moreover, they were subject to threats and resentful, hostile rejection from the recipients of humanitarian aid, and the mission was viewed as a failure. Using empirically derived cutoff scores and well-validated measures, Litz and colleagues estimated the prevalence rate of PTSD to be approximately 8 percent five months after soldiers returned home to the United States from Somalia.

Recently, Gray, Bolton, and Litz (2004) examined posttraumatic stress symptoms in a subset of these Somalia peacekeepers (n = 1,040). Four trajectories of PTSD symptoms were identified: (1) resilient cases did not meet criteria at either time point (87 percent), (2) acute-onset cases met diagnostic criteria at both time points (4.5 percent), (3) remitters met criteria only at Time 1 (2 percent), and (4) delayed-onset cases met criteria only at Time 2 (6.5 percent). Follow-up analyses revealed that the delayed-onset cases could not be explained by minor waxing and waning of symptoms, because these individuals exhibited large increases in PTSD symptoms across the two time points. This study suggests that PTSD symptoms change over time and illustrates the need for more longitudinal studies.

In contrast to Somalia, where U.S. soldiers provided humanitarian aid, enforced peace, and in some instances took part in combat operations, U.S. peacekeepers deployed to Bosnia faced a different set of challenges. The U.S. military was deployed to Bosnia after the Dayton peace accord. Thus, the Bosnia peacekeeping operation may be more representative of traditional peacekeeping missions, because there was an established peace and soldiers were not regularly faced with life-threatening situations. The mission was designed to minimize possible threats to peacekeepers: very large forces were deployed, less-restrictive rules of engagement were implemented, and troops were fortified in their attempt to assist the established peace process. Han and colleagues (2004) catalogued the experiences of U.S. Army peacekeepers deployed to Bosnia and examined the effects of mission stressors on soldiers' self-reported stress symptoms. PTSD symptoms were assessed in 3,034 soldiers prospectively, and based on a stratified-random sampling procedure, 239 soldiers were reassessed 12 to 18 months postdeployment. The assessment of PTSD symptoms prospectively represents a significant methodological strength and allows for stronger conclusions to be drawn about the impact of the mission. A total of 8 percent of soldiers assessed prior to deployment met DSM-IV criteria for PTSD, while only 1 percent met criteria during the postdeployment period. Although this was not a statistically significant drop, it suggests that PTSD related to the Bosnian mission was minimal and that preparation/anticipation for deployment may have been as stressful as the deployment itself for this mission. Another reason for the difference in PTSD rates may be the differing Criterion A events. Predeployment PTSD symptoms were assessed by asking soldiers more generally about stressful experiences in the past, while postdeployment PTSD symptoms were assessed by asking only about deployment experiences. This finding also suggests that assessing mental health immediately before deployment may not be a true baseline of psychological functioning. A more accurate baseline would likely entail assessment of mental health measures before notification of deployment. Furthermore, low levels of exposure to potentially traumatizing events were detected among Bosnia peacekeepers. Thus, it appears that the Bosnian mission did not cause a substantial amount of PTSD symptomatology. This is consistent with the findings of a study by Michel, Lundin, and Larsson (2003) conducted on Swedish peacekeepers serving in Bosnia.

Another recent prospective study assessed PTSD in a sample of Kosovo Force (KFOR) peacekeepers (Maguen, Litz, Wang, & Cook, 2004). KFOR is a peace-enforcement operation, sanctioned and mandated by the United Nations. KFOR soldiers perform a number of stressful and potentially traumatizing tasks, including providing a military presence to prevent conflict and to halt riots, acts of violence, arson, and looting. KFOR also has been a humanitarian success, allowing nearly a million refugees and displaced people to return to their homeland. In this study, 1,132 U.S. KFOR soldiers were assessed prospectively, and 203 were followed up approximately seven months after they returned. During the predeployment period, 13 percent of the sample met DSM-IV diagnostic criteria for PTSD. The prevalence of PTSD postdeployment was 4 percent, and this represented a statistically significant drop from pre- to postdeployment. This drop occurred despite the finding that the majority of peacekeepers who were evaluated were exposed to a number of potentially traumatizing events. The 4 percent PTSD postdeployment prevalence rate found in this study is considerably greater than the 1 percent rate found in Bosnia (Han et al., 2004) and less than the 8 percent rate found after the Somalia mission (Litz, King et al., 1997; Litz, Orsillo et al., 1997). The Han and colleagues and Maguen and colleagues studies illustrate the importance of assessing and controlling for predeployment PTSD when attempting to estimate PTSD symptomatology associated with deployment stress.

In sum, studies estimating the prevalence of PTSD associated with peacekeeping missions have found rates ranging from 1 to 15 percent. The most parsimonious explanation for the high variability in PTSD is method variance and differences in the type and intensity of stressors associated with diversely different missions. Furthermore, recent studies employing longitudinal designs have demonstrated the importance of assessing predeployment PTSD symptoms when determining the impact of a particular mission on soldiers' mental health and have suggested that PTSD changes over time in a complex manner following peacekeeping missions, with some soldiers developing late-onset PTSD (Gray et al., in press; Maguen et al., 2004; Michel, et al., 2003).

Cross-Cultural Military Studies of PTSD

Although PTSD arguably is a universal response to military trauma in those most at risk, very few epidemiological studies have examined differential phenomenology and rates across societies and cultures. Existing PTSD studies most frequently use samples of convenience (e.g., treatment seeking and/or inpatient samples), which makes it difficult to make cross-cultural comparisons.

Several studies have been conducted in Israel following soldiers' exposure to combat. Most studies in Israel have focused on combat stress reactions (CSR) in the war zone, rather than chronic PTSD, a conglomerate of distressing emotional reactions that may occur at any point following a traumatic event. For example, in a follow-up study of soldiers who served in the 1982 Lebanon War, Solomon, Weisenberg, Schwarzwald, and Mikulincer (1987) reported that 16 percent who did not have CSR developed PTSD, a rate that is comparable to findings of U.S. veterans. Conversely, 59 percent of those with CSR developed PTSD. Solomon and colleagues

(1994) compared the rate of PTSD in prisoners of war, veterans who had experienced CSR, and those who did not have CSR. The rate of PTSD in these veterans of the 1973 Yom Kippur War were as follows: 23 percent of the former POWs, 37 percent of the veterans who had had CSR, and 14 percent for the non-CSR group. Unfortunately, there are no formal well-controlled studies of CSR in American soldiers. The rates of PTSD for the non-CSR group in research by Solomon and colleagues (1994) is highly similar to the prevalence of PTSD found in Vietnam and Gulf War veterans.

Seedat, le Roux, and Stein (2003) surveyed 198 full-time operational members of the South African National Defence Force and found that 26 percent met diagnostic criteria for PTSD. However, it is important to note that this was not following one specific conflict and might be a conglomerate of several different operations.

Overall, the lack of rigorous and methodologically sound epidemiological studies prevent us from drawing firm conclusions about cross-cultural comparisons of the nature, development, and time course of PTSD, although existing studies seem to find similar PTSD rates as compared to U.S. military operations.

Estimating the Prevalence of PTSD: Methodological Limitations

Rates of PTSD vary considerably across study and mission. Many factors likely contribute to the varying rates of combat-related PTSD. One of the most substantial is the variety of methods employed to assess PTSD. Studies employing self-report methods used a number of different measures with varying cutoff scores. Many studies also relied on samples of convenience, limiting generalizability. Another methodological concern is that the time lapse since service in combat regions varied substantially across studies, and the few longitudinal studies documenting the rates of PTSD suggest that combat related PTSD symptomatology changes over time in a complex manner (e.g., Wolfe et al., 1999, Gray et al., in press). This state of affairs is unfortunate, because accurate estimates of prevalence are critical for informing policy decisions about resource allocation and availability of primary, secondary, and tertiary prevention efforts.

The varying nature and intensity of stressors faced by soldiers deployed to different war zones also leads to different rates of PTSD across different missions. Service in a combat zone is related to an array of intense stressors (Adler, Litz, & Bartone, 2003; Fontana & Rosenheck, 1998b; Weathers et al., 1995). Some of these stressors clearly satisfy the DSM-IV definition of a Criterion A event (actual or threatened death or serious injury that produces feelings of fear, helplessness, and/or horror), such as receiving enemy fire, witnessing the death and/or injury of others, being held hostage, and/or fearing for one's life. Other less intense, more chronic stressors (e.g., being separated from family, adverse living conditions, conflict with combat units) may not satisfy DSM-IV criteria of a traumatic event but impact soldiers' adjustment and long-term mental health (e.g., King, King, Gudanowski, & Vreven, 1995). Each war zone is characterized by a unique set of stressors that greatly colors its psychological impact.

Although war-zone stressors are substantially related to PTSD symptomatalogy, they do not fully account for the variance in PTSD symptoms in military populations. Using structural equation modeling with latent variables, King and colleagues (1995) found that a variety of Vietnam war-zone stressors accounted for 52 percent and 43 percent of the variance in PTSD symptoms in male and female veterans, respectively. Therefore, approximately half of the variance was accounted for by other factors. Over the past several years, there has been an increased effort to identify risk and resilience factors related to the development of PTSD. The next section will review this literature.

Risk and Resilience Research

In the following section, we review research on the preservice, service-related, and postservice variables that are associated with PTSD in veterans.

Preservice Risk Factors

There are a number of biological, psychological, and situational risk factors that may put soldiers at greater risk for developing mental health complications following exposure to trauma. As rates of PTSD in different contexts have been investigated and the public health implications of PTSD have become elucidated, more studies have focused on clarifying the etiology of PTSD. Biological diatheses, or constitutional predispositions toward a particular condition, have been of particular interest, given the possibility for primary prevention. Familial risk studies have received particular attention, because several investigations have found a link between preexisting familial psychopathology and risk for PTSD. Davidson, Swartz, Storck, Krishnan, and Hammett (1985) found that in Vietnam veterans diagnosed with PTSD, 66 percent had a history of familial psychopathology, most commonly alcoholism, depression, or anxiety disorders. Furthermore, studies conducted with the Vietnam Era Twin Registry, a national cohort of male twin veterans who served during the Vietnam War era, demonstrated that the association between familial psychopathology and PTSD might be partially mediated by genetic factors (True et al., 1993; Xian et al., 2000). True and colleagues found that after controlling for combat exposure, genetic factors accounted for 13 to 30 percent of the variance in reexperiencing symptoms, 30 to 34 percent of the variance in avoidance symptoms, and 28 to 32 percent of the variance in arousal symptoms. They concluded that heritability significantly contributes to susceptibility for each cluster of PTSD symptoms.

Individual biological diatheses may also act as risk factors. Results from the National Vietnam Veteran's Readjustment Study suggest that a preexisting psychiatric disorder prior to trauma exposure increased rates of PTSD (Kulka et al., 1990b). In support of this finding, using the Vietnam Era Twin Registry, Koenen and colleagues (2002) found that a diagnosis of conduct disorder, panic disorder, generalized anxiety disorder, and/or mood disorder prior to the military service were all associated with higher rates of PTSD symptoms. There is also evidence that premilitary personality traits are a risk factor for PTSD. More specifically, Schnurr,

Friedman, and Rosenberg (1993) found that Vietnam veterans who were later diagnosed with PTSD were more likely to have elevated scores on the depression, hypomania, and social introversion subscales of the MMPI prior to their military service, demonstrating that there may be some overlap between personality and premorbid psychiatric diagnoses. Another possibility is that these personality measures are really a proxy for underlying psychopathology. Furthermore, the social introversion subscale may share variance with and reflect an individual's discomfort with seeking social support, which could act as a buffer against developing PTSD. In a prospective study employing a peacekeeping sample, Bramsen and colleagues (2000) found that after controlling for level of exposure, predeployment negativism (e.g., negative, dissatisfied, and hostile attitude) and psychopathology (e.g., paranoia and unusual experiences), as measured by the MMPI, were most strongly associated with PTSD symptoms following deployment.

Personality factors may also act as buffers, protecting soldiers against the development of PTSD. In cross-sectional research, several researchers have found that the construct of "hardiness" (e.g., sense of control, viewing change as a challenge, and commitment to self) was protective against the development of PTSD in both male and female veterans in samples ranging from Vietnam to Gulf War veterans (King et al., 1999; Sutker, Davis, Uddo, & Ditta, 1995b). In their study, Sutker and colleagues also reported that among Gulf War veterans, personal resource variables were more strongly associated with resilience amidst the negative impact of war, as compared to environmental resources such as social support. However, as with all retrospective studies that do not include a prospective component, it is impossible to ascertain whether these personality factors were truly preexisting or whether they are a manifestation of PTSD.

Demographic variables, such as gender and ethnicity, may also exacerbate risk. Studies including gender as a risk factor for PTSD have yielded mixed results, and Wolfe and Kimerling (1997) suggest that differential PTSD rates may be because that type of trauma is not controlled for in many studies. When including only military-related trauma in their meta-analysis, Brewin, Andrews, and Valentine (2000) did not find that gender was a significant risk factor for PTSD; it is important to note that although they likely were exposed to many military stressors, women in these studies were not involved in direct combat, which is the most traditional measure of military trauma; this is despite the fact that sexual harassment and sexual abuse still account for many of the traumas reported by women in the military (e.g., Wolfe et al., 1998). As a result, by design, many of these studies have serious flaws that do not allow the true extent of the association between gender and subsequent trauma to be adequately reflected.

In their large cohort of Gulf War veterans, Wolfe and colleagues (1999) found that women were more likely to be diagnosed with PTSD than men, and that gender was a risk factor for PTSD immediately following return from the Gulf War and two years later. In fact, women were six times more likely than men to meet criteria for PTSD immediately following return from the Gulf and twice as likely to meet criteria two years later. At both time points, women diagnosed with PTSD far exceeded the number of men diagnosed with the disorder. One explanation for this finding is that combat exposure during the Gulf War was lower than in traditional wars and that as a result, gender differences in PTSD rates are exacerbated. A second possibility is that rates of sexual harassment and assault were inordinately high as a result of women's changing roles in the military. A third possibility for elevated rates of PTSD is that women are more likely to experience preservice sexual assault and abuse, which results in higher rates of PTSD following the service (e.g., Engel, Engel, Campbell, & McFall, 1993). Indeed, Engel and colleagues found that in a Gulf War sample, women reported higher rates of premilitary sexual and physical abuse, and women who reported premilitary abuse also demonstrated higher rates of PTSD symptoms. Findings by Wolfe and colleagues (1999) and Engel and colleagues (1993) are more consistent with those echoed in civilian samples, where women are at much greater risk for PTSD compared to men (e.g., Norris, Foster, & Weisshaar, 2002); however it is unclear if this disparity results from factors such as differential reporting, discrepancies in exposure levels, and so forth (Brewin et al., 2000).

Ethnicity has also been shown to be a risk factor for developing PTSD in Vietnam, Gulf War, and peacekeeping samples (Fontana, Litz, & Rosenheck, 2000; Fontana & Rosenheck, 1994; Kulka et al., 1990b; Sutker Davis, Uddo, & Ditta, 1995a, 1995b). Among U.S. peacekeepers deployed to Somalia, African-American ethnicity was associated with increased PTSD symptoms (Fontana et al., 2000). However, this could arguably be because African-American soldiers felt some allegiance to Somalis despite their American identity, complicating their reaction to traumatic events, such as seeing Somalis get killed. Latino ethnicity has also been found to be a risk factor for developing PTSD in Vietnam veterans (Fontana & Rosenheck, 1994). Given this group of findings, some researchers have suggested possible mediators, especially with respect to Latino veterans. Ruef, Litz, and Schlenger (2000) suggest that psychosocial factors, such as discrimination and alienation, and sociocultural variables, such as stoicism and normalization of stress, need to be explored as potential mediators of the relationship between ethnicity and PTSD.

Conversely, Brewin and colleagues (2000) suggest that ethnic minority status is not a significant predictor of PTSD, although the relationship between ethnicity and PTSD was stronger in military than in civilian samples. In this meta-analysis, however, race is dichotomized, and therefore this variable's reliability is limited. Brewin and colleagues suggest that the trend for ethnic minorities to be more at risk for PTSD in military samples washed out in studies where exposure is controlled, since higher PTSD rates may be explained by higher rates of combat exposure in ethnic minorities (see Green, Grace, Lindy, & Leonard, 1990). Indeed, Wolfe and colleagues (1999) found that ethnicity, which was also dichotomized, was not related to levels of PTSD immediately following the war or at follow up. A persistent and severely debilitating problem with the existing literature is that ethnicity is dichotomized because small samples of ethnic minorities rather than distinct ethnic groups are looked at separately. Studies that have specifically compared rates of PTSD in specific ethnic minorities have found differences; however, they have been limited because of small sample sizes.

Age is another demographic variable that has been postulated to be a predictor of PTSD (Green, Grace, Lindy, & Gleser, 1990). King and colleagues (1999) found that age of entry into Vietnam predicted PTSD for men but not for women, with younger soldiers being more susceptible. In Gulf War veterans, Wolfe and colleagues (1999) found that younger soldiers were more likely to develop PTSD following the war, but this predictor was no longer significant two years following the end of deployment.

Some researchers have also suggested that greater cognitive resources act as a buffer against the development of PTSD. For instance, Macklin and colleagues (1998), found a unique association between prewar intelligence and postwar PTSD in Vietnam veterans. More specifically, veterans with lower precombat intelligence scores were more likely to develop PTSD symptoms. Vasterling, Brailey, Constans, Gorges, and Sutker (1997) found that veterans with PTSD performed worse on verbal tasks of the Wechsler Adult Intelligence Scale-Revised (WAIS-R) than veterans without PTSD. This instrument is thought to reflect premorbid functioning when compared to veteran controls. This led to the conclusion that verbal intelligence may serve as a buffer against PTSD. No differences were found in attention or visuospatial tasks. Limitations include the fact that this was not a prospective study and that, as a result, causality is impossible to determine. McNally and Shin (1995) found that intelligence scores, as estimated by the Shipley Institute for Living Scale (a general screening measure of verbal intelligence), were a significant predictor of PTSD in Vietnam veterans. Once again, this study is limited by the lack of prospective measurement. Level of education has also been found to be associated with PTSD in some samples; those with more education are less likely to have a PTSD diagnosis (Green et al., 1990; Sutker et al., 1995b). Similarly, Koenen and colleagues (2002) reported that those not graduating from high school before entry into the military were at higher risk for PTSD.

A similarly controversial area of research has focused on brain structures of individuals with PTSD. For example, several studies have demonstrated smaller hippocampal volume in patients diagnosed with PTSD (e.g., Bremner et al., 1995); however it is unclear whether this is a preexisting risk factor or is a consequence of the high levels of cortisol that result from stress and that may cause a decrease in the volume of the hippocampus. In an MRI study of the hippocampus, Bremner and colleagues found that PTSD patients demonstrated an 8 percent decrease in right hippocampal volume, which was also associated with less short-term verbal memory resources as measured by the Wechsler Memory Scale. Vietnam veterans have also been shown to have higher corticotrophin-releasing factor (CRF) levels (e.g., Bremner et al., 1997), a hormone responsible for regulation of the hypothalamic-pituitary-adrenal axis (HPA). Additionally, CRF is responsible, in part, for regulating stress reactions, including arousal, vigilance, and behavioral inhibition. These studies are difficult to conduct because of fluctuating hormonal levels and should always be interpreted with caution.

There is also evidence that several environmental factors, including a variety of premilitary stressors, place individuals at greater risk of developing PTSD. King and colleagues (1999) reported that prewar risk factors, such as early trauma history, were associated with PTSD for both men and women. Koenen and others (2002) examined the risk factors for PTSD following trauma exposure in Vietnam and found that age at first trauma and multiple trauma exposure placed veterans at greater risk of developing PTSD. Bremner, Southwick, Johnson, Yehuda, and Charney (1993) found that after controlling for combat exposure, Vietnam veterans who experienced childhood physical abuse and veterans with a greater number of traumatic events prior to joining the military were more likely to have PTSD. Zaidi and Foy (1994) also found a significant association between childhood physical abuse and PTSD, yet they postulated that this association might be partially explained by the fact that those with a physical-abuse history report higher combat exposure. They resolve that physical-abuse history and higher combat exposure may share a great deal of variance, and that this type of trauma early in life is correlated with a higher risk for placement in high-risk situations such as combat. In a survey of 2,947 peacekeepers poised for deployment, Bolton, Litz, Britt, Adler, and Roemer (2001) found that 74 percent of soldiers reported being exposed to at least one potentially traumatic event in their lifetime and 60 percent reported being exposed to more than one across the life span. The majority of these incidents occurred prior to entry into the military. These studies highlight the importance of assessing and controlling for preexisting trauma in studies examining PTSD symptoms as a result of mission stressors.

There have been two recent meta-analyses of the risk factors for PTSD. Ozer, Best, Lipsey, and Weiss (2003) combined military and civilian studies and found that each of the following pretrauma factors significantly predicted PTSD: prior trauma, prior psychological adjustment, and family history of psychopathology. The association between history of a prior trauma and PTSD and the association between family history of psychopathology and PTSD were stronger when the trauma involved noncombat interpersonal violence than when it resulted from combat exposure or an accident. Also, the association between prior psychological adjustment and PTSD was stronger when the target trauma involved noncombat interpersonal violence or an accident than when it resulted from combat exposure. Brewin and colleagues (2000) separated military studies from civilian studies and found that for the military sample, a younger age, lower intellectual capacity, and childhood adversity were each significant predictors of PTSD. Furthermore, most of these predictors had stronger effect sizes in the military as compared to civilian samples.

Service-Related Risk Factors

The NVVRS (Kulka et al.,1990b) suggested that war-zone stressors were associated with the development of PTSD. Subsequently, several researchers have documented the relationship between increased combat exposure and risk for PTSD. In their structural equation model, King and colleagues (1995) found that four war-zone variables were differentially related to PTSD: perceived threat, malevolent environment (e.g., daily discomforts such as poor living facilities), traditional combat, and atrocities/abusive violence (exposure to deviant war-zone events such as mutilation and killing of civilians). A direct relationship between perceived threat and PTSD was demonstrated (King et al., 1995, 1999); however, perceived threat also served as a mediator between malevolent environment and PTSD and between traditional combat and PTSD (King et al., 1995). Other studies also support the relationship between perceived life threat during the trauma and PTSD (Green, Grace, Lindy, & Gleser, 1990; Ozer et al., 2003). Direct relationships between malevolent environment and PTSD for men (King et al., 1995, 1999) and atrocities/abusive violence and PTSD for both men and women have also been demonstrated (King et al., 1995, 1996, 1999). Interestingly, there was not a direct relationship between combat experience and PTSD.

Other studies have documented an association between combat exposure and PTSD during both war-zone and peacekeeping duties (e.g., Fontana et al., 2000; Fontana & Rosenheck, 1994; Litz, King, et al., 1997), and in one study combat exposure was the strongest predictor of PTSD course (Koenen, Stellman, Stellman, & Sommer., 2003). Among Gulf War veterans, Southwick and colleagues (1993, 1995) found that after one to six months, combat exposure was not significantly related to PTSD; however, after two years, the relationship between combat exposure and PTSD became significant.

One possibility for the differences in these findings is that reports of exposure may vary with symptom severity, which has been demonstrated in some studies (e.g., King et al., 2000). While exposure is necessarily a precursor for the development of PTSD, recent studies have questioned the stability of reporting military traumatic incidents over time, and some researchers have suggested that rates of reporting traumatic exposure may vary with postmilitary symptomatology (King et al., 2000; Roemer, Litz, et al., 1998; Southwick, Morgan, Nicolaou, & Charney, 1997; Wessely et al., 2003). For example, King and colleagues (2000) reported that in a longitudinal study of 2,942 Gulf War veterans, changes in reporting stressor exposure were associated with PTSD severity such that PTSD symptom severity immediately following homecoming was associated with increases in reported exposure over time. This highlights the importance of prospective designs and suggests that retrospective accounts of exposure are not necessarily objective and may be influenced by current functioning.

Another possibility is that comparing combat across wars is unreliable because of the differential rates of exposure, differences in theater, and cohort effects (i.e., Vietnam versus Gulf War). Variations in the ways that combat exposure is measured could also account for some of the difference in these studies (e.g., Combat Exposure Scale versus Desert Storm Trauma Questionnaire). Additionally, different statistical methods may yield different results (e.g., structural equation modeling accounts for both associations and mediational possibilities simultaneously). Finally, it is possible that it is not quantity but quality of combat exposure and resulting trauma that differentially predicts rates of PTSD. For example, Brewin and colleagues (2000) found that trauma severity significantly predicted PTSD in military samples. Adler, Vaitkus, and Martin (1996) found that in veterans returning from the Gulf War, those exposed to U.S. soldier casualties reported the most PTSD symptoms, followed by those exposed to civilian or Iraqi casualties, and next by those not exposed to any casualties. In a peacekeeping sample, witnessing Somalis dying was strongly associated with PTSD (Fontana et al., 2000). Similarly, in a prospective study of Kosovo peacekeepers, potentially traumatic events (e.g., patrolling in areas where there were mines, having your unit fired on, seeing dead or injured civilians, etc.) were the strongest predictors of PTSD symptoms after controlling for preservice PTSD symptoms (Maguen et al., 2004).

Yet another possibility is that it is not combat exposure per se but perception of or reaction to the exposure during military service that is associated with the development of PTSD. For example, Sutker and colleagues (1995b) found that among Gulf War veterans, there were no differences in duration of war-zone duty when those with PTSD were compared to controls; however, soldiers with PTSD reported increased perceived war stress, as compared to their counterparts. Similarly, in a sample of 15,000 Gulf War veterans representing four branches, Kang and colleagues (2003) stratified veterans by six levels of duty-related stress, ranging from serving at a home base to being involved in direct combat, a potential chemical warfare attack, and/or witnessing deaths in the Gulf region. Kang and colleagues found that rates of PTSD increased with each stress level, with about 3 percent reporting PTSD in the lowest level and 23 percent reporting PTSD at the highest level of stress. In a sample of U.S. peacekeepers deployed to Somalia, Litz, Orsillo, and colleagues (1997) found that frequency of war-zone stressors (e.g., going on dangerous patrol) and the intensity of frustration with negative aspects of the peacekeeping mission (e.g., changing rules regarding the discretionary use of force) were strongly associated with PTSD symptoms; positive aspects of peacekeeping (e.g., developing relationships with other military personnel, visiting a new country) were inversely related to PTSD symptoms. Similarly, Han and colleagues (2004) found that in Bosnia peacekeepers, after controlling for PTSD symptoms before the mission, negative aspects of the peacekeeping mission was the strongest predictor of postdeployment PTSD symptoms.

There is also some evidence that variables related to unit support concerns play a role in the development of PTSD. For example, Adler and colleagues (1996) found that reported problems with a coworker and problems with the chain of command in soldiers returning from the Persian Gulf War were strong and consistent predictors of PTSD symptoms.

Concerning peritraumatic emotional responses (e.g., fear, helplessness, horror, guilt, and shame), Ozer and colleagues (2003) found that those who had intensely negative emotional responses during or immediately after a traumatic event reported higher levels of PTSD symptoms or rates of PTSD. The authors were not able to conduct analyses for differential effects of sample or trauma type because of the small number of studies in this group. Fontana and colleagues (2000) also found that for peacekeepers, feeling fear while in Somalia was associated with greater PTSD symptoms.

Peritraumatic dissociation was also a strong predictor of PTSD in a recent meta-analytic study; those who described having dissociative experiences during or immediately after a traumatic event were more likely to report having higher rates of PTSD symptoms (Ozer et al., 2003). Among Vietnam veterans, several studies have supported an association between peritraumatic dissociation and PTSD (e.g., Marmar et al., 1994; O'Toole, Marshall, Schureck, & Dobson, 1999), although at least one study found no association (Tampke & Irwin, 1999). Marmar and colleagues found that dissociation during trauma accounted for a significant portion of the variance in PTSD diagnosis, over and above the contributions of level of war-zone stress exposure and general dissociative tendencies. Although there has been some speculation concerning differential rates of peritraumatic dissociation among ethnic groups, Zatick, Marmar, Weiss, and Metzler (1994) found that in a Vietnam sample, greater exposure to war-zone stress was related to more dissociative experiences, regardless of veteran's ethnicity.

A few studies have found an association between coping strategies employed in the war zone and subsequent development of PTSD. For example, Sutker and colleagues (1995b) found that avoidance coping was the only strategy that predicted PTSD status among Gulf War veterans. Sharkansky and colleagues (2000) found that soldiers who used higher percentages of approach-based coping (e.g., strategy directly resolving the stressor) endorsed fewer PTSD symptoms on a self-report scale immediately after returning from the Gulf War. Additionally, Sharkansky and colleagues found that the relationship between coping strategies and PTSD appears to be moderated by combat exposure, with a stronger negative association between approach-based coping and PTSD for soldiers who experienced higher levels of combat exposure. More studies assessing coping strategies in the war zone are needed. A significant limitation of existing studies is the method by which coping is measured. Sutker and colleagues (1995b) asked soldiers to rate coping with the Gulf War more generally rather than targeting a specific event that may have been traumatic. While Sharkansky and colleagues (2000) asked about specifically coping with the "most important experience or most stressful situation" during the Gulf War, this is also quite general and does not necessarily specify coping with a potentially traumatic event. Future studies should evaluate coping strategies in response to a specific traumatic event. Ideally, this would be measured either during or immediately following deployment.

For women, sexual trauma and harassment in the military has also shown to be linked to an increased risk for psychopathology. For example, Fontana and Rosenheck (1998a) demonstrated that sexual trauma in the military contributed to the development of posttraumatic stress disorder in female Vietnam veterans. Similarly, Fontana, Litz, and Rosenheck (2000) found a direct relationship between sexual harassment and PTSD symptoms in female peacekeepers. Existing PTSD studies are flawed, because many do not include women, and those that do may not specifically ask about sexual harassment. Studies that include questions about sexual harassment find high rates. In a Gulf War sample, 23 percent of women surveyed reported sexual assault, 33 percent reported physical sexual harassment, and 66 percent reported verbal sexual harassment. Sexual assault during military service had a higher impact on PTSD symptoms than did combat exposure, and more frequent sexual harassment was predictive of PTSD (Wolfe et al.,1998). Also, women who had prior combat experience were more likely to have PTSD both immediately following and at two years postdeployment; the relationship between prior combat and PTSD was not significant for men at either time point. One possibility is that the prior combat exposure variable may be a proxy for prior sexual harassment and that the effects of sexual harassment are additive for women.

Military rank and status also differentially predicted PTSD one to two years following deployment to the Gulf War (Sutker et al, 1995b; Wolfe et al., 1999). More specifically, Wolfe and colleagues found that enlisted soldiers, as compared to officers, were over five times more likely to develop PTSD, and that National Guard soldiers and reservists were three times more likely, as compared to enlisted soldiers, to develop PTSD. Similarly, in a sample of peacekeepers, Hotopf and colleagues (2003) found that junior rank was associated with greater stress symptomatology.

There is also evidence that ethnicity may moderate the impact of certain service-related variables that place individuals at higher risk for developing PTSD. For example, Litz, King, and colleagues (1997) reported that for African-American peacekeepers deployed to Somalia, there was a direct relationship between negative aspects of peacekeeping and PTSD. For non-African-American soldiers, in addition to a direct relationship between negative aspects of peacekeeping and PTSD, there was an indirect relationship with positive aspects of peacekeeping serving as a buffer. Humanitarian roles also seemed to act as a protective factor for non-African-American soldiers, mitigating stress reactions in peacekeepers. Arguably, because African-Americans may have been better able to identify with Somalis, positive experiences while peacekeeping did not have the same protective effect. However, it is difficult to decipher what this finding really means.

Postservice Risk Factors

Historically, there has been great variation in how different troops have been received upon their return home. While many Vietnam veterans described a hostile homecoming because of the controversial nature of the Vietnam War, this was not the case for Gulf War veterans or for U.S. peacekeepers, who, on the whole, are more warmly received. There is evidence that postservice factors, such as community reception, may differentially predict PTSD (Koenen et al., 2003). For example, Fontana and Rosenheck (1994) found that lack of support from family and friends upon returning from Vietnam and societal rejection at the time of homecoming were strongly associated with PTSD. Johnson and colleagues (1997) found that among Vietnam veterans, homecoming reception was the most significant predictor of PTSD symptoms, overriding combat exposure, premilitary trauma, and stressful life events. Bolton, Litz, Glenn, Orsillo, and Roemer (2002) found that among U.S. peacekeepers deployed to Somalia, family and community reception at homecoming were both significant predictors of PTSD symptoms, although these variables did not supercede variance accounted for by combat exposure.

In their meta-analysis, Ozer and colleagues (2003) found that posttrauma social support significantly predicted PTSD. The association between posttrauma-perceived social support and PTSD did not vary by the type of sample studied; however, a stronger inverse relationship was found between social support and PTSD in combat veterans compared to civilians exposed to interpersonal violence. Similarly, Brewin and colleagues (2000) found that lack of social support predicted PTSD in a military sample.

Social support may also serve as a mediator. For example, the relationship between sexual trauma and PTSD in female Vietnam veterans was strongly mediated by a lack of social support at the time of homecoming (Fontana & Rosenheck, 1998a). When comparing rates of positive and negative social contacts, Dirkzwager, Bramsen, and Van der Ploeg (2003) found that in a sample of peacekeepers, greater negative social contacts were associated with greater PTSD symptom severity. When social support was defined as the extent to which the veteran's family helped with reintegration into civilian life, Koenen and colleagues (2003) found that perceived social support significantly influences PTSD recovery. Similarly, Sutker and colleagues (1995b) found that perceived family cohesion was a consistent predictor of PTSD diagnosis. However, there was no significant relationship between PTSD and general social support and satisfaction, the degree to which family members are helpful and supportive of one another, expressiveness within the family unit, or the existence of conflict within the family. Similarly, Southwick, Morgan, and Rosenberg (2000) found that the degree of talking to family and friends about experiences in the Gulf War was not predictive of PTSD symptoms. From these studies, it appears that a more general tendency toward family cohesion may serve as a protective factor, rather than the specific ways in which the family is supportive or expressive. In support of this hypothesis, Fontana and Rosenheck (1994) found that family instability among Vietnam veterans, along with participation in abusive violence, was associated with PTSD.

Another possibility is that there are distinct gender differences with respect to social support; King and colleagues (1999) found that the social-support relationship differed for men and women. For women, functional social support, defined as perceived emotional provisions and instrumental assistance from others, was protective against PTSD. For men, structural social support, defined as the size and complexity of the social network, was negatively related to PTSD. There are a number of additional social relationship variables that are associated with PTSD. For example, reports of involvement in the community, defined as meetings or activities related to public affairs or community service, served as a protective factor in Vietnam veterans (Koenen et al., 2003).

Disclosure of military experiences is another factor that has been postulated to protect soldiers from the adverse effects of trauma exposure. In peacekeeping samples, disclosure is associated with less psychological distress (e.g., Bolton, Glenn, Orsillo, Roemer, & Litz, 2003; Greenberg et al., 2003). Here, the term disclosure refers to discussing aspects of one's deployment with a trusted other (e.g., spouse, family member, close friend). Bolton and colleagues (2003) found that among Somalia peacekeepers, disclosure to a partner/spouse, family, friends, and/or other military personnel was associated with decreased PTSD symptoms; notably, this relationship was not moderated by exposure or by other stressors. Additionally, the reactions to soldiers' disclosures were associated with PTSD symptoms, with positive reactions related to lower symptomatology; however, there was no difference in PTSD symptoms in veterans who received a negative reaction to their disclosure and those who did not disclose to anyone. Overall rates of disclosure to others vary; however, the majority of peacekeepers seem to disclose to someone, usually an individual to whom they feel close, such as a spouse or family member. Greenberg and colleagues (2003) found that two-thirds of peacekeepers disclosed their experiences to others, and Bolton and colleagues (2003) found that 69 percent of peacekeepers disclosed to a partner/spouse, 69 percent disclosed to a family member, 62 percent to friends, 78 percent to other military personnel, and 16 percent to a professional counselor or clergy; 16 percent reported not having disclosed their experiences to anyone, and 14 percent of those who disclosed reported a nonvalidating reaction. The relationship between disclosure and PTSD also seems to hold true for Vietnam veterans; those who discussed their military experiences demonstrated decreased rates of PTSD (e.g., Green, Grace, Lindy, & Gleser., 1990; Solkoff, Gray, & Keill, 1986). Koenen and colleagues (2003) found that veterans who reported discomfort in disclosing their Vietnam service experiences to friends or family demonstrated an increased risk for developing PTSD.

Upon return from the military, many soldiers are also exposed to stressors at home, including stress that results from trying to reintegrate to civilian life, employment stressors, and family stressors. These stressors may have a direct relationship with PTSD symptoms, or these stressors may act as a mediator between exposure and risk for PTSD. King and colleagues (1999) found that, for Vietnam veterans, highly stressful postwar experiences were associated with PTSD in both men and women. Wolfe and colleagues (1998) found that the relationship between sexual harassment and PTSD symptoms was mediated by number of postservice stressful life events. In peacekeepers deployed to Bosnia, poor mental health at one-year follow up was most strongly predicted by postdeployment stressors (Michel et al., 2003). Dirkzager and colleagues (2003) also found a bilateral relationship between stressful life events following deployment and PTSD symptoms in peacekeepers.

Post-war-zone coping strategies may also be associated with PTSD. A number of studies have documented a positive relationship between the use of avoidance-based coping to deal with postwar stressors and PTSD symptomatalogy (Dirkzwager et al., 2003; Fairbank, Hansen, & Fitterling, 1991; Solomon, Mikulincer, & Avitzur, 1988; Solomon, Mikulincer, & Flum, 1988). However, because these studies have not assessed prewar coping strategies, it is unclear whether the avoidant coping style was preexisting or whether it is a manifestation of PTSD. Avoidance is a hallmark symptom of PTSD, which complicates the picture to an even greater extent. Conversely, the use of approach-based strategies is less frequently found to be negatively associated with PTSD symptoms (Dirkzwager et al., 2003; Solomon, Mikulincer, & Flum, 1988). For example, Dirkzwager and colleagues reported that those using problem solving skills and seeking social-support reported less PTSD symptomatology.

Future Directions

Future research should strive for as much methodological rigor as possible to produce the most accurate prevalence rates of combat-related PTSD possible. The ideal study would measure PTSD with an empirically validated structured interview (e.g., the Clinician Administered PTSD Scale; see Weathers, Keane, & Davidson, 2001), include a large representative sample of soldiers deployed to a combat theater of operations, assess PTSD symptomatology prospectively (ideally both before and after being informed of their deployment), again shortly after soldiers return from the mission, and follow up with soldiers at multiple time points. For practical reasons (e.g., cost, unpredictability of significant combat missions, difficulties following up active-duty personnel), the ideal study is difficult to conduct. However, studies with more methodological rigor would lead to a better understanding of the prevalence of combat-related PTSD. Additionally, it would be helpful to conduct these studies both in the United States and cross-culturally, with the same measures, so that future comparisons can be made across conflicts.

While there are a multitude of studies that explore risk factors, fewer studies explore variables that act as protective factors. There is a need for studies to include more individuals who were resilient postservice and to explore the variables that contribute to resilience in this potentially at-risk group. Variables such as posttraumatic growth (i.e., the process by which an individual comes to endorse positive life changes following trauma) and personality factors that may act as buffers should be explored in scientifically rigorous and longitudinal frameworks. We need to better understand whether known protective factors are stable over time. The best way of doing this is by designing future studies with prospective and/or longitudinal designs. It has been shown that posttraumatic growth generally increases over time, although growth in various life domains follows different courses, and there is significant individual variability in these growth patterns (Frazier, Conlon, & Glaser, 2001).

Each of the reviewed preservice, service, and postservice variables should be considered when assessing an individual's risk for future mental health problems. These factors also are important to consider in the context of early intervention for trauma. Unfortunately, attention to risk factors has been virtually ignored by most mental health professionals and those designing interventions for traumatized groups (Litz & Gray, 2004). The long-held belief that everyone exposed to trauma should receive some form of intervention often results in mandatory treatment dissemination without screening for risk (e.g., critical incident stress debriefing). After empirically evaluating this assumption, studies find that overall, the majority of individuals recover from exposure to trauma over time without intervention, and that those who may require early intervention report risk factors that place them at increased chances for developing posttraumatic complications (Litz & Gray, 2004). Although there is still a lot to learn about which risk factors are most important, the variables outlined in this chapter can hopefully serve as a broad-based guide. Screening, although a challenging proposal because of methodological difficulties in setting up such a program, can ideally help identify those who are at greatest risk (Wright, Huffman, Adler, & Castro, 2002). Once early intervention is implemented, treatment should also highlight protective factors, such as social support, helpful coping strategies, and factors such as family cohesion that are known to buffer against mental health problems.

References

Adler, A. B., Litz, B. T., & Bartone, P. T. (2003). The nature of peacekeeping stressors. In T. W. Britt & A. B. Adler (Eds.), *The psychology of the peacekeeper: Lessons from the field* (pp. 149–167). Westport, CT: Praeger.

Adler, A. B., Vaitkus, M. A., & Martin, J. A. (1996). Combat exposure and posttraumatic stress symptomatology among U.S. soldiers deployed to the Gulf War. *Military Psychology, 8*, 1–14.

American Psychiatric Association (1980). *Diagnostic and statistical manual of mental disorders* (3rd ed.). Washington, DC: Author.

American Psychiatric Association (1994). *Diagnostic and statistical manual of mental disorders* (4th ed.). Washington, DC: Author.

Bolton, E. E., Glenn, D. M., Orsillo, S., Roemer, L., & Litz, B. T. (2003). The relationship between self-disclosure and symptoms of posttraumatic stress disorder in peacekeepers deployed to Somalia. *Journal of Traumatic Stress, 16*, 203–210.

Bolton, E., Litz, B. T., Britt, T., Adler, A., & Roemer, L. (2001). Reports of exposure to potentially traumatic events and PTSD in troops poised for deployment. *Journal of Traumatic Stress, 14*, 249–256.

Bolton, E., Litz, B. T., Glenn, D. M., Orsillo, S., & Roemer, L. (2002). The impact of homecoming reception on the adaptation of peacekeepers following deployment. *Military Psychology, 14*, 241–251.

Bramsen, I., Dirkzwager, A. J. E., & Van der Ploeg, H. M. (2000). Predeployment personality traits and exposure to trauma as predictors of posttraumatic stress symptoms: A prospective study of former peacekeepers. *American Journal of Psychiatry, 157*, 1115–1119.

Bremner, J. D., Licinio, J., Darnell, A., Krystal, J. H., Owens, M. J., Southwick, S. M., et al. (1997). Elevated CSF corticotropin-releasing factor concentrations in posttraumatic stress disorder. *American Journal of Psychiatry, 154*, 624–629.

Bremner, J. D., Randall, P., Scott, T. M., Bronen, R. A., Seibyl, J. P., Southwick, et al. (1995). MRI-based measurement of hippocampal volume in patients with combat-related posttraumatic stress disorder. *American Journal of Psychiatry, 152*, 973–981.

Bremner, J. D., Southwick, S. M., Johnson, D. R., Yehuda, R., & Charney, D. S. (1993). Childhood physical abuse and combat-related posttraumatic stress disorder in Vietnam veterans. *American Journal of Psychiatry, 150*, 235–239.

Brewin, C. R., Andrews, B., & Valentine, J. D. (2000). Meta-analysis of risk factors for posttraumatic stress disorder in trauma-exposed adults. *Journal of Consulting & Clinical Psychology, 68*, 748–766.

Davidson, J., Swartz, M. Storck, M., Krishnan, R. R., & Hammett, E. (1985). A diagnostic and family study of posttraumatic stress disorder. *American Journal of Psychiatry, 142*, 90–93.

Dirkzwager, A. J. E, Bramsen, I. & Van der Ploeg, H. M. (2003). Social support, coping, life events, and posttraumatic stress symptoms among former peacekeepers: A prospective study. *Personality and Individual Differences, 34*, 1545–1559.

Engel, C. C., Engel, A. L., Campbell, S. J., McFall, M. E. (1993). Posttraumatic stress disorder symptoms and precombat sexual and physical abuse in Desert Storm veterans. *Journal of Nervous and Mental Disease, 181,* 683–688.

Fairbank, J. A., Hansen, D. J., & Fitterling, J. M. (1991). Patterns of appraisal and coping across different stressor conditions among former prisoners of war with and without posttraumatic stress disorder. *Journal of Consulting and Clinical Psychology, 59,* 274–281.

Flora, C. M. (2002). A short history of PTSD from the military perspective. In M. B. Williams & J. F. Sommer (Eds.), *Simple and complex Post-Traumatic Stress Disorder* (pp. 3–8). New York: The Haworth Press.

Fontana, A., Litz, B. T., & Rosenheck, R. (2000). Impact of combat and sexual assault on the severity of PTSD among men and women peacekeepers in Somalia (2000). *Journal of Nervous and Mental Disease, 188,* 163–169.

Fontana, A. & Rosenheck, R. (1994). Posttraumatic stress disorder among Vietnam theater veterans. A causal model of etiology in a community sample. *Journal of Nervous and Mental Disease, 182,* 677–684.

Fontana, A., & Rosenheck, R. (1998a). Duty-related and sexual stress in the etiology of PTSD among women veterans who seek treatment. *Psychiatric Services, 49,* 658–662.

Fontana, A., & Rosenheck, R. (1998b). Psychological benefits and liabilities of traumatic exposure in the war zone. *Journal of Traumatic Stress, 11,* 485–503.

Fontana, A., Schwartz, L. S., & Rosenheck, R. (1997). Posttraumatic stress disorder among female Vietnam veterans: a causal model of etiology. *American Journal of Public Health, 87,* 169–175.

Frazier, P., Conlon, A., & Glaser, T. (2001). Positive and negative changes following sexual assault. *Journal of Consulting and Clinical Psychology, 69,* 1048–1055.

Gray, M. G., Bolton, E. E., & Litz, B. T. (2004). A longitudinal analysis of PTSD symptom course: Delayed-onset PTSD in Somalia peacekeepers. *Journal of Clinical and Consulting Psychology, 72,* 909–913.

Green, B. L., Grace, M. C., Lindy, J. D., Gleser, G. C., & Leonard, A. (1990). Risk factors for PTSD and other diagnoses in a general sample of Vietnam veterans. *American Journal of Psychiatry, 147,* 729–733.

Green, B. L., Grace, M. C., Lindy, J. D., & Leonard, A. C. (1990). Race differences in response to combat stress. *Journal of Traumatic Stress, 3,* 379–393.

Greenberg, N., Thomas, S., Iversen, A., Unwin, C., Hull, L., & Wessely, S. (2003). Do military peacekeepers want to talk about their experiences? Perceived psychological support of UK military peacekeepers on return from deployment. *Journal of Mental Health, 12,* 565–573.

Han, H., Litz, B. T., Wang, J. L., Britt, T. W., Adler, A. B., Bartone, P. T., et al. (2004). *Predictors of PTSD symptomatology in U.S. soldiers deployed to Bosnia.* Manuscript submitted for publication.

Hoge, C .W., Castro, C. A., Messer, S. C., McGurk, D., Cotting, D. I., & Koffman, R. L. (2004). Combat duty in Iraq and Afghanistan, mental health problems, and barriers to care. *New England Journal of Medicine, 351,* 13–22.

Hotopf, M., David. A. S., Hull, L., Ismail, K., Palmer, I., Unwin, C., et al. (2003). The health effects of peace-keeping in the UK Armed Forces: Bosnia 1992–1996. Predictors of psychological symptoms. *Psychological Medicine, 33,* 155–162.

Iowa Persian Gulf Study Group (1997). Self-reported illness and health status among Gulf War veterans: A population-based study. *The Journal of the American Medical Association, 277*, 238–245.

Johnson, D. R., Lubin, H., Rosenheck, R., Fontana, A., Southwick, S., & Charney, D. (1997). The impact of the homecoming reception on the development of posttraumatic stress disorder. The West Haven Homecoming Stress Scale (WHHSS). *Journal of Traumatic Stress, 10*, 259–277.

Kang, H. K., Natelson, B. H., Mahan, C. M., Lee, K. Y., & Murphy, F. M. (2003). Posttraumatic stress disorder and chronic fatigue syndrome-like illness among Gulf War veterans: A population-based survey of 30,000 veterans. *American Journal of Epidemiology, 157*, 141–148.

Keane, T. M., Caddell, J. M., & Taylor, K. L. (1988). Mississippi Scale for Combat-Related Posttraumatic Stress Disorder: Three studies in reliability and validity. *Journal of Consulting and Clinical Psychology, 56*, 85–90.

King, D. W., King, L. A., Foy, D. W., & Gudanowski, D. M. (1996). Prewar factors in combat-related posttraumatic stress disorder: Structural equation modeling with a national sample of female and male Vietnam veterans. *Journal of Consulting and Clinical Psychology, 64*, 520–531.

King, D. W., King, L. A., Foy, D. W., Keane, T. M., & Fairbank, J. A. (1999). Post-traumatic stress disorder in a national sample of female and male Vietnam veterans: Risk factors, war-zone stressors, and resilience-recovery variables. *Journal of Abnormal Psychology, 108*, 164–170.

King, D. W., King, L. A., Gudanowski, D. M., & Vreven, D. L. (1995). Alternative representations of warzone stressors: Relationships to posttraumatic stress disorder in male and female Vietnam veterans. *Journal of Abnormal Psychology, 104*, 184–196.

King, D. W., King, L. A., Erickson, D. J., Huang, M. T., Sharkansky, E., & Wolfe, J. (2000). Posttraumatic stress disorder and retrospectively reported stressor exposure: A longitudinal prediction model. *Journal of Abnormal Psychology, 109*, 624–633.

King, D. W., Leskin, G. A., King, L. A., & Weathers, F. W. (1998). Confirmatory factor analysis of the Clinician-Administered PTSD Scale: Evidence for the dimensionality of posttraumatic stress disorder. *Psychological Assessment, 10*, 90–96.

Koenen, K., Harley, R., Lyons, M. J., Wolfe, J., Simpson, J. C., Goldberg, J., et al. (2002). A twin registry study of familial and individual risk factors for trauma exposure and posttraumatic stress disorder. *Journal of Nervous and Mental Disease, 190*, 209–218.

Koenen, K. C., Stellman, J. M., Stellman, S., & Sommer, J. F. (2003). Risk factors for course of Posttraumatic Stress Disorder among Vietnam veterans: A 14-year follow-up of American Legionnaires. *Journal of Consulting and Clinical Psychology, 71*, 980–986.

Kulka, R. A., Schlenger, W. E., Fairbank, J. A., Hough, R. L., Jordon, B. K., Marmar, C. R., et al. (1990a). *The National Vietnam Veterans Readjustment Study: Tables of findings and technical appendices.* New York: Runner/Mazel.

Kulka, R. A., Schlenger, W. E., Fairbank, J. A., Hough, R. L., Jordan, B. K., Marmar, C. R., et al. (1990b). *Trauma and the Vietnam War generation: Report of the findings from the national Vietnam veteran's readjustment study.* New York: Brunner/Mazel.

Litz, B. T., & Gray, M. J. (2004). Early intervention for trauma in adults. In B. Litz (Ed.), *Early Intervention for Trauma and Traumatic Loss* (pp. 87–111). New York: Guilford.

Litz, B. T., Gray, M. J., & Bolton, E. (2003). Posttraumatic stress disorder following peace-keeping operations. In T. W. Britt & A. B. Adler (Eds.), *The psychology of the peacekeeper: Lessons from the field* (pp. 243–258). Westport, CT: Praeger.

Litz, B. T., Gray, M. J., Bryant, R. J., & Adler, A. B. (2002). Early interventions for trauma: Current status and future directions. *Clinical Psychology: Science and Practice, 9,* 112–134.

Litz, B. T., King, L. A., King, D. W., Orsillo, S. M., & Friedman, M. J. (1997). Warriors as peacekeepers: Features of the Somalia experience and PTSD. *Journal of Consulting and Clinical Psychology, 65,* 1001–1010.

Litz, B. T., Orsillo, S. M., Friedman, M., Ehlich, P., & Batres, A. (1997). Post-traumatic Stress Disorder associated with peacekeeping in Somalia for U.S. military personnel. *American Journal of Psychiatry, 154,* 178–184.

Macklin, M. L., Metzger L. J., Litz, B. T., McNally, R. J., Lasko, N. B., Orr, S. P., et al. (1998). Lower precombat intelligence is a risk factor for posttraumatic stress disorder. *Journal of Consulting and Clinical Psychology, 66,* 323–326.

Maguen, S., Litz, B. T., Wang, J. L, & Cook, M. (2004). The stressors and demands of peacekeeping in Kosovo: Predictors of mental health response. *Military Medicine, 169,* 198–206.

Marmar, C. R., Weiss, D. S., Schlenger, W. E., Fairbank, J. A., Jordan, B. K., Kulka, R. A., et al. (1994). Peritraumatic dissociation and posttraumatic stress in male Vietnam theater vet-erans. *American Journal of Psychiatry, 151,* 902–907.

McNally, R. J., & Shin, L. M. (1995). Association of intelligence with severity of post-traumatic stress disorder symptoms in Vietnam combat veterans. *American Journal of Psychiatry, 152,* 936–938.

Mehlum, L. (1994, June). *Positive and negative consequences of serving in a UN peace-keeping mission. A follow-up study.* Paper presented at the annual meeting of the International Congress of Military Medicine, Augsburg, Germany.

Mehlum, L., & Weisaeth, L. (2002). Predictors of posttraumatic stress reactions in Norwegian U.N. peacekeepers 7 years after service. *Journal of Traumatic Stress, 15,* 17–26.

Michel, P. O., Lundin, T., & Larsson, G. (2003). Stress reactions among Swedish peace-keeping soldiers serving in Bosnia: A longitudinal study. *Journal of Traumatic Stress, 16,* 589–593.

Norris, F. H., Foster, J. D., & Weisshaar, D. L. The epidemiology of sex differences in PTSD across developmental, societal, and research contexts (pp. 3–42). In R. Kimerling, P. Ouimette, & J. Wolfe (Eds.), *Gender and PTSD.* New York: Guilford.

O'Toole, B. I., Marshall, R. P., Schureck, R. J., & Dobson, M. (1999). Combat, dissociation, and posttraumatic stress disorder in Australian Vietnam veterans. *Journal of Traumatic Stress, 12,* 625–640.

Ozer, E. J., Best, S. R., Lipsey, T. L., & Weiss, D. S. (2003). Predictors of posttraumatic stress disorder and symptoms in adults: A meta-analysis. *Psychological Bulletin, 129,* 52–73.

Perconte, S. T., Wilson, A. T., Pontius, E. B., Dietrick, A. L., & Spiro, K. J. (1993). Psycho-logical and war stress symptoms among deployed and non-deployed reservists following the Persian Gulf War. *Military Medicine, 158,* 516–521.

Roemer, L., Litz, B. T., Orsillo, S. M., Ehlich, P., & Friedman, M. (1998). Increases in retro-spective accounts of war-zone exposure over time: The role of PTSD symptom severity. *Journal of Traumatic Stress, 11,* 597–607.

Roemer, L., Orsillo, S. M., Borkovec, T. D., & Litz, B. T. (1998). The relationship between reports of emotional response at the time of a potentially traumatizing event and PTSD symptomatology: A preliminary retrospective analysis of the DSM-IV Criterion A-2. *Journal of Behavior Therapy and Experimental Psychiatry, 29,* 123–130.

Ruef, A. M., Litz, B. T., & Schlenger, W. E. (2000). Hispanic ethnicity and risk for combat-related posttraumatic stress disorder. *Cultural Diversity and Ethnic Minority Psychology, 6,* 235–251.

Schlenger, W. E., Kulka, R. A., Fairbank, J. A., Hough, R. L., Jordon, B. K., Marmar, C. R., et al. (1992). The prevalence of posttraumatic stress disorder in the Vietnam generation: A multimethod, multisource assessment of psychiatric disorders. *Journal of Traumatic Stress, 5,* 333–363.

Schnurr, P. P., Friedman, M. J., & Rosenberg, S. D. (1993). Premilitary MMPI scores as predictors of combat-related PTSD symptoms. *American Journal of Psychiatry, 150,* 479–483.

Seedat, S., le Roux, C., & Stein, D. J. (2003). Prevalence and characteristics of trauma and post-traumatic stress symptoms in operational members of the South African National Defence Force. *Military Medicine, 168,* 71–75.

Sharkansky, E. J., King, D. W., King, L. A., Wolfe, J., Erickson, D. J., & Stokes, L. R. (2000). Coping with Gulf War combat stress: Mediating and moderating effects. *Journal of Abnormal Psychology, 109,* 188–197.

Solkoff, N., Gray, P., & Keill, S. (1986). Which Vietnam veterans develop Posttraumatic Stress Disorders? *Journal of Clinical Psychology, 42,* 687–698.

Solomon, Z., Mikulincer, M., & Avitzur, E. (1988). Coping, locus of control, social support and combat related posttraumatic stress disorder: A prospective study. *Journal of Personality and Social Psychology, 55,* 279–285.

Solomon, Z., Mikulincer, M., & Flum, H. (1988). Negative life events, coping responses and combat related psychopathology: A prospective study. *Journal of Abnormal Psychology, 97,* 302–307.

Solomon, Z., Neria, Y., Ohry, A., Waysman, M., & Ginzburg, K. (1994). PTSD among Israeli former prisoners of war and soldiers with combat stress reaction: a longitudinal study. *American Journal of Psychiatry, 151,* 554–559.

Solomon, Z., Weisenberg, M., Schwarzwald, J., & Mikulincer, M. (1987). Posttraumatic stress disorder among frontline soldiers with combat stress reaction: The 1982 Israeli experience. *American Journal of Psychiatry, 144,* 448–454.

Southwick, S. M., Morgan, C. A., Darnell, A., Bremner, D., Nicolaou, A. L., Nagy, L. M., et al. (1995). Trauma-related symptoms in veterans of Operation Desert Storm: A 2-year follow-up. *American Journal of Psychiatry, 152,* 1150–1155.

Southwick, S. M., Morgan, A., Nagy, L. M., Bremner, D., Nicolaou, A. L., Johnson, D. R., et al. (1993). Trauma-related symptoms in veterans of Operation Desert Storm: A preliminary report. *American Journal of Psychiatry, 150,* 1524–1528.

Southwick, S. M., Morgan, C. A., Nicolaou, A. L., & Charney, D. S. (1997). Consistency of memory for combat-related traumatic events in veterans of Operation Desert Storm. *American Journal of Psychiatry, 154,* 173–177.

Southwick, S. M., Morgan, C. A., & Rosenberg, R. (2000). Social sharing of Gulf War experiences: Association with trauma-related psychological symptoms. *Journal of Nervous and Mental Disease, 188,* 695–700.

Spitzer, R. L., Williams, J. B., & Gibbon, M. (1987). *Structured Clinical Interview for DSM-III-R- Patient version* (SCID-P, 4-1-87). New York: New York State Psychiatric Institute.

Sutker, P. B., Davis, J. M., Uddo, M., & Ditta, S. R. (1995a). Assessment of psychological distress in Persian Gulf troops: Ethnicity and gender comparisons. *Journal of Personality Assessment, 64*, 415–427.

Sutker, P. B., Davis, J. M., Uddo, M., & Ditta, S. R. (1995b). War zone stress, personal resources, and PTSD in Persian Gulf War returnees. *Journal of Abnormal Psychology, 104*, 444–452.

Tampke, A. K., & Irwin, H. J. (1999). Dissociative processes and symptoms of posttraumatic stress in Vietnam veterans. *Journal of Traumatic Stress, 12*, 725–738.

True, W. J., Rice, J., Eisen, S. A., Heath, A. C., Goldberg, J., Lyons, M. J., et al. (1993). A twin study of genetic and environmental contributions to liability for posttraumatic stress symptoms. *Archives of General Psychiatry, 50*, 257–264.

Vasterling, J. J., Brailey, K., Constans, J. I., Gorges, A., & Sutker, P. B. (1997). Assessments of intellectual resources in Gulf War veterans: Relationship to PTSD. *Assessment, 4*, 51–59.

Ward, W. (1997). Psychiatric morbidity in Australian veterans of the United Nations peacekeeping force in Somalia. *Australian and New Zealand Journal of Psychiatry, 31*, 184–193.

Weathers, F. W., Keane, T. M., & Davidson, J. R. T. (2001). Clinician-Administered PTSD Scale: A review of the first ten years of research. *Depression and Anxiety, 13*, 132–156.

Weathers, F. W., Litz, B. L., Herman, D., Huska, J., & Keane, T. M. (1993). *The PTSD checklist: Reliability, validity, and diagnostic utility.* Presented at the International Society for Traumatic Stress Studies Annual Meeting, San Antonio, TX.

Weathers, F. W., Litz, B. L., & Keane, T. M. (1995). Military trauma. In J. R. Freedy & S. E. Hobfoll (Eds.), *Traumatic stress: From theory to practice* (pp. 103–128). New York: Plenum.

Wessely, S., Unwin, C., Hotopf, M., Hull, L., Ismail, K., Nicolaou, V., et al. (2003). Stability of recall of military hazards over time. Evidence from the Persian Gulf War of 1991. *British Journal of Psychiatry, 183*, 314–322.

Wolfe, J., Erickson, D. J., Sharkansky, E. J., King, D. W., & King, L. A. (1999). Course and predictors of posttraumatic stress disorder among Gulf War veterans: A prospective analysis. *Journal of Consulting and Clinical Psychology, 67*, 520–528.

Wolfe, J., & Kimerling, R. (1997). Gender issues in the assessment of posttraumatic stress disorder. In J. P. Wilson & T. M. Keane (Eds.), Assessing psychological trauma and PTSD (pp. 192–238). New York: Guilford.

Wolfe, J., Sharkansky, E. J., Read, J. P., Dawson, R., Martin, J. A., & Ouimette, P. C. (1998). Sexual harassment and assault as predictors of PTSD symptomatology among U.S. female Persian Gulf War personnel. *Journal of Interpersonal Violence, 13*, 40–57.

Wright, K. M., Huffman, A. H., Adler, A. B., & Castro, C. A. (2002). Psychological screening program overview. *Military Medicine, 167*, 853–861.

Xian, H., Chantarujikapong, S. I., Scherrer, J. F., Eisen, S. A., Lyons, M. J., Goldberg, J., et al. (2000). Genetic and environmental influences on posttraumatic stress disorder, alcohol and drug dependence in twin pairs. *Drug and Alcohol Dependence, 61*, 95–102.

Zaidi, L. Y. & Foy, D. W. (1994). Childhood abuse experiences and combat related PTSD. *Journal of Traumatic Stress, 7*, 33–42.

Zatzick, D. F., Marmar, C. R., Weiss, D. S., & Metzler, T. (1994). Does trauma-linked dissociation vary across ethnic groups? *Journal of Nervous and Mental Disease, 182*, 576–582.

PART IV

ORGANIZATIONAL RESPONSES TO PSYCHOLOGICAL CHALLENGES

CHAPTER 8

HUMAN SPIRITUALITY, RESILIENCE, AND THE ROLE OF MILITARY CHAPLAINS

Thomas C. Waynick, Peter J. Frederich, David M. Scheider, Ronald H. Thomas, and Glen L. Bloomstrom

In August 2004, Chechen terrorists attacked an elementary school in Beslan, Russia, on the first day of school. For four tense days, thirty-odd terrorists held nearly 600 children, parents, and teachers hostage while Russia and the world anxiously waited outside. On the fourth day of the standoff, with negotiations failing, an explosion inside the school set off a tragic cacophony of events in which terrorists, Russian antiterror police, and even parent-vigilantes fought to regain and rescue the hostages. Nearly 400 children, terrorists, parents, and police died in the tragic mission.

One very haunting and powerful picture from that tragedy illustrates the impact of religion for people in crises.

> The photo is a close-up of a young girl's left hand. Her nails are polished, but the fingers are all covered with dirt and dried blood. There's a raw, red mark on the center of the palm; it looks like a really bad scrape. In that hand there is a small, grimy chain wrapped around the fingers and, hanging from that chain down onto the palm, is a very small golden cross. She and her brother were hostages in the school; they both survived, but the girl was hit in the head by a fragment from one of the bombs. The photograph was taken as she was lying unconscious in a first-aid tent. The cross in the picture is her baptismal cross. In Orthodox countries, when children are baptized, they are given a small cross, and they rarely take it off. But during the siege of the school, the girl had taken the cross off and wrapped the chain around her hand. (Wilcoxson, 2004, p. 2)

The cross for her was that symbol of reason and hope in the midst of an incomprehensible trauma.

The views expressed in this chapter are those of the author and do not reflect the official policy or position of the U.S. Department of Defense or the U.S. Government.

The cross in the hand of the young Beslan school survivor demonstrates something that all cultures have long known and which today's empirical research is currently validating. Human nature is innately spiritual/religious—and a sense of meaning and trust in a Divine Being helps people survive times of trouble. One excellent article from the field of medicine referencing this phenomenon indicated that there are definite links between spirituality and the overall health of individuals (Anandarajah & Hight, 2001). Though some do not embrace this concept, the reality is that most of humanity does and so do most of our soldiers. That is nowhere more true than during deployment and combat, where the crucible of separation and war tests values, beliefs, faith, and physical capabilities.

Throughout the U.S. Army's history, the chaplain has embodied that relationship between the physical and spiritual worlds. He or she has been a ready source for helping soldiers and families process the struggles of life. While this pastoral role may have been maintained in the military strictly out of tradition, there has long been anecdotal evidence that the chaplain's pastoral presence also serves a practical purpose of increasing soldier and family resilience along with personal and emotional health. This resource has usually taken two forms. First, the chaplain serves a direct, sacramental role, enabling soldiers to find connection with, and trust in their God. Second, the chaplain serves a counseling and care role, enabling soldiers to find meaning in and navigate the challenges inherent in the military lifestyle.

Building Resilience through Pastoral Care and Counseling

Chaplains in military units and the military community function as pastoral counselors. Each chaplain brings to his or her ministry in the Army a basic load of training for that work. They come into the Army with a postgraduate degree in pastoral theology, which usually includes some training in counseling basics. In addition to this, chaplains routinely receive training in conducting classes in stress management, suicide intervention, critical incident stress debriefing, sexual assault counseling, and couple communication skills during their initial entry training in the military. How he or she integrates faith and practice is very individual, but the bottom line is that the chaplain has basic skills that can be expected of a counselor to soldiers. While chaplains are not typically credentialed in the mental health community, they are able to provide meaningful help to soldiers and family members suffering from a variety of subdiagnosable mental, emotional, marriage, and family issues. Additionally, they can provide allied supportive counseling for soldiers and family members with such diagnosed mental health disorders as depression and combat stress. The *Army Family White Paper* recognized this in 2003:

> Chaplains have long been an installation—and unit-based—resource for specialized marriage and family pastoral counseling and education programs. The *Spring 2000 Sample Survey of Military Personnel* listed the chaplain as third behind family member and spouse or close friends as the person a soldier would most likely talk to about a confidential manner. (U.S. Army, 2003, p. 14)

The chaplain is unique as a counselor in that he or she is a *pastoral* counselor. His/her religious values are an integral part of his or her counseling. This whole concept of spirituality/religion and how it relates to psychology and counseling has been a topic of debate in numerous psychology and counseling articles, conferences, and books in recent years. It was first addressed in theological circles by Paul Tillich and Reinhold Neibuhr as they attempted the integration of the two disciplines. Browning (1987) discussed this interaction of psychology and theology in his book, *Religious Thought and the Modern Psychologies.* Every military minister in working with soldiers and their problems learns to integrate the relationship between psychology and religion. "In practice, every psychological confession has religious confession, and every religious confession, whether ritual and sacramental or free, its psychological effects" (Tournier, 1973, p. 204).

Because of the interconnection of these sacramental and care domains, the military's regulations have endowed the chaplain/parishioner relationship with the highest level of confidentiality. As a result, the chaplain, as pastoral counselor, has come to be seen by many military constituents as the safest place to discuss the problems, pains, and uncertainties of life. Soldiers, seamen, airmen, Department of Defense civilians, and family members count on being able to discuss problems with the chaplain without losing control of the information. Despite the presence of well-trained counselors in trauma, drug and alcohol abuse, social work, and behavioral health, soldiers today are still more likely to seek a chaplain first when confronting stressful ordeals than any other helping professional (U.S. Army, 2003). As one battalion commander from the Gulf War stated about his chaplain, "He is a spiritual leader, a soldier's friend, an informal counselor, the insight to commander's pressures" (Tyson, 1991).

Strengthening People by Connecting Them to God

Dr. Paul Tournier, the famed Swiss psychiatrist, said of the human being that it is impossible "to dissociate the physical, psychological and religious aspects of his life" (1973, p. 204). The ancients seemed to have understood this total human dimension better than we do today. The Greek concept of "body, mind, and soul" resonates with the emerging thoughts of trauma research and treatment. The literature coming out of the trauma field is replete with articles addressing these dimensions. One such article by the American Academy of Family Physicians states, "Research shows that things such as positive beliefs, comfort and strength gained from religion, meditation and prayer can contribute to healing and a sense of well-being" (2004).

What the U.S. Army chaplain brings to the table in the arena of psychological health is not just some loose recognition of the spiritual dimension of humankind, but a religious construct in which people frame their lives and find infinite meaning to life's problems. As a representative of a unique denomination, each chaplain brings to the spiritual dimension a clear set of values regarding behavior and the practice of life, as well as a developed cosmology of the world and the purpose of life. Just as significant, most religious denominations also encompass a developed community, where soldiers and families can connect in meaningful relationships.

These values and beliefs have been developed and tested over hundreds, even thousands of years. Religious traditions, when they are at their best, bring great power in helping people find order and meaning in their lives. In other words, the chaplain represents and advocates what is most valuable about religion.

The chaplain's religious role encompasses more than just addressing some vague sense of spirituality. In fact, the modern emergence of personalized, unformatted "spirituality" is a new construct with as yet an untested value in strengthening human health and resilience. Huston Smith in *Why Religion Matters* (2001), states that "spirituality" is really a relatively new word. In displacing traditional religion, the term has emerged as if people could be spiritual without being religious. He cites an interview in which

> at one point in Barbara Walter's two-hour long interview with Monica Lewinsky, Walters quoted President Bill Clinton as confessing that he had sinned in his relationship with Lewinsky, and she asked if Lewinsky thought she too had sinned. Lewinsky appeared taken back. She hesitated, shifted in her chair, and then answered, "I'm not very religious. I'm more spiritual." (Smith, 2001)

Apparently, Ms. Lewinsky associated consciousness of sin or failure with religion and decided she did not want to have anything to do with that. Instead, she claimed an apparently frameless "spirituality," which freed her from the necessity of admitting any guilt.

While it is clear that the unstructured spirituality provided Ms. Lewinsky great freedom, it is not known that it can provide meaningful help for people under stress or in crisis. What is known is that sin, redemption, guilt, grace, shame, and a host of other proven religious constructs pervade the lives of ordinary soldiers. For most soldiers, comfort and strength are connected to religious practice and religious community. Those communities embrace more than simple, vague spiritual ideas. As ordained ministers, chaplains bring hard religious practice, community, and support to soldiers' lives.

Though more and more people are devoid of particular denominational affiliations, most still frame their lives in terms of religious metaphors, words, and symbols. It is a rare soldier who does not want something of a religious nature, such as a cross, testament, or medallion from the chaplain prior to a deployment. This is especially true if there is a known period of imminent danger. Symbols of faith directly related to a person's religion can be a great source of comfort in separation and trauma. Symbols and their power are recognized in many cultures and situations. Those who are separated from their loved ones and faith communities carry religious symbols in the same way. Objects that connect us with our deepest religious beliefs can embody belief and its hope.

Religious and Interpersonal Connection Supports Resilience

We have long known that positive religious connection fosters resilience and health. However, only in the last half-century have social science and physical science researchers begun to meaningfully unpack the mechanics of that connection. In recent decades, a convergence of theories is beginning to explain how religious and interpersonal connection and resilience relate. In particular, three theories appear to "hang together" to explain this phenomena: (1) Hill's (1949) ABC-X theory of resilience, (2) the emerging field of neurobiology, and (3) attachment theory. Together, these theories are beginning to give us a look "behind the curtain" of sacred practice and resilience, as well as to suggest the activities that are most important in fostering personal health.

Life in the military presents many of the normal stresses of life, along with some that are unique to the military. Frequent moves and separation from extended family support structures represent unique stresses military families must negotiate. However, the risk of deployment and imminent danger to one or both adults in a nuclear family represents one of the most dramatic stressors military families must endure.

Deployment and possible combat disorganizes and adds greatly to the stress on individual soldiers and their family members. The equilibrium of the family is suddenly challenged when the soldier comes home and announces that he or she is leaving. The degree to which families successfully negotiate this crisis is determined by factors that are captured in Hill's ABC-X model pioneered a half century ago. In this theory "A" represents the stressor or event that has disrupted the system. "B" is the sum of the resources that are available to overcome the effects of the stress. "C" has to do with the meaning that is ascribed to the whole event and how much hope that gives. As the family system makes sense of what is happening and calls forth its resources, "the family reverses the disorganization and…may reach a new level of reorganization" (Hill, 1949).

Included in the resources a family will access in addressing the stress of military life are their religious values, practices, and beliefs. Confidence that a Supreme Being knows the family members, cares for them, and is watching out for them can be a powerful source of hope and comfort in chaotic times. This is true both for a soldier preparing to attack an enemy stronghold, and that same soldier's family, praying for him from 10,000 miles away. That is why it is a common sight in battle to see soldiers gathering for prayer before a major assault or campaign.

Religious Connection, Neurobiology, Secure Attachments, and Resilience

Studies in brain neurobiology are helping us understand how religious practice is linked with resilience. During combat and trauma, people are affected at many levels, including their brains. Rothschild, in her book *The Body Remembers* (2000), details the psychophysiology of trauma and trauma treatment. Modern PET scans and MRIs are helping us discover how the brain functions and protects itself in the midst of separation, loss, and trauma. What we are seeing in the study of the para-sympathetic nervous system is that trauma survivors, be they soldiers in combat or victims of a civil disaster, can be neurologically impaired by the experience. This physical impairment then affects the functioning of the individual.

Chaplains and religious activities can play a healing role in recovering from this physical impairment. Dr. Donald Meichenbaum, distinguished professor emeritus at the University of Waterloo, states that, "Religious activities have been found to be a support throughout the healing process of trauma and they help especially for those aspects of the situation that cannot be personally controlled and that are not amenable to problem-solving" (2002, p. 9).

These data are currently being reflected by sacred writers as well. Popular faith books have embraced what the science of neurobiology is teaching us about the human brain. Lester (2003), in *The Angry Christian,* reflects theologically on this area of brain studies and personality. Hogue, in his 2003 book *Remembering the Future, Imagining the Past: Story, Ritual, and the Human Brain,* also has integrated theology with neurobiology.

Religious communities have long known that significant healing experiences can occur in all relationships, including the community of faith and in the individual's relationship with God. The United Nations, in addressing justice for victims, declared that after crisis events: "Meaning may be found in a new relationship with God" (UNODCCP 1999, p. 29 as cited in Taylor, 2001); "Religion is known to give comfort and strength to individuals in times of extreme adversity." This may be vali-dated in the research surrounding the role of attachment, psychological well-being, and recovery from trauma. Going back as far as the groundbreaking work of Bowlby (1982) and his associates, "attachment" theorists have recognized that secure attach-ments are a protective factor, both supporting resistance to signs of trauma stress and providing venues for treatment of trauma survivors. Bowlby, in one of his lectures, once said,

> Evidence is accumulating that human beings of all ages are happiest and able to deploy their talents to best advantage when they are confident that, standing behind them there are one or more trusted persons who will come to their aid should difficulty arise. (Karen, 1994, p. 381)

For many that "one" includes their God.

Currently one of the most promising forms of treatment for trauma seems to be Emotionally Focused Therapy (EFT), where attachment bonds are recreated or newly created. As Sue Johnson, one of the founders of EFT, states:

> The therapist's goal must be not just to lessen the distress in a survivor's relationship, but to create the secure attachment that promotes active and optimal adaptation to a world that contains danger and terror, but is not necessarily defined by it. (2002, p. 10)

The process in EFT is to produce reenactments, where, in a safe container of treat-ment, significant emotional attachment can be produced. The more the sense of attachment, the more attachment figures one has, the more "social capital" gained, the greater one's ability to cope becomes. Feelings of community with "positive close relationships have been linked to immune system competence, to resilience in combat situations, and to the ability to cope with chronic stress and illness" (Kiecolt-Glasser et al., 1993, as cited in Johnson, 2002, p. 7).

One way of understanding religious activity is to see it as a series of activities aimed at helping people develop secure attachments at multiple levels, thus lowering stress and producing better coping abilities. First, religious activity facilitates a secure attachment to God, or the Divine Being. Second, the creation of vital faith communities facilitates attachment in human relationships. The resulting attachments hold the possibility of fostering individual resilience that enables people to navigate crises and recover more completely and more adequately. This may explain what has long been anecdotally known about the positive correlation between vital religious faith and trauma resilience.

This all relates back to the science of the brain. In neurobiology, the limbic system appears to be the area that monitors safety. If it determines that things are not safe, the limbic system causes a fight, flight, or freeze reaction. The thinking part of the brain can react to this in a cooperative way by calming it down if it determines things aren't that bad. Ministry to those who are overstimulated in their fight, flight, or freeze reactions involves teaching them spiritual practices such as meditation and prayer that connect people to God and that calm the limbic system. The words that caring chaplains bring can soothe the thinking brain with messages of a world that is in good hands. Barry and Connoly, in their book on spiritual direction, share the safety sentiment well. They write:

> The enjoyment of God should be the supreme end of spiritual technique; and it is in that enjoyment of God that we feel not only saved in the Evangelical sense, but safe; we are conscious of belonging to God and hence are never alone....In that relationship Nature seems friendly and homely; even its vast spaces instead of eliciting a sense of terror speak of infinite love; and the nearer beauty becomes the garment with which the Almighty clothes Himself. (1986, p. 88)

This may shed light on how a chaplain's ministry with combat soldiers becomes a religious form of safety. Soldiers who feel securely attached to people in their world and who have self-soothing skills seem to deal more effectively with combat and stress than those who lack that sense of connectedness. Individuals who lack significant connection to others, be it God, family, or community, are at a greater risk of living in a highly aroused state of fight or flight, which in its reactivity limits the ability to cope. "Indeed, current concepts of coping strategies are evolving to include spiritual beliefs and practices, along with other social, emotional, physical, and cognitive aspects, as important coping resources" (Drescher & Foy, 1995).

In summation, chaplains represent faith communities in which people have long found a sense of belonging and the ability to cope with crises by finding a sense of belonging and safety. In representing various faith (religious) groups, chaplains do not necessarily promote spirituality in a modern sense. Spirituality has come to mean a focus solely on the inward journey of an individual. Many religions, especially Christianity, reject the notion of individualism and promote communalism. Barth

(1958), in his seminal work, *Church Dogmatics,* promotes human beings as beings in encounter. We were made for relationships with both man and God. Created in that image, humanity reflects God best when engaged in loving relationships (LaCugna, 1993). Chaplains represent religions that stand in communities offering each member a sense of purpose, belonging, meaning, and safety. Those attributes are important to the emotional well-being of soldiers and their ability to cope with deployments and the resulting trauma of war. Chaplains serve the soldier's community by building and maintaining safe and nurturing environments to launch from and return to.

Promoting Resilience through Divine and Community Connection through the Crucible of Deployment and War

Current chaplain activities in the U.S. Army have both contemporary and ancient justifications. On the one hand, they are built on traditions that have developed over the course of more than two centuries of pastoral practice, care, and counseling in the U.S. Army. On the other hand, they reflect modern conceptions of attachment, resilience, and emotional well-being. An overarching theme that defines chaplain activities in the U.S. Army could be summarized by the two commonly cited mantras of the chaplain leadership: "Serve the Army by connecting soldiers and family members to God and to each other," and "Nurture the living, care for the wounded, and honor the dead."

These mandates guide chaplain activities through the cycle of deployment and in the process support resilience. However, because each stage of the deployment cycle presents different contexts and challenges, their activities vary according to the stage. Below is a summary of chaplain activities in each stage of the deployment cycle.

Predeployment

The period of time between notification of a pending deployment and actual departure is fraught with challenges for soldiers and families. First, there are massive unknowns. How long will this deployment last? Will we survive, either personally or as a family? Where will we live? Second, there is the uncomfortable process of preparing for long separation from spouses, friends, children, and parents. Third, there are inevitable questions regarding the relative meaning and value of the deployment.

With the challenge comes great opportunity for growth. Soldiers and families who prepare well and successfully navigate the challenges of predeployment commonly excel in the stages that follow. The seeds of success in life through deployment and reintegration are typically sown during the predeployment period.

Many of the personal and interpersonal challenges that must be faced in the days and weeks prior to a soldier's departure for overseas duty or war fall into the chaplain's lane. Chaplains often participate in the unit's predeployment phase both in assisting the unit to get ready for the deployment and also by getting their own unit ministry team (UMT) (at the battalion level, this is one chaplain and one chaplain assistant) ready. Once a unit is notified for deployment, the chaplain's role becomes very important. There usually are a host of personal issues the soldiers will raise. Typically, a chain of command is in full drive and relies on the chaplain at this time to take care of the people issues. During one short-notice deployment to Kuwait, I (T.C.W.) was told by the brigade commander to relocate my desk closer to his office. He fully anticipated multiple family problems and issues to arise, because the unit had received only a 48-hour notice to "wheels up."

Soldiers' families react in a variety of ways to the impending separation. Some will live in denial or hope for a change of orders, others will welcome it as some kind of break, and those who are veterans of past deployments will just want to get it over with. An additional stress in the predeployment phase is that the military member may find that he or she has to be in the field or in the motor pool for days. As a result, an additional strain is put on the family because of the soldier's inability to spend much of the remaining time with the family. This can give way to anger and resentment, which may become visible at the actual time of deployment, when arguments break out. This coping mechanism bewilders many couples. Sometimes it's easier to leave angry than it is to feel the pain of separation. Legends abound of couples who routinely experience a major fight in the week before a long deployment. Some of these families will end up in crisis and most will likely find their way to a chaplain's office before they go anywhere else.

During this phase, commanders typically identify troubled individuals or families that could be mission distracters. Because the chaplain is on the commander's personal staff, commanders see the chaplain as their "hip-pocket" mental health provider. Chaplains are frequently called in to work with these families to come up with plans for making it through the deployment.

As part of this process of helping families, chaplains usually spend time working with family readiness groups (FRGs). In the past, chaplains often were responsible for organizing the FRG. While in some units they still assume FRG leadership, with the advent of multiple deployments, units are more commonly hiring civilian FRG coordinators to organize and support the groups. However, the chaplain is still commonly seen as a supportive resource to the FRG. Often chaplains present classes on managing stress or parenting or some other personal or relational skill. A chaplain might sometimes augment what Army Community Services is doing. In my career I (T.C.W.) have also given numerous workshops at this stage for school counselors and teachers to acquaint them with the effects of deployment on children.

In the midst of extra duties to help care for soldiers and families, chaplains are confronted with their own issues regarding their own families. Chaplains, like other care providers, often spend more time taking care of others than they do themselves. These needs can add additional stress to the chaplain who may already feel a great burden from having answered the needs of so many others.

To alleviate some of this concern, another chaplain in the technical chain will be assigned to augment the ministry of the deploying chaplain. Certainly, the garrison chaplain's office will provide additional services and educational opportunities for deploying soldiers and their families. This may also include back-fill chaplains to minister to family members after the chaplain and unit deploy.

What that installation chaplain has already established in the way of faith communities becomes even more important as those congregations draw around to lend support to families. Before a deployment is ever announced, chaplain ministry is involved in creating a faith environment of support. Religious education, prayer groups, youth groups, Scripture studies, and other programs create a sense of connectedness and value for the individual, thus furthering a strong sense of attachment. The degree to which soldiers connect to these faith communities will be valuable to the soldier and his or her unit when he or she is called to deployment. Chaplain activities to build faith communities are an important deployment ministry. The *Army Family White Paper* recognized this in 2003 when it noted: "A recent command initiative conducted by chaplains is the Building Strong and Ready Families (BSRF) program, a unit-based skill training that can significantly enhance the confidence and resilience of young married couples and ease their transition into the military" (U.S. Army, 2003, p. 15).

Deployment

The deployment period is the great crucible for soldiers and military families. It is the event that gives meaning to the whole existence of the military and the military lifestyle. Armies exist to deploy, and most soldiers long for the chance, at least once, to prove their competence and mettle in the crucible of deployment and combat. It is the "great game" for which some soldiers train and prepare for decades.

However, it is also the great trial. Soldiers in wartime are often asked to risk their lives and, possibly to take life in service to their country. Many millions observe or experience traumas in the course of combat or combat-support operations. There is a psychiatric cost of war (Friedman, 2004), and it extends beyond the soldier into his or her relationships. While the soldier is away, families must live anxiously at home, watching the news and praying for the safety of their husband, wife, parent, or child. At the very least, it is a time of prolonged separation: parents from children and spouses from each other, with all the attending difficulties and challenges.

If deployment is the great test for soldiers and their loved ones, it is also the great opportunity for chaplains to make a difference. In this crucible, chaplain activities continue to aim at fostering secure connections between soldiers, God, and loved ones, as well as to provide personal and spiritual meaning to the events that are occurring.

From the beginning of our nation's history, the ministry of the "unit-centric" chaplain during a soldier's deployment away from the container of safety found at home has defined what chaplains do. Fulfilling the normalizing principle—proximity, immediacy, expectancy, simplicity (see Lewis, this volume)—the chaplain's presence with the troops in the "thick of things" has been a stabilizing force for many soldiers. The chaplain's presence in both pleasant and painful times facilitates soldier attachment, which in turn leads soldiers to seek chaplains out when they are in need.

An illustration of this comes from Iraq, where some of the well-trained members of the combat stress control (CSC) teams were not having the timely exposure with the troops that some of the chaplains had. Since grief and other emotional issues follow individual timetables, the times soldiers wanted to talk did not always coincide with the CSC team's presence. Conversely, chaplains were widely used, because they not only had shared the combat experience, but they also were present 24/7, and they had already been agents of hope in the midst of very chaotic times.

For many religions, the spiritual leader's presence is a symbol of God's nearness. As that symbol, it represents the deepest values of personal religious faith. The chaplain, for some soldiers, is an incarnational object of that congregation or fellowship back home. This is true in virtually every major religion, whether it refers to the chaplain as priest, pastor, teacher, shaman, or imam. Soldiers often see the chaplain as bringing God's blessing for the dangers of deployment. One chaplain in an Army special operations unit in Afghanistan tells the story of coming to get water from a Ranger platoon before an operation. He was with another staff officer, who approached the water supply first, only to be rebuffed by the platoon sergeant, who explained that their supply was insufficient to support nonplatoon members. As they both turned away to find another water source, the platoon sergeant recognized the chaplain and pulled him back to the water source, saying "We always have water for you, Chaplain." That bond with the chaplain is often expressed in the fond nicknames that chaplains receive during deployments—chappy, chap, and padre.

And it is not simply the chaplain's presence that is welcomed. The blessing of God is often accepted by extension and seen as lingering after the chaplain's departure. Chaplains are often asked to give a blessing at the launch of a ship, the unveiling of a new building, or before a major operation, even if they will not personally join the mission. They may even be asked to bring God's judgment on the enemy.

The converse to this can be seen when soldiers contemplate the meaning of losing their chaplain, especially to accident or enemy action. It can be seen as a sign of the withdrawal of God's blessing. My first night in Iraq I (T.C.W.) was separated from the main convoy. The next day I reconnected with the unit and observed visible relief on the faces of the unit's soldiers. Word of the chaplain's loss had quickly spread among the rank and file unit members, who had felt that the loss of a chaplain was a particularly bad omen.

Beyond the mere presence of the chaplain, the theological constructs offered by the chaplain may help soldiers make sense of the world they are encountering. Most deployments take soldiers out of their ordinary and familiar environments and place them in strange and sometimes surreal situations. In a broad sense, the chaplain's belief system may help to offer a meaningful interpretation and thus stabilize those who find themselves not only with a bit of separation anxiety, but also trying to make sense of another reality. In that way, chaplains may serve the function of a stabilizing force, because they offer alternative meanings and reframe events in terms of core values and beliefs. In a recent letter from Iraq, we see this concept as a chaplain writes, "Today I met a soldier struggling with whether or not God would condemn him for killing an insurgent during a combat operation" (St. Andrews, 2004). Of course, if the chaplain is not attuned to where a soldier is at, his attempts at helping may not help, but hurt (Baum, 2004).

That ability to wrestle with traumatic events and give them meaning is a very important part of preventing posttraumatic stress disorder (PTSD). In Iraq, as the fighting stalled because of an intense sandstorm near An Najaf, a commander commented to the chaplain, "The men are starting to talk about what they've done. I don't want them to do this because I'm afraid they may become combat ineffective." These same soldiers, upon standing down in Baghdad, were heard to say, "I guess we will need psychiatrists now." They had all been through a terrifying three weeks of combat, which was far from any reality they had ever experienced before. Intense emotions, images, and physical exhaustion had forever embedded new and disturbing memories in their minds. Grief work would follow, and the chaplain, who is the designated subject-matter expert on death and dying, was there and active in helping the soldiers integrate what had happened in combat. One battalion commander in the Gulf War wrote,

> Before the war, every guy wants to make peace with God and the chaplain must be there to alleviate fear. After the battle, every soldier wants to make peace with the actions that took place in war and the chaplain needs to be in the unit. (Tyson, 1991, p. 11)

Thus, the chaplain may play an interpretive role, helping the soldier formulate a new reality to bring sense out of chaos.

This normalizing role of affirming traumatic experiences and assisting in the creation of new meaning is a very important one for survivors of traumatic experiences. Wylie, in commenting on the work of Dr. Dan Siegel, states,

> Simply telling patients what might be going on in their brains, he discovered, could also be both deeply comforting and therapeutic. Siegel explains to patients with PTSD the difference between implicit and explicit memory and the function of the hippocampus and they feel less crazy. (2004, p. 36)

When we can affirm to soldiers that they are not crazy and that their experiences are part of the human condition, it has a powerful effect. Coming from their "pastor," that effect might be magnified, because it is perceived to be part of God's message to them.

The role of chaplain as worship leader serves another significant function. Hymns, liturgies, and sacred readings allow the transcendent qualities of God and man to be present in what is often an obscure and sparse environment. Desert wanderings have often been associated in the history of man with deep spiritual encounters. Deployments often provide the physical dimensions of that; the chaplain can provide the catalyst for that spiritual growth. The things of God for many soldiers provide a sense of safety when far from home. God is portrayed as that nurturing parent, the ultimate object constant, who accompanies them no matter how far they are away from their relational objects.

Another important function of the chaplain is to provide the "first responder" counseling that soldiers seek. Whether it is bad news from home, an impending

Uniformed Code of Military Justice (UCMJ) action, discrimination, sexual assault, an illness, suicidal ideation, or a scene of an accident or death, the chaplain is usually the soldier's first resource in a deployment environment. Interestingly, the chaplain is often called to help even if the soldier is known to have no religious beliefs. Part of this is explained by the conventional wisdom that crises bring out whatever religious core exists even in people who profess no faith—there is an old saying commonly repeated that "there are no atheists in foxholes." This demonstrates that the chaplaincy is the one entire system recognized as the clearinghouse for all soldier related problems. In the history of our Army, it has been chaplain programs that ultimately led to the establishment of more formal organizations (i.e., Army Community Services, drug and alcohol, social work, etc.). In deployments, where other agencies are not as available or are far from the field, the chaplain becomes the sole "helping agency" available. If that chaplain has special skills in pastoral care or counseling, either as a result of personal study or other education, that chaplain may become a referral source from other chaplains in the area of operations. I (T.C.W.) received several PTSD-related cases during the Iraqi invasion because of those credentials. I was able to help counsel and do appropriate referrals because of my training. Nevertheless, the majority of soldiers trust the chaplain, regardless of counseling expertise, simply because the chaplain symbolizes the deepest relationship possible—that of God and man.

Implicit to the definition of the chaplain is the role of father confessor. The UCMJ protects the priest-penitential privilege. This role remains very important. Whereas at home a soldier may have his or her local congregation or a favored priest to go to and relieve his or her burden of guilt and shame, in a deployed environment, any chaplain may be asked to play that role.

Often chaplains become aware of troubles and trends through these confessions. Without revealing any confidence, the chaplain can aid the overall health of the organization in the field by advising commanders of the general morale and morals prevalent in the organization. Significantly, it was a chaplain who first officially reported the massacre at Mei Lai during the Vietnam War. The significance of this role for chaplains is also demonstrated by the frequency with which chaplain shortage or underfunctioning is reported as a factor in command failures. For example, reports from the 1980s sexual abuse of basic training soldiers at Aberdeen Proving Ground (Federal Advisory Committee, 1997) and the 2002 Fort Bragg string of family violence murders (U.S. Army Surgeon General, 2002) both identified a shortcoming in either chaplain presence or functioning. Likewise, anecdotal reports from the investigation of prisoner mistreatment at Abu Ghraib suggest that the units involved were underserved by chaplain resources.

Chaplains and trauma are intricately related in the deployment arena. Tragedy is recognized as the "chaplain moment." Chaplains are trained at military training sites such as the National Training Center (NTC), Joint Readiness Training Center (JRTC), and Combat Maneuver Training Center (CMTC) to respond to accidents and loss. One of my (T.C.W.) first important chaplain experiences in a field exercise occurred at 0200 while maneuvering with the brigade at Fort Hood. I received the radio message, "Chaplain, come to grid coordinate such and such, we have had a fatality." Upon arrival, I was told a soldier had been killed while standing between two trucks, the one trying to tow the other out of a ditch. The poor driver had put the lead truck in reverse instead of forward. That driver was lying alone in the dark, in a fetal position, unable to speak. No one was around him. All were angry with him. No one knew what to do with him. It was a chaplain moment, as I held and rocked him in my arms as he wept uncontrollably.

Chaplains are often asked to do Critical Incident Stress Debriefings (CISD). Proficiency in the use of these debriefings is also important to assure that no one is retraumatized by CISD itself. The knowledge of shock, individual timetables, hope, and encouragement to get on with the routines of life are all things chaplains who are embedded in the unit can do and do well. This was recognized recently in a report from Behavioral Health where it was stated that, "The workplace-centric chaplaincy methods of care represent an ideal model for delivery of behavioral health services" (U.S. Surgeon General, 2002).

A preliminary report to the Army on Operation Iraqi Freedom (OIF) noted that the chaplain's role in combat operations is more central than ever. The findings read,

> In OIF the chaplain's role is seen more in spiritual and counseling terms. The chaplain, even if a stranger, is regarded as one who gives honest advice without any hidden agenda. From a soldier's viewpoint, seeing a chaplain about a personal problem carries much less stigma than seeing a mental health counselor. As one soldier put it, seeing a mental health counselor means, "You're a nut job in the file." (Moskos, 2003, p. 3)

Rear-Detachment Ministry

The chaplain and assistant left behind during a deployment have a significant job working with the families of deployed soldiers and the rear-detachment command. This often means being present when difficult news is received or sensitive situations are dealt with. The unit ministry team frequently will be very busy in the community working with the other "helping professions" in addressing a myriad of problems confronted by those left behind to keep the post running. This may include counseling soldiers who have just arrived and are being sent downrange to take a wounded soldier's place. It may mean helping the family readiness group quell the latest rumor from downrange, working with a spouse who is ready to call it quits, or just helping a family find answers to practical questions.

This nurturing of the living will almost always involve crisis and grief counseling. It involves reminding people of their religious values and the secure attachment they have to each other and God through their faith. The comfort of the wounded might mean hospital or home visits, again offering the sense of community and safety in the care of others. The rear-detachment chaplain is called on to honor the dead. This requires speaking to the Army family through memorial or funeral services. It entails accompanying the body of a soldier killed downrange back to his or her family. In so many ways that chaplain symbolizes the greater community and care of God, adding to the sense of attachment so necessary for healthy functioning.

Postdeployment

At the end of *The Odyssey,* Homer tells how Odysseus returns from a decade-long deployment to the Trojan War to find his wife married to another man and his farm preempted by ruffians. Surprisingly, the last battle of the war for Odysseus is the battle to win back his family and his former life. Some modern soldiers returning from extended deployment sense, in one way or another, that their experience parallels that ancient story.

Whether overcoming the simple distance and mutual independence necessitated by long separation or the hurt brought on by mistakes and injuries committed while apart, soldier families find that, in contrast to their dreams for a honeymoon reunion, reintegration into families is a challenge. Moreover, the results of injury, whether physical or emotional, often require soldiers to fight great battles simply to regain their healthy selves. A physically wounded soldier will require family adaptations in ways no one could have imagined beforehand.

In this new and sometimes unexpected context of challenge, chaplains and their assistants act in ways to support healthy reintegration of soldiers into families, communities, and, ultimately, themselves. While these activities are still guided by the goal of fostering Divine and interpersonal connection, the new context and challenges result in a discrete, though connected set of helping activities.

After the deployment, chaplains help soldiers and their families reunite and reintegrate with each other. Soldiers who are married and/or are parents receive specialized ministry during the postcombat phase. After a deployment, each family must reorganize in order to reintegrate the soldier (see also Wiens & Boss, Volume 3, this set). Couples need information so that they can anticipate this stress and normalize it. As the soldier reenters home life after a combat experience, he or she may have difficulty managing emotions and the complications of relationships with children. Sexual activities may also be awkward. Soldiers and family members who aren't suffering PTSD need to know that these things are normal. They typically receive information on how to cope from the unit ministry team. Unit ministry teams offer workshops, retreats, formal pastoral counseling, and informal pastoral conversations to assist the reconciliation for families in this postcombat phase.

Since not all soldiers are married with families, chaplains offer creative ministry initiatives to help single soldiers reattach to life and significant relationships when they return from combat. Again, this involves activities to help quiet the limbic system, in hopes that the soldier relaxes enough to enjoy relationships and other activities. Traditionally, chaplains have offered adventure outings for this part of their unit. Chaplains often invite a speaker or offer a short class to build relationships and encourage healthy lifestyles.

Chaplains can also help normalize the symptoms of PTSD that affect soldiers returning from war. A new chaplain once asked a retiring chaplain who wore a combat patch how long he had been in Vietnam. He replied, "All my life." Wives of soldiers also lose years of intimacy and sometimes their entire marriage as a result of the debilitating effects of the limbic system going awry and creating the need for fight, flight, or freeze. Some children raised by combat veterans also feel as if they have lost their childhood and more because of the war. These people are some of the many clients family life chaplains often counsel.

Many chaplains look at helping marriages and families as part of their Divine calling. As representatives of God within various religions, chaplains unite in a common ministry activity to restore love and intimacy for the families of combat veterans. Unit ministry teams, ministering to PTSD victims and their families, offer workshops on family relationships, pastoral counseling for the soldier and family, and pastoral care for those who need a confidential listener to discuss troubling symptoms of PTSD. Chaplains with special training may also provide specialized PTSD workshops and pastoral counseling. Hospital chaplains offer specialized pastoral care for those diagnosed with and in treatment for PTSD. Unit chaplains offer ongoing pastoral care for soldiers and families for all issues, including PTSD.

According to Dr. Gary Hill, who worked with many of the 9/11 survivors, taking trauma victims out for fun with other people may be more effective than forcing them to debrief their trauma around others. He advocates simply having fun together as a way to reconnect with the safe part of life and to engage emotions that are not dominated by fear and anger (Hill, 2004). Unit ministry teams sponsor, or cosponsor recreation services and fun activities that get soldiers laughing, enjoying, and connecting with others to help alleviate ruminations of past traumatic events.

In the current Deployment Cycle Support Plan, UMTs offer marriage workshops and retreats after the soldiers return from leave with their families. This is an opportune time for commanders and NCOs to assess whether or not a soldier is successfully integrating into the family. Hill suggests that six weeks after the traumatic incident is an optimal time for caregivers to see how the person is readjusting. If symptoms persist or increase after six weeks, then the individual may need a behavioral health referral. The UMT retreat is not considered treatment for PTSD, but it can offer skills and experiences that may assist other medical interventions.

Chaplains also provide or perform religious education before, during, and after combat. The intent is the general growth in knowledge and relationship with God for soldiers and family members. However, in this phase, religious education may address more specifically the need to integrate new and powerful experiences into the soldiers' worldview. Soldiers have been exposed to new cultures, religions, values, and experiences. Many of these exposures challenge their precombat worldview. For many, combat and the effects of war may have resulted in disillusionment because expectations and core beliefs have been attacked. Processing these images and their meanings in the presence of a chaplain who serves as a spiritual director, Bible study teacher, or group leader allows the soldiers and their families to process troubling aftereffects of the war.

Soldiers may feel disconnected from God as a result of combat. There may be feelings of isolation, guilt, shame, and alienation from anything spiritual. For some, sacraments and ordinances of their religion will help reconnect them to God and the faith community. As they join in rituals of confession, hearing the Word of God, receiving absolution or forgiveness, and participating in the symbols of God's love provided in communal meals, they can regain a sense of being connected to God and community (Prey-Harbaugh, 2003). The sights, smells, touch, hearing, and music of worship help soldiers remember who they are and where they belong. Worship often restores a sense of safety as well as meaning and purpose as people acknowledge where we come from, where we are going, and why we are here on this Earth. Worship within a military community avoids shaming soldiers for serving their country and performing their duties.

Chaplains in all phases of the deployment cycle continue to advise their commanders on both morals and morale after a combat deployment. This responsibility includes updating the commander on trends in the unit that are warning signs of soldiers not taking care of themselves or others. Suicide prevention and classes advocating healthy lifestyles fit within chaplain activities to counter poor morale. The UMT cannot divulge confidential information if a soldier confesses. However, UMTs are often told second- and thirdhand information that may warrant the chaplain to speak with the commander as part of his or her duties to advise on morale and morals.

Present Challenges and Future Directions

Chaplains, like all caregivers in this time of war, are being faced with multiple challenges. The current rate of burnout in the global war on terrorism operational environment is a concern at the highest levels in the Chaplain Corps. The very issues surrounding PTSD, spoken of earlier in this chapter, are now being addressed among the chaplains themselves. Questions about skill level and connectedness are leading the Chaplain Corps to ask questions about how it will train future chaplains and chaplain assistants.

The Chaplains Corps has tread this ground before. War is always an affront to mankind's spiritual well-being. It calls to the chaplaincy to do its work and to do it well. Probably the last time the Chaplain Corps was so challenged was in Vietnam. One article on the pastoral response there gave the chaplains a mixed review:

> A religious or spiritual vacuum was created by the Vietnam War. Many soldiers sought to theologize their experience (that is, bring spiritual significance to them), but found it futile; emptiness engulfed their attempts for theological meaning, which, itself, was challenged by demonic interpretations. Many looked to the chaplain for meaning and strength. (Some veterans readily affirmed the importance of the chaplain and the relationship he gave; meaning and strength were caringly incarnated in his presence.) Others recall negative memories of the chaplain. (Jacob, 1987, p. 52)

The intent today from the Chief of Chaplain's Office down is to raise the corps and thus the Army to a higher spiritual level, so that soldiers receive the best in pastoral care and counseling from their chaplain and chaplain assistant.

Recognizing that chaplains enter the Army with very diverse skills and experiences, there are initiatives in the works to raise the pastoral care and counseling skills of all chaplains, to have a set standard of care. This will require continuing education so that chaplains and their assistants do not fall behind in current trends and technologies of pastoral care. Current demands are asking chaplains and their assistants to develop specialized skills in a variety of pastoral care contexts. These include sexual assault, suicide prevention, domestic violence, and combat operational stress.

Other areas of current discussion that will demand additional attention and training center around self-care, avoiding secondary trauma in war-time scenarios, and recognizing when the chaplain and his or her assistant need to seek behavioral health resources themselves. Open discussions about boundary issues regarding the needs of command, the downrange pull to become involved in civilian affairs issues, and over-identifying with combatants are needed. This also entails overcoming any confusion regarding confidentiality and privileged communication. It means having a clear understanding of the role of confession and the role of informed consent.

Chaplains have an old phrase that speaks of their role: "Bringing soldiers to God and God to soldiers." They do this through their priestly offices as spiritual leaders, and they do it one-on-one as they counsel soldiers on a daily basis. As religious leaders, they mystically connect people with the blessing, community, and presence of God, strengthening their hope and consequently their resilience. As caregivers and counselors, chaplains provide personal care, helping soldiers and military constituents build personal skills, manage crises, overcome problems, and find meaning in life.

Chaplains are mandated by the laws of the United States to ensure that military service does not deny the religious rights of soldiers. Chaplains either perform or provide for that free exercise of religion through their ministries. That ministry model is at its best when it fits the latest sciences, what we moderns know about the functioning of the mind, and what the ancients believed about a man's spirit. Human nature is innately religious.

References

American Academy of Family Physicians. (2004). *Spirituality and Health*. Retrieved October 1, 2004, from http://www.Familydoctor.org

Anandarajah, G., & Hight, E. (2001). Spirituality and medical practice: Using the HOPE questions as a practical tool for spiritual assessment. *American Family Physician, 63*, 81–89.

Barry, W. A., & Connoly, W. J. (1986). *Practice of spiritual direction*. San Francisco: Harper Collins.

Barth, K. (1958). *Church dogmatics, volume III/2*. London: T. and T. Clark International.

Baum, D. (2004, July 12). The price of valor: We train our soldiers to kill for us. Afterward, they're on their own. *The New Yorker*, 50.

Bowlby, J. (1982). *Attachment*. New York: Basic Books.

Browning, D. S. (1987). *Religious thought and the modern psychologies: A critical conversation in the theology of culture*. Philadelphia: Fortress.

Drescher, K. D., & Foy, D. W. (1995). Spirituality and trauma treatment: Suggestions for including spirituality as a coping resource. *National Center for PTSD*. Retrieved October 1, 2004, from http://www.ncptsd.org/publications/cq/v5/n1/drescher.html

Federal Advisory Committee. (1997). *Report of the Federal Advisory Committee on gender-integrated training and related issues to the Secretary of Defense*. Washington, DC: Author.

Friedman, M. S. (2004). Acknowledging the psychiatric cost of war. *The New England Journal of Medicine, 351*, 75–77.

Hill, G. R. (Speaker). (2004, September). *Post 9/11: New developments for treatment of trauma.* Presented at the annual meeting of the American Association for Marriage and Family Therapy, Atlanta, GA.

Hill, R. (1949). *Families under stress.* New York: Harper and Row.

Hogue, D. (2003). *Remembering the future, imagining the past: Story, ritual, and the human brain.* San Francisco: Pilgrim Press.

Jacob, M. (1987). A pastoral response to the troubled Vietnam veteran. In T. Williams (Ed.), *Post-Traumatic Stress Disorders* (pp. 51–74). Cincinnati, OH: Disabled American Veterans.

Johnson, S. M. (2002). *Emotionally focused couple therapy with trauma survivors: Strengthening attachment bonds.* New York: Guilford.

Karen, R. (1994). *Becoming attached: First relationships and how they shape our capacity to love.* New York: Oxford University Press.

LaCugna, C. M. (1993). Freeing theology. In C. M. LaCugna (Ed.), *God in communion with us: The Trinity* (pp. 86–87). New York: Harper Collins.

Lester, A. D. (2003). *The angry Christian: A theology for care and counseling.* Louisville, KY: Westminister John Knox Press.

Meichenbaum, D. (Speaker). (2002, April). *Trauma, spirituality and recovery.* Presenter notes (pp. 1–20) from the annual meeting of the American Association for Pastoral Counselors, Newport, RI.

Moskos, C. (2003). Preliminary report on Operation Iraqi Freedom (OIF) in *Memorandum to Hon. Lee Brownlee, Acting Secretary of the Army – dated 14 Dec. 2003,* p. 3.

Prey-Harbaugh, J. (2003). A Lord's Supper liturgy for survivors of trauma: On sacramental healing. *Journal of Religion and Abuse, 5*(4), 29–49.

Rothschild, B. (2000). *The body remembers: The psychophysiology of trauma and trauma treatment.* New York: W. W. Norton.

RTI International. (2003). *2002 Survey of health related behaviors among military personnel.* Research Triangle Park, NC: Author.

Saint Andrews Presbyterian Church—Columbus, GA. (2004, November). *Mission News & Opportunities,* p. 7.

Smith, H. (2001). *Why religion matters: The fate of the human spirit in the age of disbelief.* San Francisco: Harper Collins.

Taylor, A. J. W. (2001). Spirituality and personal values: Neglected components of trauma treatment. *Traumatology, 7*(3), 111–118.

Tournier, P. (1973). *Guilt and grace.* San Francisco: Harper & Row.

Trover, R. H. (1985). Military. In R. J. Wicks, R. D. Parsons, & D. E. Capps (Eds.), *Clinical handbook of pastoral counseling* (pp. 440–451). Mahwah, NJ: Paulist Press.

Tyson, G. E. (1991, Summer). Chaplains in the Gulf War: A collage. *Military Chaplains' Review Gulf War,* 7–11.

U.S. Army. (2003). *The Army family white paper.* Washington, DC: Author.

U.S. Army Surgeon General. (2002). *Fort Bragg epidemiological consultation.* Washington, DC: Author.

Wilcoxson, A. (2004). The cross is a reminder of our connection with Christ. *HCN Column.* Retrieved October 23, 2004, from http://www.theforerunner.org/pages/aidancolumn.htm

Wylie, M. S. (2004). Mindsight. *Psychotherapy Networker, 28*(5), 29–39.

CHAPTER 9

TOWARD A LIBERAL THEORY OF MILITARY LEADERSHIP

Carl Andrew Castro, Jeffrey L. Thomas, and Amy B. Adler

One of the trademarks of a strong organization is an emphasis on identifying and developing its leaders. This is especially true in the military, where all senior leaders arise from the ranks within the military. Unlike civilian businesses, in which proven managers and leaders at all levels can be hired from outside the organization (see Chambers, Foulton, Handfield-Jones, Hankin, & Michaels, 1998; Sessa & Campbell, 1997), the military can only hire managers and leaders at the entry level, before their abilities have been demonstrated. Thus, the military has the tremendous responsibility of identifying and developing its junior leaders for advancement within the organization. This commitment to developing leaders from within is reflected in the immense resources militaries around the world dedicate to developing their leaders (see Bass, 1996; Taylor & Rosenbach, 1992).

Despite the fact that the emphasis on developing *future* leaders presupposes that leaders in their *current* position are effective, that assumption is, in fact, premature. While it may be true that intermediate and more senior-level leaders are effective (witness their promotion to positions of higher leadership), it is questionable for junior leaders, because they assume positions of leadership based primarily on appointment, not on the basis of proven leadership ability. For instance, second lieutenants, who serve as platoon leaders/commanders, are typically recent college graduates, and noncommissioned officers at the junior level, who serve as team or squad leaders, usually have only two to four years of active-duty experience. Indeed, a common concern voiced by senior leaders in the U.S. Army is that junior leaders (both officers

The views expressed in this chapter are those of the authors and do not necessarily represent the official policy or position of the U.S. Army or the U.S. Department of Defense.

and noncommissioned officers) are advanced too quickly to the next leadership position before they obtain the skills necessary to perform effectively at the higher level. Thus, it is likely that insufficient leader development has taken place prior to their assumption of junior leadership positions (see Katz & Kahn, 1966).

The emphasis on developing junior leaders to assume future leadership positions is ironic, given that comparatively little attention is paid to the development of their effectiveness in their current position. Arguably, the most junior leaders in the military are the ones who need the most training, because they have primary responsibility for the direction and supervision of those military personnel executing the essential day-to-day activities of the unit in garrison and in leading teams and squads in combat. While garrison activities are crucial to the smooth running of a unit and to preparing the unit for military operations, combat is the ultimate test for military units.

A recent monograph by Wong (2004) underscores the importance of focusing on junior officers and the significant impact they have on the mission and their subordinates in combat. Through a series of structured interviews conducted in Iraq with junior officers, Wong found that the deployed environment, characterized by ambiguity, constantly changing demands, and complexity, bred innovative, flexible, and seasoned leaders at the "boots on the ground" level who had a profound impact on the reshaping of postwar Iraq. His assessment of the impact of these junior officers provides evidence for the fundamental point that junior-level leaders are the linchpin of the Army and that their impact on the mission and their subordinates is profound. This impact, while described as positive by Wong, also has the potential to be negative. Thus, any discussion of junior leader's attitudes and behaviors needs to be geared toward both positive and negative attitudes and behaviors that influence the effective functioning of the small unit, especially during a combat deployment.

Combat makes extraordinary demands on every individual, particularly the junior leader. Many of the significant stresses placed on individuals in combat are unknown in garrison and civilian life. The cumulative demand of combat may affect the leader's ability to lead his or her unit and has the potential to ultimately tempt military personnel to quit. This temptation would be almost irresistible if the mental fortitude of the individuals had not been tempered to the ordeal (see Stouffer et al., 1949). Similarly, the junior leader must be tempered to the ordeal of command, both in peacetime and in war. The behavior of the junior commissioned and noncommissioned officers in combat is critical to the survival, performance, and morale of the unit. One way in which the morale and well-being of the unit can be improved or enhanced is through thoughtful and flexible leadership, whether in combat or in garrison (see Britt & Dickinson, Volume 1, this set). The importance of leadership in mitigating the demands of military life has been the subject of leadership theories (e.g., cognitive resources theory, Fiedler & Garcia, 1987), stressor–strain theories (the Soldier Adaptation Model, Bliese & Castro, 2003), and supervisory support theories (e.g., Thomas, Bliese, & Jex, in press), to name a few.

Regardless of the research orientation taken in investigating leadership and its helpful and unhelpful effects on soldier morale and well-being, measuring leadership by focusing on specific, observable behaviors simultaneously sets the groundwork for potential leadership training and intervention approaches. These behaviors do not necessarily have to be extraordinary, and indeed, often they are not. It is the everyday behaviors the junior leaders perform that enable their combat teams to carry on in the face of the ever-present dangers of war. Despite the importance of junior leaders to units during combat, there have been very few studies that have focused on the junior leader. The few studies that have been conducted have focused on junior officers (i.e., lieutenants and captains), with most of our knowledge concerning leader behaviors in combat coming from war memoirs (see Fussell, 1989; MacDonald, 1947; McDonough, 1985; and see Sledge, 1981 to obtain the perspective of a junior enlisted soldier during World War II). Wong's study of junior officers in combat marks one of the few scientific departures from this model, although even this approach was more qualitative in nature.

Given the importance of junior leadership to the military organization, the focus of this chapter is to review junior leader behaviors that contribute to the success and health of subordinates in combat. Our basic precepts regarding military leadership are not new. Elements of every precept discussed can be found in either official Department of Defense or Department of Army publications, or in one of the documents listed in the U.S. Army's recommended reading list on leadership (see Department of Army, 1990, 1999). As this reading list demonstrates, numerous books and articles have been written on leadership. Such volumes address a range of leadership theories and ways of conceptualizing leadership, including leadership traits (e.g., Mann, 1959), the role of the situation (e.g., Hersey & Blanchard, 1974), contingency theory (e.g., Fiedler, 1971), cognitive resources theory (Fiedler, 1986), charismatic leader theories (e.g., House, 1977), transactional/transformational views (e.g., Bass, 1997; Yammorino & Bass, 1990), and leader–member exchange (Dienesch & Liden, 1986). A complete review of the leadership literature has been presented elsewhere (see Bass, 1990). These approaches to leadership have had profound influences on leader theory and practice; our approach in this chapter is to examine the leadership field and compile a description of essential behaviors junior leaders need to perform to meet the challenges of combat.

The leader behaviors we discuss in this chapter should not be viewed as representing a new angle on leadership but rather a "greatest hits compilation" of what junior leaders need to be, know, and do to lead their subordinates successfully through the stress of combat. To this end, we present research findings collected from soldiers serving or who have served in combat or peacekeeping deployments, highlighting those behaviors that junior leaders perform that contribute to the health and well-being of deployed soldiers.

We begin our discussion by distinguishing between two general approaches to leadership: the rigid institutional approach and the flexible pragmatic approach, demonstrating how those leaders who view the leader role as part of a responsive, flexible, open system tend to naturally engage in leadership behaviors and actions advocated by the U.S. Army (Department of Army, 1990, 1999). Next, we discuss the theory of the social contract, illustrating how leader behaviors can either strengthen or weaken the relationship between the leader and subordinates and thereby dramatically influence unit effectiveness. Following an analysis of how social contract theory drives the fundamental approach of the two contrasting leadership types, a discussion of the cultural aspect of leader behaviors is presented. We then present two lists of behaviors. The first list contains those behaviors and actions that junior leaders *should* employ in leading their subordinates in combat, while the second list includes those actions and behaviors that junior leaders *should not* engage in. The chapter concludes with a discussion of proposals for future research in the area of junior leader development.

The Flexible Pragmatic and Rigid Institutional Approaches to Leadership

While the flexible pragmatic and rigid institutional approaches to leadership differ in terms of attitudes and behaviors, there are fundamentals of military leadership to which both approaches subscribe. First, both the flexible pragmatic and rigid institutional approaches to leadership believe in the primacy of the mission. Both types of leaders recognize that military life is hard and that personal sacrifices are often necessary to accomplish the mission. In times of war, both flexible pragmatic and rigid institutional leaders acknowledge that one of these sacrifices might involve giving up one's life. This fact of military life transcends leadership style.

Second, both leadership approaches assume that controls need to be placed on the behavior of subordinates. That is, rules and regulations are acceptable and necessary in order for the organization to function. Without such structures, it is not certain if individuals would conform to the dictates of reason and justice. Americans, in particular, are imbued with a strong belief in the virtues of rugged individualism and the right to engage in any activity so long as it does no harm to others or society. Both flexible pragmatic and rigid institutional leaders believe that regulations and policies are essential for prescribing behavioral conduct. In addition, flexible pragmatic and rigid institutional leaders accept as necessary the requirement for every recruit to undergo a period of indoctrination in order to instill discipline and group cooperation among military personnel (see McGurk, Cotting, Britt, & Adler, this volume).

Finally, both the flexible pragmatic and rigid institutional perspectives on leadership believe in the virtues of the military chain of command as the decision-making authority, subject to overall civilian control. When problems or issues arise, both flexible pragmatic and rigid institutional leaders expect the decision to be made by someone within the chain of command. Thus, actions or decisions made outside of or contrary to the directives of the chain of command are viewed as one of the most serious of offenses and deserving of severe punishment.

Despite the importance of the similarities between the flexible pragmatic and rigid institutional approaches to leadership, these two views differ in three important aspects. First, flexible pragmatic leaders believe in a system of mutual obligation. They believe unbreakable obligations exist between the leader and the subordinate, and although these obligations are not legally binding, flexible pragmatic leaders believe they are duty bound to uphold these obligations. In fact, flexible pragmatic leaders would consider it a failure in leadership not to adhere to these obligations. From the perspective of the subordinate, these nonbinding obligations are ones they expect their leaders to fulfill. In contrast, rigid institutional leaders feel no obligation to perform functions other than the ones they are specifically directed to perform. For the rigid institutional leader, the carrying out of these unwritten responsibilities or meeting subordinate expectations is not part of the essential construct of leadership and is viewed as simply optional. If the rigid institutional leader does fulfill these nonbinding, optional obligations, then the rigid institutional leader expects the subordinate to be grateful. However, flexible pragmatic leaders expect no gratitude from their subordinates when they discharge a nonbinding obligation because, from their perspective, they were only following through on a commitment inherent to the assigned position.

The second significant difference between flexible pragmatic and rigid institutional perspectives on leadership is how leaders acquire and maintain power and authority. While flexible pragmatic leaders hold that their power and authority derive from both their leadership position and the content of their decisions, rigid institutional leaders believe that their power and authority are based solely on their position as a leader. For flexible pragmatic leaders, the respect that subordinates show them is a direct reflection of the validity of their decisions irrespective of their position in the organization; that is, respect from subordinates is earned by the leader not awarded from superiors. Flexible pragmatic leaders, in fact, view their position in the organization as a means toward the end, rather than the end itself. Rigid institutional leaders, however, believe that subordinates should respect them because they are the leaders. For the rigid institutional leader, respect is not earned from subordinates but from superiors who appointed them to their current leader position. Rigid institutional leaders believe they are entitled to be respected by subordinates.

The final important difference between flexible pragmatic and rigid institutional views on leadership concerns criticism. Flexible pragmatic leaders permit and encourage criticism from their subordinates, while rigid institutional leaders forbid any criticism of their policies or decisions and consider such criticism a type of insubordination. From the flexible pragmatic leader's perspective, to deny subordinates an opportunity to criticize their leaders denies leaders an opportunity to gain knowledge of matters and issues, which, if they knew about, they would rectify themselves. Permitting criticism aids the flexible pragmatic leader in (a) avoiding inconsistent or contradictory rules and policies; (b) nipping potential crises in the bud; and (c) allowing leaders the opportunity to remedy their own blunders or mistakes. Without positive and negative input from subordinates, leaders put themselves in a stultifying position in which they inevitably appear inconsistent, ridiculous, or, worse, incompetent. By allowing criticism, leaders become fact-minded and critical of themselves, which tends to prevent them from engaging in what amounts to unit- or self-destructive behaviors. Such openness to feedback from subordinates ensures that decisions are made in the interests of all concerned, the subordinates', the unit's, and the military's.

In summary, flexible pragmatic leadership is an approach that affects the attitude and the behaviors of the leaders. We label this style "flexible pragmatic" because the leader views the unit, whether a platoon, company or other military group, as an organism that changes as a result of forces from below as well as from above and that strives to reach homeostasis, a stable adaptation to demands. The system respects structure and hierarchy and yet is elastic in structure when it comes to accepting feedback from subordinates. The flexible pragmatic military system is not an unstructured system but one in which the mission is paramount, rules and hierarchy are fundamental, and unit relationships are built with input informed by experience. The flexible pragmatic leader, as the head of this relatively flexible pragmatic system, sees the intertwined obligations between leader and subordinate as bidirectional, rather than exclusively top-down driven. The respect accorded the flexible pragmatic leader is not considered to occur in a vacuum, as only a function of assigned position, but one that emerges from a series of interactions. These sets of beliefs undoubtedly influence behavior of the leaders and the response of subordinates and may well, in fact, affect job performance.

It is important to point out that there are similarities between the flexible pragmatic leader and what is known as the transformational leader. Transformational leaders (Bass, 1997) instill a sense of purpose in, motivate, and transcend the expectations of their followers through creating a vision and culture within their organization. This vision is one in which subordinates can believe. In comparison, the flexible pragmatic leader can have a similar effect but may not have or even need the charisma and "cult of personality" that the transformational leader has. Flexible pragmatic leaders need not be charismatic; flexible pragmatic leaders need only be thoughtful and reflective in their choice of leader actions and adaptive and attentive to both the mission and their followers.

One of the challenges in defining the approach that successful leadership takes is that the extent to which those behaviors and attitudes associated with success in garrison lead to success on the battlefield is not known. Those individuals who view the relationship with subordinates as hierarchical but also as a flexible pragmatic system in which bidirectional communication and earned respect are vital, have the potential to succeed in an operational environment. The rigid institutional leader has this same potential. Both leaders are mission driven. Thus, categorizing leaders as flexible pragmatic or rigid institutional in their perception of the leader–subordinate relationship does not indicate that one will necessarily achieve mission goals and the other won't. The important distinction between these two leadership approaches is that flexible pragmatic leaders will achieve mission success much more efficiently and effectively than rigid institutional leaders.

The Nature–Nurture Debate of Leadership

Regardless of leadership type and its relationship with leader effectiveness, a natural follow-on question to address is the degree to which a leader style can be trained or is "inside the skin" of the individual. Before proceeding to our discussion of leader behaviors, there is a critical question that is almost always asked when talking about leadership: Are effective leaders born or made? From a theoretical perspective, there is not a single skill, attitude, or behavior that defines the effective leader that any man or woman cannot master. Unfortunately, from a practical perspective, it does not follow that everyone can be taught to lead.

In the majority of aspiring leaders, success or failure is caused more by mental attitude than by mental capacity. There are aspiring leaders who are unwilling to face the ordeal of thinking for themselves and accepting responsibility for others, without which they can never be effective leaders, despite any other talents they might possess. This notion is similar to Bennis and Thomas's (2002) contention that most effective leaders undergo a crucible experience that summons their abilities and forces them to make difficult choices. Leaders who withstand this crucible experience develop or broaden their adaptive capacity to handle difficult and ambiguous situations. Leaders who do not pass through this crucible may be unable to develop an influence with others that is proportionate to their talents and capacity for work. After all, the accolade of leadership is not inherent in the individual but is conferred on the individual by the group. Leadership in work-related tasks is a main requirement, but if the group does not warm toward the appointed leader, if its members cannot feel any enthusiasm about their assigned leader, they will be hypercritical of whatever he or she does.

The Social Psychological Contract

One critical aspect of effective leadership—whether using a flexible pragmatic or rigid institutional style—is the degree of trust and respect that leaders instill in their subordinates. At the very center of earning and keeping subordinate trust and respect is the explicit and implicit "contract" of expectations agreed upon between leader and follower. A constructive psychological contract is a set of shared obligations and expectations that exist between employers and employees in regard to their working relationships (Dabos & Rousseau, 2004; Rousseau, 1989, 2000; Rousseau & Tijoriwala, 1999). From a military standpoint, psychological contracts consist of promises and commitments that leaders and subordinates make to each other. Significantly, psychological contracts are present in every leader–subordinate relationship, whether they are desired or not. In other words, psychological contracts are obligatory, not voluntary. It is this fact that makes the style of leadership adopted so important in the development of leader–subordinate bonds.

The value of a psychological contract lies in leaders and subordinates agreeing on the terms of the contract. When there is agreement between leaders and subordinates on the interpretation of the promises and commitments, future interactions become more predictable, resulting in effective planning, coordination, and execution (cf. Dabos & Rousseau, 2004). It is important to appreciate that it is only when the level of agreement between the leader and subordinate (i.e., mutuality) is high that the benefits of a psychological contract are realized. When agreement, or mutuality, is low, that is, when there is a lack of agreement between leaders and subordinates in the meaning of promises and obligations, current and future exchanges between the leaders and subordinates become strained, culminating in subordinates distrusting and lacking confidence in their leaders.

For example, when soldiers join the U.S. Army, they give up certain rights, including control over their work and personal time. Indeed, it is not uncommon for soldiers to be required to work 60–70 hours per week. Soldiers do not receive direct monetary compensation for these additional hours. In exchange, soldiers expect their leaders to ensure that the soldiers' time is not wasted because of poor planning, coordination, or some other inefficiency that could have been prevented. Further, given that they will not be receiving payment for the additional work hours, soldiers expect their leaders to recognize and reward them through some other mechanism, typically by giving them additional time off at some future point.

The response of leaders in this case will depend on whether they adopt a flexible pragmatic or rigid institutional viewpoint. While both the flexible pragmatic and rigid institutional leaders will demand that their subordinates work the additional hours until the mission is accomplished, flexible pragmatic leaders will feel obligated to reward the soldiers for imposing this extra demand, even if the requirement was initiated by higher ups. That is, even though the soldiers were required to work the additional hours, flexible pragmatic leaders will respond to their subordinates' performance as representing a personal commitment on their part to ensuring that the mission is accomplished and deserving of recognition. By recognizing their subordinates in this manner, flexible pragmatic leaders ensure that the level of agreement or mutuality remains high (see Britt, Davison, Bliese, & Castro, 2004).

In contrast, rigid institutional leaders will feel no obligation to compensate their subordinates for the extra hours worked, because there is no legally binding requirement for them to do so. In fact, rigid institutional leaders might respond by telling their subordinates that if they wanted a 40-hour-a-week job, they should not have joined the military. And when these rigid institutional leaders do compensate their subordinates for working the unusually long hours by giving them extra time off from work, they are surprised when their subordinates do not respond toward them in an appreciative and enthusiastic manner. The reason for this reaction is simple; the subordinates view the added time off as just compensation for their hard work, not something extra that their rigid institutional leaders have done for them. Thus, the rigid institutional leaders' response in this situation serves to decrease the mutuality of the psychological construct, resulting in strained relationships between the leaders and the subordinates.

As can be seen from the example above, there are inherent dangers associated with the presence of psychological contracts. First, psychological contracts involve expectations of binding promises between leaders and/or subordinates in which there might not be agreement. The consequences of this lack of agreement are strained leader–subordinate relations, resulting in lower morale, cohesion, and retention, which tend to degrade unit performance. Another danger of psychological contracts is that neither the promises nor the expectations are written down or always clearly communicated. Instead, these promises and expectations are assumed to exist based on individual values, motives, and cultural norms (Rousseau, 1995). Finally, even when there is agreement regarding promises and commitments, these promises can unilaterally be broken by either the leaders or the subordinates. Since promises create prima facia obligations to fulfill them, broken promises naturally lead to resentment and lack of trust. However, our contention is that leaders who adapt a flexible pragmatic approach not only will engage in behaviors that build constructive leader–subordinate relationships, but also will engage in behaviors that serve to help them avoid these pitfalls inherent in all psychological contracts.

Leader Actions that Transcend Nationality and Culture

Another leadership issue that needs to be considered is determining whether perceptions of leader actions are idiomatic of a particular culture. This issue must be considered, given the prevalence of multinational military operations. One need only look at the recent deployment of U.S. forces in Iraq and at the numerous peacekeeping missions that the United States continues to be involved in to see how much junior leaders are involved in nation building and working within a multinational task force to understand that cultural aspects of leadership are critical to mission success (see Wong, 2004; see also Soeters, Poponete, & Page, Volume 4, this set). For example, it would be important for a deployed junior leader working with local nationals or other alliance partners to have an understanding of differences that may exist between cultures in order to avoid unnecessary confusion, conflict, or misunderstandings during the mission.

In the sociological and organizational literature, researchers interested in how leadership varies across cultures have found that there are indeed differences in what cultures value in leaders (e.g., Bass, 1990; Gerstner & Day, 1994; Hofstede, 1993). While studies such as these find that leadership styles can vary by culture, a recent multinational study that gathered data from over 61 countries, the Global Leadership and Organizational Behavior Effectiveness (GLOBE) research project, found that although there are differences across countries in terms of preferred leadership behaviors and styles, there also are many similarities that transcend culture. For a recent review of the project, see House, Javidan, Dorfman, and Hanges (2004).

In an earlier GLOBE study (Den Hartog et al., 1999), researchers found that expressed leader behaviors (both good and bad) associated with charismatic/transformational leadership were, by and large, universal and not idiomatic to particular cultures. Specifically, they found that universal leader attributes and behaviors centered on having integrity (e.g., trustworthiness, fairness, honesty), having charisma and vision (e.g., giving encouragement, being positive and motivational, building confidence), and being team focused (e.g., team building, communicating, coordinating). Conversely, there also were leader attributes and behaviors that were found to be universally disliked. These included "going it alone" and being uncooperative, ruthless, nonexplicit or vague, irritable, and dictatorial in style.

Many of the leader behaviors and attitudes found to be universal in the GLOBE study can be used to influence the development of a set of guidelines, such as those presented in the next section, which can distill the essence of flexible pragmatic leadership. Such leadership does not have to be contingent on personality but can entail specific behaviors and attitudes that can be targeted for training. For this reason and because it is more constructive to lay out leader behaviors as the ties that bind us in the military community regardless of culture, we have chosen to focus on leader behaviors, which we also believe are universally transcendent as opposed to culturally contingent (i.e., idiomatic to U.S. forces).

Leader Behaviors and Attitudes

Recommendations for What Leaders Ought to Do

Lists of "Do's and Don'ts" by their very nature constrain behavior, and the lists below are no exception. Further, leaders naturally don't like their behavior constrained. However, not all constraints are bad. No leaders at any level can lead effectively unless they focus their attention and channel their efforts to performing only those behaviors that maximize the performance of their subordinates toward mission accomplishment. Constraints do not lessen authority as much as they direct leaders to their proper interests, for example, the welfare of their subordinates. Restraints strengthen. Paradoxically, lists of "Do's and Don'ts" then do not limit the leader's power; they create and organize a leader's power as well as give it direction.

This organizing principle, of course, assumes that the lists of recommended leader behaviors are based on practical experience and that the list of leader behaviors has been shown to be useful in leading subordinates in garrison as well as in combat. The lists of leader behaviors presented below are, indeed, based on such practical experience. In developing this list, we have borrowed from numerous sources: the scientific literature, the war literature, Department of Defense publications, and our own research examining leader behaviors during deployments and combat. In particular, we draw heavily from scientific surveys and interviews conducted with U.S. military personnel during and following combat duty in Iraq (Castro & McGurk, 2003/2004) as part of our systematic assessment of the impact of combat and deployment stressors on the mental health and well-being of U.S. personnel (Castro & Hoge, 2003).

Be Fair and Just

Leaders should never issue an order they cannot enforce. They should promise nothing they cannot deliver. Leaders should be as good as their word, at all times and in any circumstance. Intellectual honesty demands that leaders energetically strive to refute their own convictions. If the leader has not played devil's advocate, attempting vigorously to disprove his or her own opinions, then the leader should not feel confident in his or her own particular position.

The importance of fairness and justness extend also to the treatment of unit members. All members of a unit must share a common objective; they must be willing to make sacrifices for the sake of this objective, but they will only do so if they can be assured that others too will do their part. It is the leader's responsibility to make sure that all members of the unit assume equal risks and make equal sacrifices in pursuit of the unit's mission. Despite the obvious importance for leaders to treat their subordinates fairly and justly, when junior enlisted soldiers who had served in combat in Iraq were surveyed about the behaviors of their noncommissioned officers (NCOs), only 41 percent of these junior enlisted soldiers reported that their NCOs set a single standard that everyone was expected to meet, with 43 percent of them reporting that their NCOs showed favoritism to certain members in the unit (Castro & McGurk, 2003/2004). Thus, from findings obtained from junior enlisted soldiers in combat, the tendency of NCOs to be just and fair is an area that the flexible pragmatic leader must master in order to become an effective leader. Soldiers will be motivated to make personal sacrifices when they can be assured of equal treatment.

Admit Mistakes

The best thing leaders can do when they are wrong is to admit it, publicly. Naturally, no one likes being contradicted and refuted, so this is best done by the leaders themselves. Contrary to what many leaders may think, when leaders admit mistakes in the presence of their subordinates, their credibility and authority is enhanced, because their subordinates see them as someone who is interested in the truth and who is honest and sincere. When leaders are wrong, they should not be afraid to contradict their previous decisions. Failing to admit obvious mistakes only lowers the leader's prestige in the eyes of their subordinates.

Indeed, it is a common complaint among junior enlisted soldiers and NCOs that they are blamed when things go wrong even when they were following the orders they were given by their supervisors (Castro & McGurk, 2003/2004). Leaders should never use their subordinates as scapegoats to avoid accepting responsibility for the outcome of their decisions. Pragmatic flexible leaders accept personal blame when things go wrong, even if it wasn't their fault, yet they credit all successes to their subordinates.

Underwrite Honest Mistakes

Organizations only improve when members of the organization are allowed to make mistakes. When subordinates make mistakes, but not from any lack of good will or effort, it is best for the leader to take the rap for them or to "fly high cover" for them, as it is sometimes called in the military. The last thing a leader wants to do is disaffect an honest, hardworking subordinate needlessly. Not underwriting honest mistakes is a very quick way to squander any capital that leadership has brokered in the eyes of subordinates.

In interviews conducted with junior enlisted soldiers (and NCOs), we frequently hear that leaders have a hard time underwriting mistakes, with the result being that initiative is stifled. When leaders refuse to support their subordinates' honest mistakes, their subordinates will eventually stop taking the risk of demonstrating initiative and simply wait to be told what to do. As one junior noncommissioned officer deployed to Iraq noted, "Why stick your neck out, if they [the unit leadership] are just waiting to chop it off?" Flexible pragmatic leaders know the value of maintaining subordinate initiative and are willing to take the hits from time to time from their superiors in order to ensure that their subordinates' initiative is sustained.

Protect Subordinates

The protection of subordinates takes two forms. First, it is the duty of leaders to intervene and protect their subordinates against any manifest injustice, whatever its source. This includes abuse or harassment from other members of the unit. In fact, this trust is so implicit between leaders and subordinates that all leaders should be willing to risk their professional reputation on it, when they are convinced that their subordinate is being unfairly assailed, or that due process is not being followed. This protection does not extend to cheating or thwarting justice for the sake of their subordinates simply because they are their subordinates. Occasionally, higher authority overreaches; leaders must stand as a shield, protecting their subordinates against unfair treatment. However, in a survey of junior enlisted soldiers who served in combat in Iraq, 53 percent reported that their NCOs seldom or never fought for the welfare of soldiers if it might harm their own career (Castro & McGurk, 2003/2004).

Second, in combat it is the duty of leaders to ensure that their subordinates do not assume unnecessary risks. Every soldier has the right to expect that their leaders will provide them the greatest opportunity of surviving on the battlefield. Indeed, junior leaders were rated higher in this area, with 52 percent of junior enlisted soldiers reporting that their NCOs ensure that they do not assume unnecessary risks when conducting combat missions in Iraq. A total of 59 percent of these same soldiers also reported that their NCOs were concerned about their personal safety (Castro & McGurk, 2003/2004).

Communicate

Tell subordinates what is going on. Every individual in military service is entitled to the why and the wherefore of what he or she is expected to do. The individual's efficiency, confidence, and enthusiasm will wax strong in response to the leader's communication about the mission or task. Leaders who believe in the importance of giving full information in a straightforward manner, and who continue to act on that principle, will benefit over the long term by their subordinates' efforts. Here NCOs do a good job, with nearly 80 percent of soldiers surveyed reporting that their NCOs provide clear guidance on how tasks or missions are to be accomplished (Castro & McGurk, 2003/2004).

The problem besetting some leaders is to talk to their subordinates naturally, without yelling or screaming. Yet, the skill of flexible pragmatic communication requires both sending and receiving. If subordinates can talk naturally to their leaders, the product of their resourcefulness becomes available to all. Taking counsel of subordinates in any enterprise or situation is therefore a matter of giving them full advantage of one's own information and reasoning, weighing with the intellect whatever thought or argument they may contribute to the sum of the considerations, and then making, without compromise, a clear decision as to the line of greatest advantage. To know how to command obedience is very different from making subordinates obey. Obedience is not benefited by fear, but by understanding, and understanding is based on knowledge. Subordinates should be encouraged to present their views as it is the surest way for leaders to win the confidence of their subordinates.

Visit the Troops

Meaningful contact with subordinates goes beyond merely sending information down the chain of command for dissemination. It is also absolutely critical for leaders to be with their subordinates when their subordinates are enduring hardship (e.g., deployment, rigorous training, long hours on task, being in remote sites, functioning as part of detachment). Subordinates will become discouraged and will lose their sense of direction unless the leader has face-to-face contact with them, looking in on them periodically. During visits, leaders should ask their subordinates whether they can be of help and thus get their subordinates to open up and discuss problems that might exist. Another benefit of this type of contact is that the leader demonstrates by example that he or she is not above experiencing hardship and will personally sacrifice time, comfort, convenience, and energy to support the troops.

Surprisingly, many leaders fail to perform this simple task. In interviews with NCOs in Iraq during the first year of the war, a common complaint was that their leaders (i.e. junior officers) never visited the troops, especially if the troops were located in a very austere environment. Naturally, the assumption was that their leaders did not want to be inconvenienced by having to travel from their air-conditioned headquarters buildings to where the troops were located in 120-degree heat. Impressively, these NCOs did not resent their leaders having air-conditioned working environments, although they themselves did not, but they did take exception to their leaders' apparent unwillingness to sacrifice a little by refusing to visit them (Castro & McGurk, 2003/2004).

Encourage Involvement

Leaders must encourage their subordinates to become involved in recognizing and solving problems. As Den Hartog and colleagues' (1999) multicultural study points out, a universally disliked attribute of leaders is a dictatorial style. Making subordinates a part of the solution instead of a victim of the problem is a way to instill confidence, innovation, and adaptability in a unit. If the problem is such that the subordinates cannot solve it, then the problem needs to be brought to the attention of the leader. Leaders should decentralize information and imagination.

This focus on developing independent thinking in junior leaders is something the former chief of staff of the Army, retired General Eric Shinseki, was very concerned about. In fact, Shinseki commissioned a study examining the degree to which the U.S. Army was actually *stifling innovation* in its junior ranks (Wong, 2002). As Wong argued, when subordinates are provided the support to be proactive, innovative, and flexible, a leader is likely to ensure mission success. Thus, leaders should encourage fact-mindedness and create incentives for constructive criticism and learning that are focused on solving problems. When given a task, subordinates should be encouraged to develop alternate courses of action and to select one. When orders are unclear or ambiguous, leaders should demand that their subordinates seek and obtain clarification before executing them. No leader is on firm ground when he or she is impatient with questions that are to the point, or resentful of the subordinates who ask them.

One of the best means available to leaders to encourage involvement in the unit is to recognize and reward their subordinates. Yet, in our survey of junior enlisted soldiers who served in combat in Iraq, only 29 percent of junior enlisted soldiers reported that their NCOs told them when they had done a good job. And only 26 percent of these junior enlisted soldiers believed that their NCOs ensured that all deserving soldiers received military awards for their performance in Iraq (Castro & McGurk, 2003/2004). Acknowledging the contributions and sacrifices of subordinates is a relatively simple way of encouraging involvement and represents one set of leader behaviors that can be taught and developed.

Team Build

Team building is the sole responsibility of the leader. The unity that develops from recognizing one's dependence on others is the mainspring of every movement by which society and the military moves forward. One set of key leader attributes and behaviors valued across cultures is for a leader to be a team builder (Den Hartog et al., 1999). Team building by its very nature must be inclusive to be effective; therefore, it should never be undertaken at the expense of excluding other unit members or other units. In Iraq, for instance, it was common practice to post signs limiting access to morale and welfare facilities to only "permanent" party, meaning that only soldiers assigned to that particular base camp or unit could use the phones or gymnasium facilities on that base camp. What made such exclusions infuriating to the nonpermanent party soldiers was the fact these soldiers were typically combat arms soldiers who were located at remote sites where phone or gym facilities had not yet been set up. In other words, those soldiers who were assuming the greatest risks were the very ones being denied these important morale and welfare facilities. Flexible pragmatic leaders ensure that such exclusionary policies are not established, or when confronted with such policies, they quickly move to abolish them.

While the benefits of being a team builder are obvious in their positive effects on both group and individual performance and well-being, the leader who builds teams must also be vigilant against possessive individualism and splinter factions within the unit. Both are counterproductive to group goals. Factions that can arise within a group may split the unit and subvert unit integrity and command authority and bring about animosities among unit members. Often, individuals of these factions will voluntarily sacrifice themselves in the interest of their subgroup over that of the larger unit. If "me first" or "we first" factions emerge in a military unit, leaders must take action and deal with them swiftly even if that means transferring offending individuals to another unit. By many accounts (e.g., Taguba, 2004), the Abu Ghraib prisoner abuse incidents represented actions of such a splinter faction.

Instill Discipline

The level of discipline should at all times be according to what is needed to get the best results from the majority of the subordinates. There is no practical reason for any sterner requirement than that. There is no moral justification for countenancing anything less. Discipline destroys the spirit and working loyalty of the general force when it is pitched to the minority of malcontented, unproductive individuals within the organization, whether to punish or to appease them. Discipline within the military should not be viewed as a ritual or form, but simply as the best course of conduct most likely to lead to efficient performance of an assigned responsibility. Subordinates are able to recognize right and reasonable discipline as such, even though it causes them personal inconvenience. But if the discipline is unduly harsh or unnecessarily lax, subordinates' morale will fall.

One of the most contentious actions that leaders can take is to create rules or policies for subordinates by which they themselves do not abide. In studies we have conducted of soldiers deployed on peacekeeping or combat operations, this has been a consistent complaint of junior enlisted soldiers and noncommissioned officers (Castro & McGurk, 2003/2004). Typically, these "double standards" are seen in uniform wear and phone use, where junior officers fail to maintain the uniform standard and overuse their phone privileges, without any apparent adverse consequences. Subordinates obviously resent rules and policies when they are expected to follow them, but their leaders do not. Flexible pragmatic leaders understand that while rules and policies are important for maintaining discipline and good order, rules should not be established that they themselves do not intend to follow.

Use Punishment Judiciously

Before meting out punishment, it is necessary to judge the subordinate, and judgment means to think over, to compare, to weigh probable effects on the subordinate and on the command, and to give the offender the benefit of any reasonable doubt. Before any punishment is given, the question must be asked: What good will it achieve? If the answer is none, then punishment is not in order. Punishment of a vindictive nature is a crime of leadership; when it is given uselessly or handed out in a strictly routine manner, it is an immoral act. To punish a body of subordinates for offenses committed by two or three of their members, even though the offense is obnoxious and it is impossible to put the finger on the culprits, is no more excusable within a military organization than in civilian society. Any leader who resorts to this practice of "mass punishment" is likely to forfeit the loyalty of the best in his or her team.

An exemplar of this type of mass punishment was seen during the early years of the peacekeeping mission in Kosovo. Telephone banks were established for soldiers to use to call home to their families. However, because the telephone switching capacity was severely restricted, soldiers were required to limit their telephone calls to 15 minutes twice a week. This was such an essential restriction in order to maintain operational effectiveness that actual telephone use was monitored by higher headquarters for compliance. Unfortunately, a few soldiers discovered a way to exceed these time limits for telephone use, resulting in phone calls exceeding two hours in duration. Unable to locate the offending soldiers, whom the leadership knew numbered fewer than 10 soldiers from a battalion of over 700 soldiers, phone privileges were revoked for the entire battalion for one week. From the perspective of the 690 or so soldiers who followed the telephone use rules, this punishment was seen as extremely unfair and inappropriate, especially given that this was their primary means of communication with their families. Flexible pragmatic leaders know that mass punishment for the actions of a few only serve to lower unit morale and increase subordinate distrust in the unit's leadership.

Recommendations for What Leaders Ought Not to Do

Just as examples of flexible pragmatic leader attributes and behaviors can be identified that actively support subordinates and the unit, so can the attributes and behaviors of rigid institutional leaders be identified that are unhelpful in terms of leading subordinates. In fact, some may argue that negative leader attributes and behaviors serve as better guideposts for leadership than do positive ones, because they are more salient. Here, we cite negative leader behaviors that are particularly egregious and demoralizing to subordinates.

Embarrass Subordinates

In general, leaders should not embarrass or humiliate their subordinates in front of others. One of the strongest passions individuals are subject to is their aversion to being criticized, contradicted, and exposed as a fool before an onlooking crowd. Making clever remarks that casually denigrate the worth of subordinates only serves to lower their self-worth as a member of the unit, while at the same time eroding respect other subordinates may have in the leader. Remarkably, noncommissioned officers tend to routinely engage in this type of behavior. In our survey of junior enlisted soldiers who served in Iraq, 79 percent of them reported that NCOs routinely embarrassed them in front of others (Castro & McGurk, 2003/2004).

While it is a serious error to reprimand subordinates in the presence of any other person because of the unnecessary hurt to their pride, circumstances moderate the rule. If the offense for which the reprimand is being given involves injury of any sort to some other person or persons, it may be wholly proper to apply the treatment in their presence. For example, the bully or the smart aleck who wantonly humiliates fellow service members is not entitled to have his or her own feelings spared.

Hide behind Rules and Regulations

Rules and regulations constrain individuals for the good of the group, but the excuse that one was only following rules or regulations is never an acceptable answer when committing an injustice toward another human being. Receiving orders of instruction does not relieve the leader from the obligation to exercise common sense. When leaders limit their thinking to questions about "What is the policy, what is the rule, what is the regulation?" rather than "What should the policy be for the good of the service, for the good of the country?" they have set their sights too low. Rules only exist for the good of the service and the good of the country. Rules that do not achieve at least these objectives should be at least questioned and considered carefully in terms of their guidance. That said, leaders should remember that when there is doubt about a regulation or policy, if it benefits service members, such as earning a pass for reenlistment, it should be assumed to be just and equitable.

Abuse Privileges

In the military, rank has its privileges. However, it is out of the abuse of privileges that much of the friction between leaders and subordinates arise. With increased rank, also comes increased responsibility. In fact, ranks only exist to facilitate leaders in fulfilling their responsibilities. What puts most of the grit into the machinery is not that privileges exist, but that they are exercised by those leaders who are not motivated by a passionate sense of duty and responsibility toward their subordinates.

An incident that occurred in Iraq illustrates this point. The junior officers from the companies of a battalion were put in charge of the morale and welfare funds of the unit, with the responsibility of using these funds to purchase televisions and fans, as well as other amenities to improve the quality of life of the soldiers. Indeed, these junior officers did a remarkable job of procuring televisions, with satellite dishes, as well as fans from the local Iraqi economy. However, rather than place the fans and televisions in locations where all the soldiers from the company could benefit from their use, these junior officers placed them in their private living quarters, where only they had access to them (Castro & McGurk, 2003/2004). While the battalion commander quickly rectified this situation when he became aware of it, the damage done by these junior officers to the relationships between them and their subordinates is nearly impossible to repair. Subordinates will not be resentful of the rightful privileges of their leaders so long as their leaders are also concerned about their welfare as well.

Future Directions

The model of flexible pragmatic and rigid institutional leadership proposed here provides a framework for viewing leader actions, for understanding the belief system of leaders that drives their behaviors, and for establishing a starting point from which research can be designed to assess helpful leader behaviors in a profoundly applied arena, namely combat. These leader actions can be summarized into three cardinal leader principles (see Table 9.1). However, numerous questions remain and the framework must ultimately incorporate these remaining questions in order to be optimally useful:

1. What influence does predisposition play in determining what approach a junior leader will play? Does this predisposition evolve from genetics, temperament, early childhood experiences, experience with leadership and authority models, and/or one's personal family system?

Table 9.1
Cardinal Principles of Leadership

Cardinal Principle
First Leader Principle—Leaders are personally responsible for the safety and well-being of their subordinates.
Second Leader Principle—When a regulation or policy is in the favor of the service member, it is always just and equitable.
Third Leader Principle—It is the duty of all leaders to take care of the needs of their subordinates before caring for themselves.

2. Can rigid institutional leaders be viewed positively by subordinates, or are they basically viewed negatively? Does the perception of the leader depend on what kind of subordinate one has or what the task is?

3. Assuming leadership style can be trained, and this is a fundamental assumption of Army training manuals and the flexible pragmatic leadership style described in this chapter, what should training look like to be effective? When should such training be conducted with the junior officer?

4. Can a leader be neither a fully flexible pragmatic leader nor a fully rigid institutional leader but one who straddles the two approaches?

Despite the fact that many organizations, to include military organizations the world over, assume that leaders' behaviors can be developed and indicate the need to do so through their investment in leadership development programs, research evidence is simply lacking to inform organizations how to tailor, improve, or overhaul leader training and development programs most effectively. Despite this lack of research, there continues to be strong interest in developing tools and methods for how junior leaders should behave to make a positive impact on unit performance and their subordinates' well-being. This interest is driven by the recognition that the well-being of subordinates and units are deeply affected by leadership decisions at all levels. As illustrated by a U.S. Army report based on an assessment of the mental health of deployed forces in Iraq (U.S. Army Surgeon General, 2004), leader behaviors are seen as a critical way to influence the adaptation and functioning of military personnel (see also Britt et al., 2004). Thus, there is support for the ecological validity of prioritizing the development of effective leader behaviors.

Leader Behaviors

Determining what the effective (and ineffective) leader behaviors are in deployed environments would be beneficial for junior leaders who may lack life and work experiences but find themselves in roles of tremendous responsibility in combat operations. For instance, because leaders high in adaptability have been found to be effective and are a valued commodity in Iraq (Wong, 2004), researchers need to determine what aspects of adaptability are important, what makes leaders adaptable, and how best to measure it and model it within a stress and performance framework.

In terms of measurement, the pool of scale items addressing leader behaviors used in leadership scales should be expanded to make certain that the correct leader behaviors are being ascertained. Military researchers should continue to listen to leaders and soldiers using surveys, interviews, and focus groups so that the full range of effective and ineffective leadership behaviors are identified.

Another critical area of leadership behavior research that needs to be examined is the multinational setting of military operations. While research has demonstrated the existence of cross-cultural leadership behaviors, there are also leadership behaviors that are idiomatic to particular cultures. These culture-specific behaviors need to be examined, especially because of the multinational reality of many deployed settings.

While the focus of this chapter has been on the development of junior leaders, the different roles assumed by junior officers and junior noncommissioned officers in a military unit may require different emphases in terms of encouraging flexible and pragmatic leader behaviors and attitudes. Traditionally, the doctrinal role of officers in a unit is to define the unit's mission and develop a strategy for executing that mission. In contrast, the traditional role of noncommissioned officers is to execute the mission. Thus, both levels of leaders influence the well-being of military personnel and the perceptions of unit morale and readiness. Given their differing roles in guiding subordinates, however, systematic research is needed to assess the impact of these two groups of leaders in terms of distinctive optimal leadership behaviors.

How the question of military leadership is addressed is ultimately a reflection of the priorities of the organization. The organizational culture sets a climate of expectation regarding acceptable leader behaviors and attitudes. Thus, not only are flexible and pragmatic leadership behaviors the responsibility of the individual leader, junior or otherwise, but they also are the responsibility of the organization itself. The military organization sets policy and procedures that affect whether positive leadership behaviors are promoted or abandoned. Thus, the future of military leadership lies in the current behaviors of the junior military leader and the system in which they are indoctrinated and sustained.

References

Bass, B. M. (1998). *Transformational leadership: Industrial, military, and educational impact.* Mahwah, NJ: Erlbaum.

Bass, B. M. (1997). Does transactional-transformational paradigm transcend organizational and national boundaries? *American Psychologist, 52,* 130–139.

Bass, B. M. (1996). A new paradigm of leadership: An inquiry into transformational leadership. Alexandria, VA: U.S. Army Research Institute for the Behavioral and Social Sciences.

Bass, B. M. (1990). *Bass and Stogdill's handbook of leadership: Theory, research and managerial applications* (3rd ed.). New York: Free Press

Bennis, W. G., & Thomas, R. J. (2002). *Geeks and geezers: How era, values, and defining moments shape leaders.* Boston: Harvard Business School Press.

Bliese, P. D., & Castro, C. A. (2003). The soldier-adaptation model (SAM): Application to peacekeeping. In T. W. Britt & A. B. Adler (Eds.). *The psychology of the peacekeeper: Lessons from the field* (pp. 185–203). Westport, CT: Praeger Publishers.

Britt, T. W., Davison, J., Bliese, P. D., & Castro, C. A. (2004). How leaders can influence the impact that stressors have on soldiers. *Military Medicine, 169*, 541–545.

Castro, C. A., & Adler, A. B. (2000, November 6–9). *The impact of operations tempo: Issues in measurement.* Paper presented at the Annual Conference of the International Military Testing Association. Edinburgh, UK.

Castro, C. A., & Hoge, C. W. (2003). *Impact of PERSTEMPO on deployment experiences on the mental health and functioning of soldiers and their families.* Washington, DC: Walter Reed Army Institute of Research.

Castro, C.A., & McGurk, D. (2003/2004). [Junior enlisted soldiers' and noncommissioned officers' views of unit leadership]. Unpublished raw data.

Chambers, E. G., Foulton, M., Handfield-Jones, H., Hankin, S. M., & Michaels, E. G. (1998). The war for talent. *The McKinsey Quarterly, 3*, 44–57.

Dabos, G. E., & Rousseau, D. M. (2004). Mutuality and reciprocity in the psychological contracts of employees and employers. *Journal of Applied Psychology, 89*, 52–72.

Den Hartog, D. N., House, R. J., Hanges, P. J., Ruiz-Quintanilla, S. A., Dorfman, P. W., Field, R. H. G., et al. (1999). Culture specific and cross culturally generalizable implicit leadership theories: Are attributes of charismatic/transformational leadership universally endorsed? *Leadership Quarterly, 10*, 219–256.

Department of Army (1990). *Military leadership* (FM 22-100). Washington, DC: Author.

Department of Army (1999). *Army leadership: Be, know, do* (FM 22-100). Washington, DC: Author.

Dienesch, R. M., & Liden, R. C. (1986). Leader-member exchange model of leadership: A critique and further development. *Academy of Management Review, 11*, 618–634.

Fiedler, F. E. (1986). The contribution of cognitive resources and leader behavior to organizational performance, *Journal of Applied Social Psychology, 16*, 532–548.

Fiedler, F. E. (1971). Validation and extension of the contingency model of leadership effectiveness: A review of the empirical findings. *Psychological Bulletin, 76*, 128–148.

Fiedler, F. E., & Garcia, E. (1987). New approaches to effective leadership: Cognitive resources and organizational performance. New York: Wiley.

Fussell, P. (1989). Wartime: Understanding and behavior in the Second World War. New York: Oxford University Press.

Gerstner, C. R., & Day D. V. (1994). Cross-cultural comparison of leadership prototypes. *Leadership Quarterly, 5*, 121–134.

Hersey, P., & Blanchard, K. H. (1974). So you want to know your leadership style? *Training and Development Journal, 28*, 22–37.

Hofstede, G. (1993). Cultural constrains in management theories. *Academy of Management Executive, 7*, 81–94.

House, R. J. (1977). A 1976 theory of charismatic leadership. In J. G. Hunt and L. L. Larson (Eds.), *Leadership: The cutting edge* (pp. 189–207). Carbondale: Southern Illinois University Press.

House, R. J., Javidan, M., Dorfman, P. W., & Hanges, P. J. (2004). GLOBE research program. In G. R. Goethals, G. J. Sorenson, & J. M. Burns (Eds.). *Encyclopedia of Leadership* (Vol. 2) (pp. 577–581). Thousand Oaks, CA: Sage.

House, R. J. (1996). Path goal theory of leadership: Lessons, legacy, and a reformulated theory. *Leadership Quarterly, 7*, 323–352.

Katz, D., & Kahn, R. L. (1966). *The social psychology of organizations.* New York: Wiley.

Mann, R. D. (1959). A review of the relationship between personality and performance in small groups. *Psychological Bulletin, 56*, 241–270.

MacDonald, C. B. (1947). *Company commander.* Washington, DC: Infantry Journal Press.

McDonough, J. (1985). *Platoon leader.* Novato, CA: Presido Press.

Robinson, S. L., & Rousseau, D. M. (1994). Violating the psychological contract: Not the exception but the norm. *Journal of Organizational Behavior, 15*, 245–259.

Rousseau, D. M. (2000). *Psychological contract inventory technical report.* Unpublished manuscript.

Rousseau, D. M. (1995). *Psychological contracts in organizations. Understanding written and unwritten agreements.* Thousand Oaks, CA: Sage.

Rousseau, D. M. (1989). Psychological and implied contracts in organizations. *Employee Rights and Responsibilities Journal, 2*, 121–139.

Rousseau, D. M., & Tijoriwala, S. A. (1999). What's a good reason to change? Motivated reasoning and social accounts in promoting organizational change. *Journal of Applied Psychology, 84*, 514–528.

Sessa, V. I., & Campbell, R. J. (1997). *Selection at the top: An annotated bibliography.* Greensboro, NC: Center for Creative Leadership.

Sledge, E. B. (1981). *With the old breed.* New York: Oxford University Press.

Stouffer, S. A., Lumsdaine, A. A., Lumsdaine, M. H., Williams, R. M., Smith, M. B., Janis, I. L., et al. (1949). *The American soldier: Combat and its aftermath* (Vol. 2). Princeton, NJ: Princeton University Press.

Taguba, A. (2004). Article 15-6 investigation of the 800th Military Police Brigade. Retrieved April 25, 2005, from http: www.agonist.org/annex/taguba.htm

Taylor, R. L., & Rosenbach, W. E. (1982). *Military leadership: In pursuit of excellence* (2nd ed.). Boulder, CO: Westview Press.

Thomas, J. L., Bliese, P. D., & Jex, S. M. (in press). Interpersonal conflict and organizational commitment: Examining two levels of supervisory support as multi-level moderators. Manuscript accepted for publication at *Journal of Applied Social Psychology.*

U.S. Army Surgeon General. (2004). Operation Iraqi Freedom (OIF) Mental Health Advisory Team (MHAT) Report. Retrieved May 3, 2005, from http://www.globalsecurity.org/military/library/report/2004/mhat.htm

Van Fleet, D. D. (1996). *Online bibliography of military leadership.* Retrieved May 4, 2005, from http://www.west.asu.edu/vanfleet/milbib/milbib.htm

Wong, L. (2004). *Developing adaptive leaders: The crucible experience of Operation Iraqi Freedom.* Retrieved October 14, 2005, from http://www.strategicstudiesinstitute.army.mil/pdffiles/PUB411.pdf

Wong, L. (2002). *Stifling innovation: Developing tomorrow's leaders today.* Carlisle Barracks, PA: Strategic Studies Institute.

Yammarino, F. J., Bass, B. M. (1990). Long-term forecasting of transformational leadership and its effects among naval officers: Some preliminary findings. In K. E. Clark & M. B. Clark (Eds.), *Measures of leadership* (pp. 151–170). West Orange, NJ: Leadership Library of America.

CHAPTER 10

SOCIAL CLIMATES: DRIVERS OF SOLDIER WELL-BEING AND RESILIENCE

Paul D. Bliese

As members of Army units interact and encounter common experiences, they develop shared perceptions of their social environments. These shared perceptions represent distinct "social climates." Social climates are important factors influencing how soldiers interpret and react to events. For instance, Shils and Janowitz (1948) wrote a compelling article examining the remarkable resilience of German soldiers in the *Wehrmacht*. In their work, they claimed that soldier resilience was a function of the social climates actively managed in *Wehrmacht* units. Shils and Janowitz wrote that "German officers saw that solidarity is fostered by the recollection of jointly experienced gratifications and that accordingly the groups who had gone through a victory together should not be dissolved but should be maintained as units to the greatest extent possible" (p. 287).

In military research, however, the empirical study of social climates has tended to lag behind the theoretical development. The most compelling information about social climate comes from rich qualitative work by authors such as Shils and Janowitz rather than from empirical analyses of military data. Rich qualitative analyses certainly have an important role in behavioral science research; nonetheless, it is necessary to build on qualitative studies with quantitative work. Among other things, doing so will help researchers and planners more effectively incorporate social climate variables into military models of human and organizational well-being, performance, and resilience (Pew & Mavor, 1998).

This material has been reviewed by the Walter Reed Army Institute of Research. There is no objection to its presentation and/or publication. The opinions or assertions contained herein are the private views of the author, and are not to be construed as official, or as reflecting true views of the Department of the Army or the Department of Defense.

The purpose of this chapter is to discuss findings from empirical studies of social climate in military settings. Much of this work has been conducted by researchers at the Walter Reed Army Institute of Research (WRAIR) in the period from the early 1990s to 2005. Most of this research centers on the role that shared social climates play in the well-being of soldiers. Well-being is a broad concept incorporating (but not limited to) factors such as depression, morale, job satisfaction, and physical health. Results from studies of well-being have implications for soldier performance and resilience in that well-being is presumed to be a driver of both (see for instance, Bliese, Thomas, & Jex, 2002).

Studies of climate and well-being conducted at WRAIR have revealed two important things: (1) the existence of specific social climates can be empirically demonstrated using a variety of statistical tools; and (2) some specific types of social climate, most notably climate as related to unit leadership, directly and indirectly affect soldier well-being. Within these two broad themes, however, are a number of important nuances that help advance the theoretical understanding of the measurement properties of climates, and the role social climates play in individual and organizational outcomes.

Climate and Culture in the Army

In considering social climates, it is useful to begin by defining climates and specifying how social climates differ from related concepts such as culture. In research conducted at WRAIR, the concept of social climates is considered to be theoretically distinct from the concept of organizational culture on three dimensions: (a) how the two concepts originate, (b) the level at which both constructs operate, and (c) the time span it takes to change climate versus culture.

In terms of concept origination, social climates are viewed as evolving from day-to-day interaction patterns and shared experiences among group members. Because the concept of social climate depends on social interaction, it meets the definitional criteria of a concept that applies to "groups"—groups being defined as interacting individuals working together toward some common goal (McGrath, 1984). Indeed, Shils and Janowitz (1948) discussed the existence of social climates as evolving from characteristics of a "primary group"—a primary group being characterized by face-to-face association and cooperation and involving mutual identification.

The view that climates originate from interactions and shared experiences among primary group members relates directly to the level at which we see the concept operating in the U.S. Army. Specifically, social climates are seen as applying to smaller Army units such as companies, platoons, and squads, because army groups at this level are comprised of sets of interacting individuals working toward common goals. Presumably, any group (military or otherwise) working together toward some common goal and engaging in face-to-face communication and cooperation would be expected to develop shared social climates.

In terms of time span, social climates are seen as malleable and quickly changed. For instance, we would not find it surprising for the social climate of a unit to change dramatically within two or three months as a function of changes in key unit leadership or as a function of targeted leadership development. The speed at which social climates develop may be impacted by the intensity of the shared experiences among group members. A newly formed group might be expected to develop a strong shared social climate around the facet of unit leadership within days if the group were exposed to a particularly dramatic experience (either positive or negative) involving their leaders. In contrast, a shared social climate regarding unit leadership might take months to evolve in the absence of any particularly strong event involving unit leadership.

Unlike social climate, we conceptualize culture as evolving from shared exposures to salient aspects of large entities such as entire organizations or nations. The culture of a nation, for instance, is driven by signs and symbols transmitted through media such as television and speeches of elected officials. In organizational theory, the culture of an organization is hypothesized to be largely determined by the actions of what Hunt (1991) calls systems leaders. Systems leaders represent the highest levels of leadership within an organization; therefore, in the U.S. Army, systems leaders are three- and four-star general officers (Wong, Bliese, & McGurk, 2003). Hunt (1991) argues that one of the primary tasks of leadership at the systems level is to ensure that the culture within the organization is congruent with cultures of organizations outside of the Army. For example, the culture of the U.S. Army is expected to be congruent with the vision and goals of the executive branch of the U.S. Government, and proper alignment at these levels are a principal concern of systems leaders.

Given that we conceptualize organizational culture as originating from the actions of systems-level leaders, it should not be surprising that we consider culture to be difficult to change. Changes that do occur happen gradually over extended periods of time—consider the cultural changes in the U.S. Army from a "drug culture" (Ingraham, 1984) to a professional army. Systems leaders were able to drive changes in the culture of the Army in the late 1970s and early 1980s, but these changes took years to fully achieve.

In summary, climate and culture differ in terms of the three dimensions in the following ways. First, climate evolves from shared interactions among members; culture evolves primarily from shared exposure. Second, climate operates at the level of small primary groups; culture operates within large social entities such as entire organizations. Third, climates can be rapidly changed; cultures evolve relatively slowly over time.

While this section has focused on how climate and culture differ, it can also be helpful to consider how the concepts are related. First, climates within a work group may be influenced by broader social properties related to the culture of an organization or even to the culture within the nation. That is, culture can exert a top-down influence on climate. For instance, Shils and Janowitz (1948) claim that the social climate within smaller units of the *Wehrmacht* was partially driven by a small cadre of "hard core" members. The "hard core" element was comprised of

> young men between 24 and 28 years of age who had had a gratifying adolescence in the most rewarding period of National Socialism. They were imbued with the ideology of

Gemeinshaft (community solidarity)…and accordingly placed a high value on 'tough-ness', manly comradeliness and group solidarity. (p. 286)

This is a prime example of a national culture exerting a top-down process on the cli-mates within units.

The second similarity is that climate, like culture, is most meaningful when con-sidered with respect to specific referents. That is, the power of using either climate or culture as explanatory variables is dependent on linking these constructs to specific dimensions. For instance, the value that researchers such as Hofstede (1980) added to the study of culture was that they defined specific dimensions such as masculinity versus femininity; individual versus collective orientation; low- versus high-power distance. This, in turn, helped quantify differences among nations. In a similar fash-ion, studies of unit climate in the Army are most valuable when they focus on con-structs such as safety, leadership, citizenship behavior, and collective efficacy climates (Bliese & Britt, 2001; Bliese & Castro, 2000; Bliese & Halverson, 2002; Erhart, Bli-ese, & Thomas, in press; Hofmann, Morgeson, & Gerras, 2003; Jex, & Bliese, 1999).

It is important to study distinct forms of climate when understanding how climate relates to specific outcomes. For instance, in nonmilitary organizational research, Schneider and colleagues (Schneider 1990; Schneider & Bowen, 1985; Schneider, White, & Paul, 1998) have repeatedly shown that group members' climate for serv-ice (group members' shared attitudes toward serving customers) is related to custom-er satisfaction. A central argument in this line of research is that other types of cli-mate should *not* be expected to relate to customer satisfaction. As another example, studies of safety climate are typically conducted in research predicting accidents (e.g., Zohar, 2002). Finally, in Army well-being and resilience research, focus has been centered on understanding shared perceptions of leader support (Bliese & Cas-tro, 2000; Britt et al., 2004). The focus on leadership is based on the theoretical proposition that social support is a key driver of well-being (Cohen & Wills, 1985) and that leaders provide one of the most important forms of social support in occu-pational settings (see also Leather, Lawrence, Beale, Cox, & Dickson, 1998). In sum, it is necessary to have a theoretical framework dictating which specific forms of cli-mate are likely to be related to specific outcomes when examining the role of climate.

With a clear definition of social climate, it is now possible to discuss the research paradigm employed at WRAIR in studying social climate in Army units.

Paradigm for Studying Climate

Empirical data supporting the existence of social climates come from surveys. One of the key factors having made social climate research possible at the WRAIR has been the sampling scheme employed during survey data collections. In the majority of behavior science health research conducted by WRAIR, data has been collected so as to maintain the hierarchical group structure of the organization. A typical strategy has been to survey every available member of a large unit such as a brigade (roughly 3,000 soldiers). Statistically, surveying every member is neither the most efficient way to estimate attributes of the brigade (a random sample one-tenth the size would accomplish this goal); nor does surveying every member of a single brigade help us understand much about the larger Army population as a whole. That is, we cannot draw any inferences about levels of morale in the entire Army based on the results from 3,000 soldiers from the same brigade, because health outcomes and other outcomes of interest vary significantly among units (Bliese & Jex, 2002).

The positive side to sampling entire units, however, is that this data collection strategy allows for constructing data sets that maintain individual responses within the nested hierarchy characterizing the brigade. Specifically, the strategy permits coding of soldiers' unit membership in terms of battalion, company, platoon, and squad and thereby permits understanding of individual responses from soldiers within the context of the groups to which they belong. By collecting and maintaining data in this fashion, we are able to examine empirically the existence and influence of social climates.

In behavioral science health research at WRAIR, we have been primarily interested in how social climates operate at the company level. As background, a company represents a group with between 50 and 200 members, depending on the specific type of company. Combat arms units such as armor companies tend to be at the lower end of the size continuum, and headquarters companies tend to be at the upper end of the size continuum.

The company has traditionally been considered an important source of social influence for soldiers. Moskos, for instance, contended that a soldier's "social horizon is largely circumscribed by activities occurring at the level of the company" (cited in Ingraham, 1984, p. 208). The social influence of the company comes from the fact that as an autonomous group working toward a common mission or goal, soldiers in the company tend to have a great deal of intragroup interaction and relatively little intergroup interaction. In addition, companies have distinct and influential leadership in the form of a company commander and first sergeant. All in all, these conditions form an ideal situation for unique and powerful social climates to develop within companies.

Embedded underneath the company are platoons and squads. We believe these smaller groups also develop distinct climates; however, we currently have little empirical information about social climates in platoons and squads. All else being equal, work by Latané (1981) would suggest that smaller groups such as platoons and squads would exert more influence on individuals than larger groups such as companies. At the same time, however, squad and platoon membership tends to be more permeable, with considerable intergroup contact among different platoon and squad members, and this permeability would work against the development of distinct social climates at these lower levels. Therefore, we simply conclude that while squads and platoons are likely to develop distinct social climates, the lack of empirical evidence allows us only to speculate about the relative strengths of climate at different levels.

Parenthetically, the relative importance of companies, platoons, and squads to impact climate may be context specific. For instance, in combat settings, smaller units may develop stronger climates, because many of the acts associated with war fighting, such as patrolling, are small-unit endeavors. In contrast, in garrison the focus is on training, and major training events tend to be company-level experiences. Thus, stronger platoon- and squad-level climates might be expected in combat than in garrison. Work of this nature is an important area for future research.

Having defined our terminology regarding social climates, and having introduced the research paradigm used in this line of research, it is possible to discuss the two core basic findings in detail. Recall, the two core findings are: (1) groups develop social climates that can be empirically demonstrated, and (2) some specific types of social climate affect soldier well-being both indirectly and directly.

Empirically Demonstrating Climates

The logic behind empirically demonstrating social climate is rooted in the theoretical notion that climates evolve from the shared interaction patterns of group members. Consequently, to show empirically that a group has a social climate, the group members must be shown to have a shared sense of social reality. Historically, Larry James and colleagues can be credited with most clearly articulating this basic argument (see James, 1982; James, Demaree, & Wolf, 1984; James & Jones, 1974). More recent work by Bliese (2000) and Kozlowski and Klein (2000) have further clarified some of the distinctions surrounding whether group members "agree" and/or whether group members provide ratings that reliably differentiate one group from another. Details of the distinction between agreement and reliability are beyond the scope of this chapter; nonetheless, empirical demonstrations of the existence of climate need to show that group members agree, and practically speaking, the empirical evidence should also show that measures of social climate reliably vary across groups.

Present but Subtle

Perhaps one of the most interesting aspects of studying social climates in the Army has been that the empirical evidence for the existence of climate has been rather subtle. That is, soldiers' responses to items on surveys show agreement and allow differentiation among companies, but these differences are not blatantly obvious. For example, consider a simple question asking soldiers in a company, "How many hours do you usually work in a day?" Responses to this item might reasonably be used to develop a measure of workload climate if it could be shown that (a) group members agree when it comes to ratings of work hours, and (b) group means reliably differ from one another. Note that even though the item asks soldiers about their individual work hours, it is theoretically reasonable to expect detectable differences among groups, because unit leadership typically sets uniform work hours in response to unit-based work requirements.

Interestingly, when responses to questions of work hours are examined, considerable variability is observed within groups. Figure 10.1 shows a histogram of individual ratings of work hours across nine randomly selected Army companies taken from data reported in Bliese and Halverson (1996). Notice how four of the nine companies have clear modal responses centered around 12 hours (companies 1, 2, 4, and 7). The remaining companies have a much broader range of responses. The histograms suggest that agreement about work hours is apparent in four companies, but absent or weak in the remaining five companies.

There potentially are a number of reasons why some groups agree about work hours and others do not—some companies may do a better job of stipulating and enforcing work hours; some companies may delegate work hour decisions to the platoon level, and platoon leadership may set different rules; some companies may have highly diverse functional task areas (e.g., a maintenance platoon or a finance section),

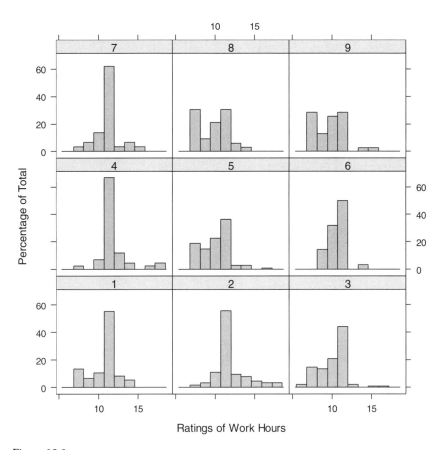

Figure 10.1
Histogram of Work Hours, by Company

and these task areas may have different work hours because they have different work-loads. Nonetheless, the key observation to draw from these data is that even though we know that companies generally dictate work hours to their members based on unit-based work requirements, we still find considerable variability in agreement about work hours among members of the same groups.

The example with work hours raises at least one other issue relevant to measuring climate. Specifically, the concept of individual work hours has a factual basis in that it potentially can be objectively measured (using time clocks, for instance). Thus, individual ratings of work hours (even if biased) do have an objective foundation. In many cases, however, climate reflects shared social realities, and assessments of shared social reality are likely to have a high degree of subjectivity. Consider, for instance, questions that attempt to assess the leadership climate within a unit. Recall, leadership climate can be defined as group members' shared perceptions about the degree of support provided by leaders. It is almost a certainty that soldiers' responses to leadership climate items will be influenced by numerous individual factors such as personal response biases, individual dyadic experiences with leaders, and individual mood states. This, in turn, suggests that it may be quite difficult to demonstrate agreement.

Figure 10.2 shows ratings of leadership from the same nine companies as those providing work hour ratings. Leadership was assessed using an 11-item scale, with response options ranging from (1) strongly disagree to (5) strongly agree. In effect, the scale ranges from very poor perceptions of leadership to very positive perceptions of leadership. Notice the wide range of variability in responses within the companies. On the basis of the visual evidence alone, it is unclear whether soldiers show any agreement about their leadership.

The histograms for leadership (and to a lesser extent for work hours) make it clear that empirical decision tools are needed to help determine when agreement is and when it is not present. And indeed a statistical analysis of the 99 groups and 7,382 soldiers representing the complete data reported in Bliese and Halverson (1996) reveals that both work hours and ratings of leadership show significant within-group agreement. In the following paragraphs, we discuss the statistical evidence for agreement, with a particular focus on how agreement can be visualized.

Research conducted at WRAIR has centered on the measurement and visualization of within-group agreement. A nontechnical overview of how agreement is assessed must begin by noting that statistical analyses of agreement are fundamentally based on examinations of the levels of variance within groups. A variance of zero (no variability) constitutes perfect agreement, because it indicates that everyone in the group gave the same response; however, variances of zero are never observed in practice; rather, what one observes in analyses of within-group variance are values associated with distributions such as those presented in Figure 10.2.

Consider, for instance, company number two in the bottom middle panel of Figure 10.2. This company has relatively low variability in the ratings of leadership with a variance of 0.35, reflecting that a high number of soldiers give ratings around 2.5. In contrast, the variance in ratings of leadership associated with the responses from

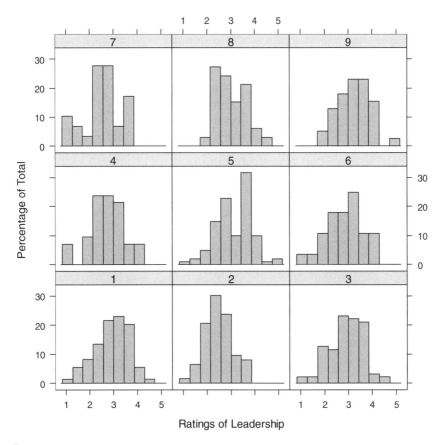

Figure 10.2
Histogram of Soldiers' Perceptions of Leadership, by Company

company number seven in the top left corner is 0.60. This relatively high value is driven by the fact that about 10 percent of the company gave the leadership very negative ratings around 1, while around 20 percent gave moderately positive ratings around 4. High and low splits in ratings within a group are associated with high variance. Clearly, there is less agreement (more variance) in company seven than in company two.

The problem with looking at variances to make determinations of agreement is that it is not exactly clear how a particular variance value should be interpreted; is a variance of 0.35 low enough to provide proof that group members agree? Likewise, is a value of 0.60 large enough to suggest a lack of agreement or even disagreement? James and colleagues (1984) proposed solving this problem by contrasting observed variances with theoretically expected random variances; however, in practice, determining the correct expected random variance can be problematic (see Bliese,

2000). Thus, researchers at WRAIR developed a technique to compare observed variances to expected random variances generated from pseudo groups. Basically, computer algorithms were developed to randomly create thousands of groups. Each time a random group was created, the variance for that group was calculated, and these random variances were compared to actual group variances (Bliese, 2005; Bliese, Halverson, & Rothberg, 1994).

Figure 10.3 uses the statistical foundation of pseudo group variance to provide a visualization of within-group agreement surrounding leadership. The small

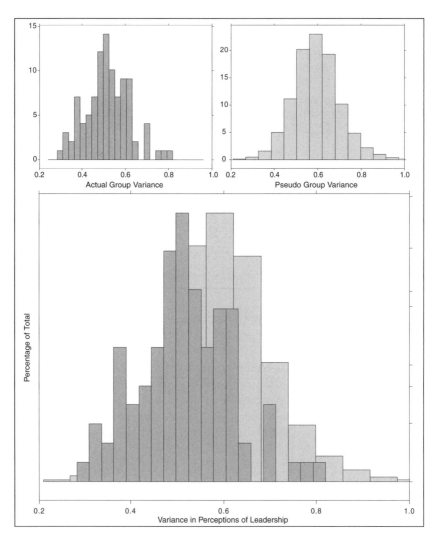

Figure 10.3
Random Distribution Versus Actual Distribution for Perceptions of Leadership

histogram on the left shows variances from actual groups, and the small histogram on the right shows variances from 9,999 pseudo groups. The big histogram provides an overlay of the two smaller histograms on an aligned X-axis. Notice in the big histogram that variances from the actual groups fall on the lower end of the pseudo group variances. That is, variances about leadership from actual groups are smaller than the variances about leadership in pseudo groups. This provides visual evidence of agreement for the entire sample of 99 groups. Probability-based statistics (see Bliese, 2005; Bliese & Halverson, 2002) can be used to confirm that within-group variances from actual groups are statistically smaller than within-group variances from pseudo groups. Based on the statistical analyses, we conclude social climates related to leadership exist among the 99 companies as a whole.

Another innovation developed to visually demonstrate the existence of social climates is to contrast group means with pseudo group means. The analysis of this type attempts to determine whether group means from actual groups are more extreme than means from random groups. This is done to show, in essence, that something about being members of intact groups causes soldiers to respond either more positively or more negatively than would be expected by chance.

Figure 10.4 contrasts actual group means (gray bars from 99 companies) with expected random group means presented as a black line. These data are the ratings of leadership climate from the Bliese & Halverson (1996) study. The graphic assigns the 7,382 soldiers assigned to 99 random groups 250 times. The means from each of

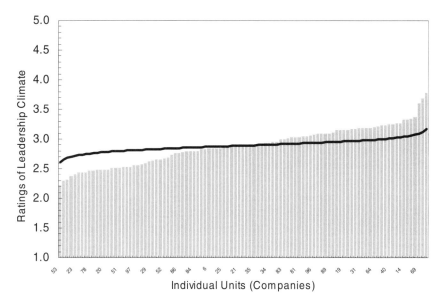

Figure 10.4
Random Group Means (Line) Versus Company Means (Bars) for Perceptions of Leadership

the 250 iterations were sorted from lowest to highest, and average sorted values were used to create the random group mean line. An automated program to conduct this analysis is included in Bliese (2005).

In Figure 10.4, average company ratings of leadership are more extreme than would be expected by chance. Specifically, companies on the left of the figure show ratings of leadership lower than chance levels, and companies on the right of the figure show ratings of leadership that are more positive than chance levels. It may not be obvious immediately that contrasts of group means and contrasts of group variances are different variants of the same test. When within-group variances are smaller than would be expected by chance, group means are caused to have more variance than would be expected by chance. This logic is behind the basic Analysis of Variance (ANOVA) test. Thus, it is not surprising that the results for the variance analyses composing Figure 10.3 tell a similar story to the results of the mean analysis in Figure 10.4.

Both Figure 10.3 and Figure 10.4 confirm the existence of social climates surrounding leadership by demonstrating that a specific pattern of results for either within-group variances or between group means is unique to actual groups. Interestingly, however, both graphs also illustrate the somewhat subtle nature of social climates. In Figure 10.3, it is clear that the distribution of variances from the actual groups falls into the small tail of the distribution of variances from pseudo groups —the actual group variances, however, display a great deal of overlap with pseudo group variances. Likewise, Figure 10.4 reveals that a completely random range of group responses varies between 2.60 and 3.18, but the actual group responses are not that different in that they range from 2.23 to 3.78.

Generalizability

Because the examples used in the previous section used data from an Army sample, it is worth considering whether the examples are likely to be similar to results from data collected in other types of organizations or even to other Army samples. With regard to comparability of Army and non-Army findings, the evidence clearly suggests Army climate data are similar to climate data from other organizations. James (1982) has argued that one potential measure of agreement is the Intraclass Correlation Coefficient 1 or ICC(1). In retrospect, the ICC(1) may actually be best conceptualized as a measure of reliability (see Bliese, 2000); however, regardless of how the ICC(1) is conceptualized, one advantage associated with examining ICC (1) is that the measure provides effect-size estimates directly comparable across studies. James (1982) reported that the median ICC(1) value from a number of studies was 0.12. A value of 0.12 can be interpreted as meaning 12 percent of the variance in any one individual's rating of the target construct can be explained by his or her group membership.

James's (1982) estimate of 0.12 is almost certainly inflated, because James did not draw a distinction between eta-squared and ICC(1) values (see Bliese, 2000; Bliese & Halverson, 1998b), and eta-squared values are nearly always inflated estimates of the

ICC(1); nonetheless, it is worth noting that the ICC(1) values for leadership and work hours in the Bliese and Halverson (1996) data set provided in the preceding examples are 0.15 and 0.13, respectively.[1] We have found that values around 0.15 tend to be on the high side—more typical values tend to be between 0.05 and 0.10 (see Jex & Bliese, 1999, for an example). Given that (a) observed values in Army data are generally between 0.05 and 0.10, and (b) the estimate of 0.12 provided by James (1982) was most likely inflated, it is reasonable to conclude that the group-level properties associated with Army data are comparable to the group properties of data from other organizational settings.

It is also worth reiterating that Latané (1981) proposed an inverse relationship between group size and group effects. The hypothesized inverse relationship is based on theoretical and not mathematical foundations. That is, there is no mathematical reason why group effects estimated with the ICC(1) should decrease as group size increases (Bliese, 2000). On theoretical grounds, however, Latané proposed that small groups exert more influence on individuals than do large groups, and this would result in high ICC(1) values for small groups. Thus, the claim that Army data display typical ICC(1) values in the range of 0.05 to 0.10 should be interpreted in the context of analyzing company-level data. Analyses of squad or platoon-level data may be accompanied by higher ICC(1) values. Along this line, it appears fairly common for leadership variables assessed in smaller groups to have ICC(1) values at or above 0.20 (see Van Engen, Van der Leeden, & Willemsen, 2001; Zohar, 2002).

Why Are Effects Subtle?

Finally, in this section it is interesting to consider some of the theoretical reasons why measures of climate are not more pronounced. In addition to the argument that group size is inversely related to group effects, one can identify at least two other logical explanations for why climate is not more pronounced. First, as indicated earlier, there is almost always a large amount of individual difference in perceptions of climate as a result of factors such as response biases and mood states. These individual differences reduce the ability to detect group differences. Second, and perhaps more interesting, is the notion that organizations actively work to maintain many types of climate within acceptable ranges. For instance, if members of a specific Army company were experiencing a crisis in unit leadership, the organization would, in all likelihood, intervene and find a solution designed to improve unit leadership. This act of monitoring climate and working to ensure that it stays above some minimal levels is a standard part of organizational functioning, but it serves the point of reducing overall variance among groups. This, in turn, reduces the range of unit climate scores and makes climate more subtle than it would be if it were permitted to freely develop.

Section Summary

Several conclusions can be drawn from examining the empirical existence of climates. First, the evidence shows that while climates exist, their manifestation (at least as exhibited through survey items) tends to be relatively subtle. This was evident in the Army examples used here and appears consistent with other examples from the literature. As a consequence, it may be valuable to use advanced statistical techniques to empirically demonstrate the existence of climates. In this regard, statistical tools and visualization techniques developed at the WRAIR may be helpful in understanding the exact nature of agreement within groups.

Leadership Climate and Well-Being

Having discussed the ways to empirically demonstrate the existence of social climates, we can now turn to the second goal of the chapter—to show how social climates affect soldier well-being. In this discussion, both direct and indirect effects are addressed using examples drawn from leadership climate. It is critical to acknowledge that the ability to study the direct and indirect effects of any type of social climate (leadership climate or otherwise) has been greatly enhanced by the development of a class of statistical techniques specifically designed to model nested data. This class of techniques, broadly defined as Random Coefficient Models, or RCMs, allows the direct and indirect inclusion of group-level variables such as climate into explanatory models. Details of these techniques are beyond the scope of this chapter (see Bliese, 2002; Hox, 2002); however, the theoretical notions of direct and indirect effects illustrated in the following sections are central to understanding what can be accomplished using RCM techniques. Thus, the particular example of leadership climate can be used to illustrate direct and indirect multilevel effects.

As previously noted, leadership climate centers on the degree to which soldiers perceive that unit leaders are concerned about their well-being (Bliese & Castro, 2000). Leadership climate is important, because it is likely to be the proximal factor driving other forms of social climate and unit functioning. For instance, in an Army setting, Chen and Bliese (2002) found that leadership climate contributed to soldiers' perceptions of strain and role clarity, which, in turn, led to perceptions of self and collective efficacy. Thus, the results were congruent with a model where leadership climate was the driver of strain, role clarity, and efficacy. As another example, Zohar (2002) operationalized leadership climate as group members' ratings of leaders on five transformational leadership dimensions. These five ratings of climate were then used as predictors of safety climate, and safety climate was subsequently used as a predictor of accidents. Zohar found evidence to suggest that safety climate mediated the link between leadership climate and accidents. Thus, Zohar's work also supports the idea of leadership climate being a key driver of other forms of social climate and unit functioning.

While leadership plays a central role in almost all aspects of unit functioning, the notion of modeling and conceptualizing leadership as a climate variable is a relatively new idea (see Britt et al., 2004). This is because leadership has often been viewed as a dyadic relationship between two individuals. In the military, however, leadership has less of a one-to-one interactive nature than it does in other settings. For instance, Shamir, Zakay, Breinin, and Popper (1998) argue that the nature of leadership in

Army companies is such that leaders direct actions and behaviors toward the members of the unit as a whole—leaders develop relatively few dyadic relationships with subordinates. Because actions and behaviors are targeted to entire units and shared among unit members, they result in the development of leadership climates.

Direct Effects

Direct effects involving leadership climate and well-being are commonly identified in survey data collected at WRAIR. The most convincing evidence for the direct effect of leadership climate comes from statistical RCM analyses that contrast individual-level findings with group-level (climate) findings in what Hofmann and Gavin (1998) refer to as an "incremental prediction multilevel model." In an incremental prediction RCM model, individual-level relationships (based on individual data) are simultaneously contrasted with group-level relationships (based on group means). The purpose of an analysis of this nature is to show that relationships between group means (climate variables) differ from relationships between individual variables. By demonstrating that group-level relationships differ from individual relationships, one can convincingly argue that social climate is important and the effects of social climate are independent of individual-level effects (Lincoln & Zeitz, 1980).

When applied to leadership variables, incremental prediction multilevel models typically reveal that the relationship between individual soldier perceptions of leadership and individual soldier well-being is weaker than the relationship between a company's average perception of leadership and a company's average well-being. In practical terms, this means that the average unit well-being can be estimated from average perceptions of leadership with a high degree of accuracy, while (perhaps ironically), predicting an individual soldier's well-being using an individual soldier's rating of leadership is done with less accuracy.

Figure 10.5 shows a specific visual example of an incremental prediction model. The figure is a scatter plot, with soldiers' ratings of noncommissioned officer (NCO) leadership behaviors on the X-axis (bottom) and average depression on the Y-axis. In terms of leadership, soldiers are rating the degree to which NCOs engage in negative behavior such as (a) embarrassing soldiers in front of other soldiers and (b) trying to look good to higher-ups by assigning extra missions or details to soldiers. For simplicity, depression is coded as average responses to a nine-item scale such that higher values correspond to more symptoms of depression. The points in the graph represent 33 companies.

Figure 10.5 reveals that, as perceptions of negative NCO behaviors increase, ratings of depression also increase. Notice, however, that the dotted line representing the relationship between group average ratings of NCO behavior (leadership climate) and group average depression is steeper than the solid line representing the relationship between individual perceptions of NCO leadership and individual depression. This visual evidence is confirmed in analyses showing that the correlation between group means is 0.72 (very strong), while the adjusted individual correlation is 0.32

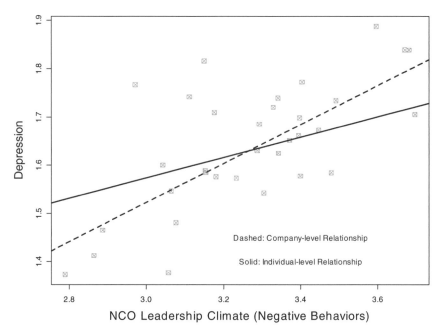

Figure 10.5
Leadership Climate and Depression at the Individual and Group Levels

(moderate). Again, these results emphasize that the average well-being of a unit can be predicted from leadership climate with much more accuracy (r=0.72) than individual well-being can be predicted from individual leadership ratings (r=0.32).

It is not surprising that the statistical evidence also shows that the 33 companies can be reliably differentiated from each other in terms of NCO leadership climate. This is evident because the ICC(2) value is 0.72. To detect differences between individual-level results and group-level results, reliable group mean differences (Bliese, 1998) are needed. In short, these 33 companies have clear differences in leadership climates, and these climate differences are related to the average levels of depression in the unit.

Tests of incremental prediction models demonstrate the direct impact of leadership climate variables on well-being outcomes. Results from these models are important, because they suggest ways in which the Army can act to directly impact well-being in Army units. The Army's strong emphasis on leadership development of NCOs, for instance, should have a direct positive effect on soldier well-being. In another example, strategies to routinely assess unit leadership and provide feedback and guidance to unit leaders would almost certainly help improve soldier well-being, because such actions would help create strong, healthy leadership climates.

Indirect Effects

Because the military cannot eliminate certain stressors, it must consider other ways to lessen their impact. One promising way to do so is to work to develop supportive social climates. As previously noted, we suspect supportive leadership climates, in particular, may play an important indirect role in soldier well-being by ameliorating or attenuating relationships between stressors and strains. One example of an indirect effect can be demonstrated using data collected from soldiers deployed to Haiti in 1994. In these data, we surveyed soldiers' perceptions of task significance, psychological hostility/anger, and perceptions of leadership climate. We were interested in task significance, because in interviews soldiers expressed concern about the types of tasks they were required to perform on peacekeeping missions. An opinion expressed by some soldiers was that the tasks they were asked to perform had little or no significance to the accomplishment of the overall mission.

In any deployment, task significance is likely to be a stressor, because soldiers at lower levels may not know or appreciate higher-level strategic considerations for why certain tasks are performed. In addition, many deployments tend to have long periods of inactivity resulting in boredom, and so leaders may come up with tasks that have little significance other than serving the purpose of occupying soldiers' time.

Analyses of the data collected in Haiti reveal there is a significant relationship between soldiers' perceptions of task significance and their reports of hostility and anger. Specifically, soldiers who reported low task significance tended to report high hostility and anger. Interestingly, however, this overall trend showed considerable variability when examined on a company-by-company basis. Figure 10.6 shows scatter plots and regression lines representing the relationship between individual ratings of task significance and individual ratings of hostility for 25 different companies. Notice the variability in the regression slopes across companies.

For instance, in the company in the top left corner (company 20), the relationship between task significance and hostility was very strong. Soldiers who reported high task significance tended to report low hostility—soldiers who reported low task significance tended to report high hostility. In contrast, consider company 18. In this company, a number of people reported low task significance, yet the overall rates of hostility were low, and the slope representing the relationship between task significance and hostility was flat in comparison to company 20.

Complete analyses of these data demonstrated that leadership climate attenuated the relationship between task significance and hostility. A special issue of the journal *Leadership Quarterly* was devoted to the analyses of these data, and three different groups of researchers, using three different analytic techniques, all confirmed that companies with positive leadership climates were less affected by the stressor of low task significance than were companies with negative leadership climates (Bliese & Halverson, 2002; Gavin & Hofmann, 2002; Markham & Halverson, 2002). To visually represent the findings, consider that company 18 probably had a positive leadership climate, while company 20 had a negative leadership climate. Indeed, in company 20, the mean rating of leadership climate was 2.80, and in company 18, the

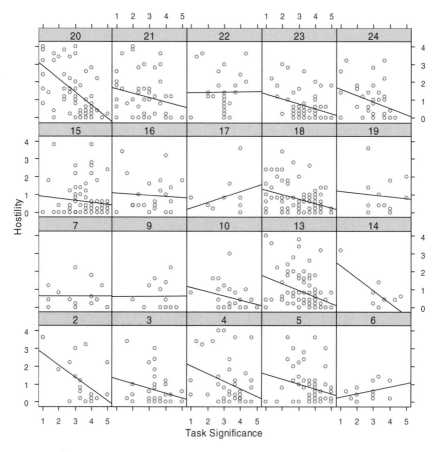

Figure 10.6
The Relationship between Task Significance and Hostility across Companies

mean rating was 3.10. In both companies, some soldiers reported low task significance, but only in company 20 did this lead to high levels of hostility.

Section Summary

Social climate has both direct and indirect effects on soldier well-being, and the ability to detect these has been made available by a new class of statistical models (RCM). In this section, the focus was primarily on leadership climate. Leadership climate, however, is only one specific type of climate likely to be important in terms of soldier well-being and job attitudes. For instance, Jex and Bliese (1999) showed that collective efficacy had direct and indirect effects involving job satisfaction. Collective efficacy is relevant to the military, because it represents a unit's overall belief in their ability to perform their mission. Another area of importance in modern military settings is social climates related to how the unit balances work and family demands. Within this context, Cabrera and colleagues (2004) showed that a unit's family work climate played a role in soldiers' marital satisfaction. Finally, while we have emphasized the protective role of positive social climates, it is important to realize that groups that fail to develop shared social climates may put their members at risk. Research by Bliese and Halverson (1998a) and Bliese and Britt (2001) have shown that climate strength itself is an important direct and indirect predictor of well-being outcomes over and above the absolute mean ratings. Groups strive to reach agreement among members, and a failure to do so is clearly a risk factor.

Future Directions

Social climates exist, and their existence can be empirically demonstrated using a variety of statistical techniques. In many organizations such as the Army, social climates are likely to be relatively subtle; nonetheless, climates play an important role in soldier well-being and, by implication, in their resilience and performance as well.

It has been over 50 years since Shils and Janowitz (1948) published their qualitative findings demonstrating the importance of social climates to the *Wehrmacht* in World War II. From an empirical basis, however, we know little about the role of social climates in combat situations, because our current work is based on studies conducted in garrison, training, and peacekeeping operations. Nonetheless, as this chapter is being written, the U.S. military is engaged in prolonged direct combat. Thus, one of our current research agendas is to understand the role of shared social climate during and following combat. The goal of this research is to find ways to develop strong and protective social climates to enhance soldier well-being, adaptation, and resilience.

Note

1. The values of 0.17 and 0.16 reported in the article are incorrect.

References

Bliese, P. D. (1998). Group size, ICC values, and group-level correlations: A simulation. *Organizational Research Methods, 1*, 355–373.

Bliese, P. D. (2000). Within-group agreement, non-independence, and reliability: Implications for data aggregation and analysis. In K. J. Klein & S. W. Kozlowski (Eds.), *Multilevel theory, research, and methods in organization* (pp. 349–381). San Francisco: Jossey-Bass.

Bliese, P. D. (2002). Multilevel random coefficient modeling in organizational research: Examples using SAS and S-PLUS. In F. Drasgow & N. Schmitt (Eds.), *Measuring and analyzing behavior in organizations: Advances in measurement and data analysis* (pp. 401–445). San Francisco: Jossey-Bass.

Bliese, P. D. (2005). *Multilevel modeling in R: A brief introduction to R, the multilevel package, and the NLME package*. Unpublished manuscript, Walter Reed Army Institute of Research.

Bliese, P. D., & Britt, T. W. (2001). Social support, group consensus and stressor-strain relationships: Social context matters. *Journal of Organizational Behavior, 22*, 425–436.

Bliese, P. D., & Castro, C. A. (2000). Role clarity, work overload and organizational support: Multilevel evidence of the importance of support. *Work and Stress, 14*, 65–73.

Bliese, P. D., & Castro, C. A. (2003). The Soldier Adaptation Model (SAM): Applications to behavioral science peacekeeping research. In T. W. Britt & A. B. Adler (Eds.), *The psychology of the peacekeeper: Lessons from the field* (pp. 185–203). Westport, CT: Praeger Press.

Bliese, P. D., & Halverson, R. R. (1996). Individual and nomothetic models of job stress: An examination of work hours, cohesion, and well-being. *Journal of Applied Social Psychology, 26*, 1171–1189.

Bliese, P. D., & Halverson, R. R. (1998a). Group consensus and psychological well-being: A large field study. *Journal of Applied Social Psychology, 28*, 563–580.

Bliese, P. D., & Halverson, R. R. (1998b). Group size and measures of group-level properties: An examination of eta-squared and ICC values. *Journal of Management, 24*, 157–172.

Bliese, P. D., & Halverson, R. R. (2002). Using random group resampling in multilevel research. *Leadership Quarterly, 13*, 53–68.

Bliese, P. D., Halverson, R. R., & Rothberg, J. M. (1994). Within-group agreement scores: Using resampling procedures to estimate expected variance. *Academy of Management Best Paper Proceedings*, 303–307.

Bliese, P. D., & Jex, S. M. (2002). Incorporating a multilevel perspective into occupational stress research: Theoretical, methodological, and practical implications. *Journal of Occupational Health Psychology, 7*, 265–276.

Bliese, P. D., Thomas, J. L., & Jex, S. M. (2002). *Job strain as a mediator between stressors and performance: Evidence from the field.* In G. A. Adams (Chair) and C. S. Smith (Discussant), Performance: The forgotten criterion variable in occupational stress research. Symposium conducted at the 17th Annual Conference of the Society for Industrial and Organizational Psychology, Toronto, Canada.

Britt, T. W., Davison, J. Bliese, P. D., & Castro, C. A. (2004). How leaders can influence the impact that stressors have on soldiers. *Military Medicine, 169*, 541–545.

Cabrera, O. A., Bliese, P. D., Hoge, C. W., Castro, C. A., Messer, S. C., & McGurk, D. (2004, August). *Adverse childhood experiences, family-friendly work environment and marital satisfaction.* Poster session presented at the annual meeting of the American Psychological Association, Honolulu, HI.

Chen, G., & Bliese, P. D. (2002). The role of different levels of leadership in predicting self and collective efficacy: Evidence for discontinuity. *Journal of Applied Psychology, 87*, 549–556.

Cohen, S., & Wills, T. A. (1985). Stress, social support and the buffering hypothesis. *Psychological Bulletin, 98*, 310–357.

Ehrhart, M., Bliese, P. D., & Thomas, J. L. (in press). Unit-level OCB and unit effectiveness: Examining the incremental effect of helping behavior. *Human Performance*.

Gavin, M. B., & Hofmann, D. A. (2002). Using hierarchical linear modeling to investigate the moderating influence of leadership climate. *Leadership Quarterly, 13*, 15–34.

Hofmann, D. A., & Gavin, M. (1998). Centering decisions in hierarchical linear models: Theoretical and methodological implications for research in organizations. *Journal of Management, 24*, 623–641.

Hofmann, D. A., Morgeson, F. P., & Gerras, S. J. (2003). Climate as a moderator of the relationship between leader-member exchange and content specific citizenship: Safety climate as an exemplar. *Journal of Applied Psychology, 88*, 170–178.

Hofstede, G. (1980). *Culture's consequences: International differences in work-related values.* Beverly Hills, CA: Sage.

Hunt, J. G. (1991). *Leadership: A new synthesis.* Newbury Park, CA: Sage.

Hox, J. (2002). *Multilevel analysis techniques and applications.* Mahwah, NJ: Lawrence Erlbaum.

Ingraham, L. H. (1984). *The boys in the barracks: Observations on American military life.* Philadelphia: Institute for the Study of Human Issues.

James, L. R. (1982). Aggregation bias in estimates of perceptual agreement. *Journal of Applied Psychology, 6,* 219–229.

James, L. R., Demaree, R. J., & Wolf, G. (1984). Estimating within-group interrater reliability with and without response bias. *Journal of Applied Psychology, 69,* 85–98.

James, L. R., & Jones, A. P. (1974). Organizational climate: A review of theory and research. *Psychological Bulletin, 81,* 1096–1112.

Jex, S. M., & Bliese, P. D. (1999). Efficacy beliefs as a moderator of the impact of work-related stressors: A multi-level study. *Journal of Applied Psychology, 84,* 349–361.

Kozlowski, S. W. J., & Klein, K. J. (2000). A multilevel approach to theory and research in organizations: Contextual, temporal and emergent processes. In K. J. Klein & S. W. Kozlowski (Eds.), *Multilevel theory, research, and methods in organizations* (pp. 3–90). San Francisco: Jossey-Bass.

Latané, B. (1981). The psychology of social impact. *American Psychologist, 36,* 343–356.

Leather, P., Lawrence, C., Beale, D., Cox, T., & Dickson, R. (1998). Exposure to occupational violence and the buffering effects of intra-organizational support. *Work and Stress, 12,* 161–178.

Lincoln, J. R., & Zeitz, G. (1980). Organizational properties from aggregate data: Separating individual and structural effects. *American Sociological Review, 45,* 391–408.

Markham, S. E., & Halverson, R. R. (2002). Within- and between-entity analyses in multilevel research: A leadership example using single level analyses and boundary conditions (MRA). *Leadership Quarterly, 13,* 35–52.

McGrath, J. E. (1984). *Groups: Interaction and performance.* Englewood Cliffs, NJ: Prentice-Hall.

Pew, R. W., & Mavor, A. S. (1998). *Modeling human and organizational behavior: Application to military simulations.* Washington, DC: National Academy Press.

Schneider, B. (1990). The climate for service: An application of the climate construct. In B. Schneider (Ed.), *Organizational climate and culture* (pp. 383–412). San Francisco: Jossey-Bass.

Schneider, B., & Bowen, D. (1985). Employee and customer perceptions of service in banks: Replication and extension. *Journal of Applied Psychology, 70,* 423–433.

Schneider, B., White, S. S., & Paul, M. C. (1998). Linking service climate and customer perceptions of service quality: Test of a causal model. *Journal of Applied Psychology, 83,* 150–163.

Shamir, B., Zakay, E., Breinin, E., & Popper, M. (1998). Correlates of charismatic leader behavior in military units: Subordinates' attitudes, unit characteristics, and superior appraisals of leader performance. *Academy of Management Journal, 41,* 387–409.

Shils, E. A., & Janowitz, M. (1948). Cohesion and disintegration in the Wehrmacht in World War II. *Public Opinion Quarterly, 3,* 281–282.

Van Engen, M. L., Van der Leeden, R., & Willemsen, T. M. (2001). Gender, context and leadership styles: A field study. *Journal of Occupational and Organizational Psychology, 74,* 581–598.

Wong, L., Bliese, P. D., & McGurk, D. (2003). Military leadership: A context specific review. *Leadership Quarterly, 14,* 657–692.

Zohar, D. (2002). The effects of leadership dimensions, safety climate, and assigned priorities on minor injuries in work groups. *Journal of Organizational Behavior, 23,* 75–92.

PART V

FUTURE DIRECTIONS

CHAPTER 11

OPERATIONAL STRESS: COMMON THEMES AND FUTURE DIRECTIONS

Amy B. Adler, Carl Andrew Castro, and Thomas W. Britt

When U.S. Navy psychiatrist Robert Koffman deployed to Iraq, he met a surreal combination of hope and despair—life-affirming graffiti and the desperation of calculating one's odds of survival in a war zone. In his final analysis, Koffman writes that America's military personnel embody resilience in the face of a new and challenging landscape of military operations.

This compelling introductory chapter outlines the goal of this volume—to understand the psychological underpinnings that support military personnel as they confront deploying on modern military operations. Whether such deployment is characterized by combat, peacekeeping, or humanitarian missions, the stressors military personnel encounter can tax even the most resilient.

The question of how to prepare military personnel psychologically for deployment is addressed in the first section of the volume. McGurk, Cotting, Britt, and Adler discuss the issue of entry into the military organization, the social psychology behind indoctrination, and the psychological challenge of adapting to a demanding organization. Salas, Priest, Wilson, and Burke then review the latest information on scenario-based training. Once military personnel have developed a military identity, what is the best way to prepare them using realistic training? The need for such training to enhance adaptability and resilience is then explored by Thompson and McCreary in their chapter on stress inoculation.

The second section of the volume highlights the psychological impact of deployment and mirrors closely the struggles that Koffman describes. Clinical experts write about the challenge of deployment-related mental health problems and interventions that accompany them. Lewis reviews the current research, the military's doctrine, and his own real-world experience in a chapter on combat stress control. Steffian, Bluestein, Ogrisseg, Doran, and Morgan provide unique insight into the psychology of prisoners of war. They outline the stages of captivity, the psychological impact of being held as a prisoner of war, and the psychological consequences that may arise after repatriation, in a behind-the-scenes look into the practice of working with repatriated prisoners of war. Finally, Maguen, Suvak, and Litz detail the nature of one of the most difficult and common psychological problems following exposure to combat: posttraumatic stress disorder. In each chapter, coming to terms with the experiences of deployment and integrating these experiences successfully into one's worldview is not an easy process, as Koffman foreshadows in his first-person account.

The third section of the volume takes a different approach to the question of the psychology of operational stress. Instead of focusing on how to prepare for deployment stress or how to treat deployment stress, this section reviews other organizational initiatives that influence the psychological well-being of military personnel both in garrison and on deployment. In their chapter on human spirituality and religion, military chaplains Waynick, Frederich, Schneider, Thomas, and Bloomstrom offer a groundbreaking description of the importance of spiritual strength and religion in the military. Their personal account of serving God while serving in the military recognizes a critical component of well-being for military personnel: spiritual well-being. In the next chapter of the section, Castro, Thomas, and Adler discuss another important influence on the relationship between military stressors and well-being outcomes, the military leader. In the final chapter of this section, Bliese places the experience of service members in the context of their unit. The impact of unit climate on corresponding outcomes can affect individuals over and above the influence of individual variables.

Thus, the military provides a context in which service members experience operational stress, and it is this context that has tremendous potential to moderate the impact of operational stress on the well-being of military personnel. The task of optimizing organizational factors, from leadership to policy, provides hope and yet is fraught with the reality of competing priorities. As Koffman humorously describes, military leaders, with their policies and directives, have the potential to provide structure that can protect or inhibit healthy adjustment. What role the policies, leaders, and support structures play will ultimately determine the well-being of the individual and the units.

Core Principles of Operational Stress

A review of the individual, leader, and organizational efforts designed to increase adaptation to military demands yields a set of core principles. These core principles underscore the fundamental responsibility the military has for helping military personnel cope with operational stress. Such principles can serve to guide efforts designed to reduce the impact of operational stress and to enhance adjustment of military personnel, a task that military psychiatrists such as Koffman may find themselves addressing in remote and dangerous places.

1. Exposure to traumatic events during military operations affects the mental health and well-being of service members. Traumatic experiences can shatter the assumptions of invincibility, predictability, and personal control.

2. Preparation for exposure to traumatic events on deployment can protect service members from the ensuing psychological consequences. Preparation begins with indoctrination and continues throughout the service member's career. This training includes fundamental military skills, as well as specific training in dealing with the stressors of combat and deployment.

3. Spirituality enables service members to process their operational experiences within a personally meaningful framework. Deriving meaning from traumatic experiences is a critical task for recovering from deployment.

4. Early intervention following exposure to stressful events can be effective. Applying the principle of far-forward mental-health care on the battlefield ensures those military personnel needing help get it.

5. Leader behaviors focused on meeting the needs of military personnel are the best way to build psychological resilience. By demonstrating their commitment to the well-being of their subordinates, military leaders can help reduce the psychological problems resulting from exposure to traumatic events.

Future Directions

The consistent themes across each chapter in this volume demonstrate the fundamentally human endeavor of preparing, supporting, and caring for military service members. Deployed military personnel may confront numerous challenges, but the assumption underlying most of the chapters is that the more prepared and the more supported, the better off military personnel will be in terms of performance and recovery. The identification of common challenges also points the way for common areas of future research.

One area for future research is the need to identify the best methods for preparing military personnel psychologically for operational stress. Despite the assumption that military personnel need preparation for military operations, there is very little empirical evidence regarding the best method for providing that support. Questions such as whether training should be geared toward the individual or the unit, or whether military personnel can benefit from better preparation for the psychological stressors encountered by those in combat remain unanswered. Future research should assess the effectiveness of systematic attempts to train military personnel in what to expect from particular deployments and how they might best handle the stressors of such deployments.

Another research gap is the evidence for the efficacy of mental health interventions provided during deployment as well as those provided following deployment. The lack of early intervention research is well established, and in the case of the military, such research efforts face major ethical and logistical hurdles. Yet, the interventions that are delivered may not be the best and the timing may not be the most effective. Furthermore, although it is clear that good leadership can moderate the impact of operational stressors on the health and performance of military personnel, identifying exactly what comprises good leader behavior is another area for future research.

In addition, the degree to which the findings reported in this volume are descriptive of the challenges faced by the militaries of other nations has not been systematically examined. While efforts to develop an agreement among NATO partners about the psychological needs of military personnel and the supports that should ideally be available to them have been initiated through NATO research groups, many research questions remain. For example, what impact does conscription have on the dynamics of operational stress and interventions discussed here? What impact does spirituality have on the well-being of military personnel from nations with different religious foundations, or for those nations that do not have clergy in uniform? What impact does culture have on the course and nature of mental health problems following combat? These questions are critical for understanding the degree to which the information presented here can be adapted for use in the militaries of other nations. Taken together, these core principles and areas for future research create both a foundation and a blueprint for addressing operational stress issues.

Military personnel get exposed to horrific events. They can be asked to kill, to risk being killed, and to witness hostilities against enemy and friendly forces. These experiences can lead to a range of problems from temporary adjustment difficulties to profoundly debilitating mental health problems. Leaders at all levels have the responsibility to take care of their military personnel and to provide an optimal context for healthy adaptation to extreme and harsh conditions. This context needs to encompass a systematic approach that integrates mental health support in initial training and the phases of the deployment (before, during, and after), extending across the individual's military career into retirement.

INDEX

Koffman, Robert L., on psychological coping mechanisms exhibited in Iraq War combat zone, 3–9, 237

Korean War (1950–1953), 122; establishment of Code of Conduct during, 85; Kilroy graffiti in, 3–4; prisoners of war in, 85, 91, 93, 95, 102, 108

Kosovo, peacekeeping mission in, 150, 162, 206–7

KSAs. *See* Knowledge, skills and attitudes (KSAs)

Leadership, military, 192–212; actions of universal, transcending nationality and culture, 200–201; behaviors and attitudes of, 201–8, 209–10; cardinal principles of, 208, 209*t*; combat stress control and role of, 129; flexible pragmatic versus rigid institutional approaches to, 194, 195–200; future directions on research and modeling of, 208–10; importance of junior officers for, 193, 194; literature on, 194; measuring, 193–94; mental readiness in soldiers and role of, 72; nature–nurture debate on, 197–98; social climate and perceptions of, 220, 221*f*, 222*f*, 223*f*, 224; transformational, 197; well-being of soldiers and effects of, 226–31

Learned helplessness in captives, 94

Learning experts, cooperation with subject-matter experts in scenario-based training, 47

Line Operational Safety Audits (LOSA), 44

Long-term stage of captivity, 90–91

Loss of routine in captivity, 100

Marine Corps, U.S., training programs for, 13, 67

Marine Corps Boot Camp, 13

Master Scenario Event List (MSEL), 42

Meichenbaum, D., on stress inoculation, 59–60

Mental health programs: mental readiness training in, 72–73; stigma against seeking help from, 57–58, 137

Mental readiness training, 54–79; applications of, 68–69; conclusions on, 73; within continuum of therapeutic techniques, 72–73; graded stress inoculation as, 64–65; military training programs and, 56–58; modeling adaptive coping as, 65–66; organizational context of, 66–67; psychological spectrum of modern military operations and, 55–56; stress exposure training and, 63–64; theoretical foundations of, 58–63; training issues relevant to, 69–72

Military leadership. *See* Leadership, military

Military mission: commonality of approaches to leadership regarding primacy of, 195; repatriation of captives as, 103–4

Military personnel: Code of Conduct for, 83–84; training (*see* Indoctrination, military; Mental readiness training; Training, military)

Military unit: combat stress control and survey of, 129, 130*f*; role of chaplain in normalizing conditions in, 182–86; support from, and risk of posttraumatic stress disorder, 158

Mindlessness (compliance) in captives, 94

Mistakes: leader's admission of, 202; leader's underwriting of subordinates' honest, 202–3

Modification of future scenario-based training programs, 38*f*, 45

Morale survey, 130*t*

Movement stage of captivity, 90

National Guard, posttraumatic stress disorder (PTSD) in, 147, 160

Nationality, leader actions that transcend, 200–201

National militaries, posttraumatic disorder among veterans of select, 148, 150–51

About the Contributors

AMY B. ADLER is a research psychologist with the U.S. Army Medical Research Unit–Europe, Walter Reed Army Institute of Research (WRAIR), in Heidelberg, Germany. She is science coordinator at the unit, has deployed in support of peacekeeping operations, and is interested in deployment-related stress and early interventions. She and Thomas Britt edited a book published by Praeger Press in 2003, *The Psychology of the Peacekeeper: Lessons from the Field*.

PAUL D. BLIESE is the Commander of the U.S. Army Medical Research Unit–Europe, a special foreign activity of the WRAIR, an organization with which he has been affiliated since 1992. Lieutenant Colonel Bliese is an industrial-organizational psychologist and has published extensively in the area of leadership, occupational stress, and multilevel modeling.

GLEN L. BLOOMSTROM is a military chaplain and colonel in the U.S. Army. He is the director of the Ministry Initiatives Directorate at the U.S. Army Chief of Chaplains Office in Washington, DC. His service includes assignments at the battalion and brigade levels in infantry and special operations units and combat service with the 75th Ranger Regiment in Operation Just Cause in 1989–90. He is a clinical member in the American Association for Marriage and Family Therapy, as well as a fellow in the American Association of Pastoral Counselors. He is ordained and endorsed by the Baptist General Conference.

BRENDON W. BLUESTEIN is a captain in the U.S. Army and a Survival, Evasion, Resistance and Escape (SERE) psychologist. He is also involved in the assessment and selection of Special Forces candidates. Current work and research interests include the psychological support of interrogations, biomarkers of extreme stress within Army survival training, and development of Special Forces situational reaction exercises.

THOMAS W. BRITT is an associate professor in the Department of Psychology at Clemson University. He was a uniformed research psychologist in the U.S. Army from 1994 to 1999 and deployed in support of peacekeeping, humanitarian, and contingency operations. His research interests include the search for factors that enhance resiliency and morale among soldiers serving on different types of military operations. Together with Amy Adler, he edited the book, *The Psychology of the Peacekeeper: Lessons from the Field* (Praeger Press, 2003).

C. SHAWN BURKE is a research scientist within the Institute for Simulation and Training (IST) at the University of Central Florida. While at IST, Dr. Burke has worked on several military projects which examine such issues as team adaptation, multicultural team performance, team performance under stress, and development of training tools for multicultural team leaders.

CARL ANDREW CASTRO is a lieutenant colonel and research psychologist in the U.S. Army. He is chief of the Department of Military Psychiatry at the WRAIR. He has served tours of duty in Bosnia, Kosovo, and Iraq. His research interests include understanding the impact of deployments on the health and well-being of soldiers and families and how values improve individual performance.

DAVE I. COTTING is a social and personality psychologist and chief of research technical operations in the Department of Military Psychiatry at the WRAIR. He served in the Swiss Army for eight years and now serves as a captain in the U.S. Army. He has deployed to the Middle East in support of Operation Iraqi Freedom as part of the Army's Surgeon General's Mental Health Advisory Team (MHAT). His research interests include the study of the impact of combat experiences on war fighters, with an emphasis on appraisals and coping strategies that either improve or impair military performance and well-being.

ANTHONY P. DORAN is a commander and clinical psychologist for the U.S. Navy. He presently works as a special assistant for the Navy on exceptional family member and suicide prevention issues at Navy Headquarters in Millington, Tennessee. Dr. Doran was previously stationed in Brunswick, Maine as the Survival Evasion Resistance Escape (SERE) psychologist, and his academic interests include ethics, human performance under stress, and the physiological effects of stress.

PETER J. FREDERICH is a chaplain and lieutenant colonel in the U.S. Navy. He directs the Family Life Chaplains' Training Center and School at Fort Benning, Georgia. He is an approved supervisor and clinical member in the American Association for Marriage and Family Therapy, a diplomate in the American Association of Pastoral Counselors, and is licensed as a marriage and family therapist. Chaplain Frederich began his career in the Army as an infantry officer, serving in that capacity for five years before transitioning to the Chaplain Corps, where he has served for 15 years. He has led or ministered to soldiers in deployments to Grenada,

Panama, and the Middle East. He is ordained by the Conservative Baptist Association of America.

ROBERT L. KOFFMAN is a captain in the U.S. Navy and board-certified psychiatrist with extensive operational experience. With additional specialization in aerospace medicine and an area of concentration in occupational medicine, he currently serves as the force surgeon for Naval Construction Forces (the Seabees) based in Little Creek, Virginia. Having deployed to Iraq multiple times in the capacity of a mental health provider, he functioned as the senior combat stress control consultant during Operation Iraqi Freedom I for Naval forces ashore. The mental health issues associated with nontraditional combat roles (support staff, health care providers, and construction workers) are his areas of interest and expertise.

BRETT T. LITZ is a professor in the Department of Psychiatry at Boston University School of Medicine and the Psychology Department at Boston University College of Arts and Sciences. He is also the associate director of the Behavioral Sciences Division of the National Center for Posttraumatic Stress Disorder (PTSD) at the VA Boston Health Care System. Dr. Litz is internationally recognized for his research on traumatic stress and early intervention for trauma.

STEVE J. LEWIS is a major and social worker in the U.S. Army. He has deployed to both peacekeeping and combat operations providing mental health services to soldiers. His research interests include the prevention and treatment of PTSD, occupational stress, coping, and moderators of occupational stress.

SHIRA MAGUEN is a behavioral science fellow at the National Center for PTSD, VA Boston Health Care System. Dr. Maguen has been involved with a series of projects examining prevalence and predictors of mental health variables in peacekeepers deployed to Kosovo and Bosnia. She has also examined barriers to mental health treatment and the associations between physical health symptoms and stress symptoms in these peacekeeping samples. Additional research interests include coping with the threat of terrorism and posttraumatic growth.

DONALD R. MCCREARY is a defense scientist with the Stress and Coping Group at Defence R&D Canada–Toronto, as well as an adjunct professor of psychology at both York University (Toronto) and Brock University (St. Catharines), and a fellow of the American Psychological Association. Dr. McCreary's research interests lie in the general area of occupational health psychology and focus on the stress–health relationship.

DENNIS MCGURK is a major and research psychologist in the U.S. Army where he serves as the chief of combat and operational studies in the Division of Psychiatry and Neuroscience at the WRAIR. He has deployed to Haiti and has conducted research while deployed to Kosovo and Afghanistan. His primary research interest is on the effects of combat and deployments on soldier well-being.

C. A. MORGAN III is an associate professor of psychiatry at Yale University and is the director of the Human Performance Laboratory at the National Center for PTSD, VA Connecticut. He has conducted psychological and neurohormonal research within the operations community in order to better characterize how uncontrollable stress affects human memory, cognition, and behavior. Dr. Morgan's interests include forensic psychiatry and history of medicine.

JERRY OGRISSEG is a major in the U.S. Air Force, where he serves as a clinical psychologist and chief of Survival, Evasion, Resistance, and Escape research for the Human Factors Directorate of the Joint Personnel Recovery Agency. He chairs an international survival psychology research panel through the Technical Cooperation Program, and his research interests include human performance under extreme stress and social anxiety.

HEATHER A. PRIEST is a graduate research assistant at the Institute for Simulation & Training and a Ph.D. candidate in applied experimental and human factors psychology at the University of Central Florida. She is the lead graduate student on two separate projects funded by the Army Research Office and the Army Research Institute examining team performance under stress and multicultural team leadership. Her research interests include teams, training, distributed teams, and team performance under stress.

EDUARDO SALAS is trustee chair and professor of psychology in the Department of Psychology and the Institute for Simulation & Training at the University of Central Florida. He has over 20 years of research experience on team training, simulation-based training, and training effectiveness, and he has published over 300 articles, chapters, and papers on those topics.

DAVID M. SCHEIDER is a chaplain and lieutenant colonel in the U.S. Army. He is the director of the Family Life Chaplains' Training Center and School at Fort Hood, Texas. He is an approved supervisor and clinical member in the American Association for Marriage and Family Therapy, as well as a diplomate in the American Association of Pastoral Counselors. Chaplain Scheider is an Episcopal priest serving on active duty for 17 years. He holds master's degrees in divinity, mental health, and family life education and consultation. Currently he is working toward a doctor of ministry in Christian nurture.

GEORGE STEFFIAN is a clinical psychologist and commander in the U.S. Navy where he is assigned to the Survival, Evasion, Resistance and Escape (SERE) school, Naval Air Station, Brunswick, Maine. His research interests include human performance and extreme stress.

MICHAEL SUVAK is pursuing his Ph.D. in clinical psychology at Boston University and is working as a graduate research assistant at the National Center for PTSD located in the Boston VA Health Care System. His research interests include emotional processes underlying psychopathology and the impact of trauma on individuals' mental health and well-being.

JEFFREY L. THOMAS is a U.S. Army major and research psychologist assigned to the WRAIR. He has conducted psychological research for the U.S. Army in deployed, training, and garrison military environments. His research interests span occupational health psychology, clinical intervention, and industrial and organizational disciplines in support of soldiers, leaders, and military units.

RONALD H. THOMAS is a chaplain and lieutenant colonel in the U.S. Army where he serves as the family ministry staff action officer at the U.S. Army Chief of Chaplains Office. He has experience as a chaplain in combat, peacekeeping, humanitarian, and other operations. His research interests include spiritual and relationship implications of combat operational stress.

MEGAN M. THOMPSON is a defense scientist with Defence Research and Development Canada in Toronto, Canada. She is a social psychologist and is the group leader of the Stress and Coping Group within the Command Effectiveness and Behavior Section. Her present research foci include stress, coping, and psychological resiliency in the military and other high-risk occupations, and the role of individual differences in stress, coping, and decision making.

THOMAS C. WAYNICK is a chaplain and lieutenant colonel in the U.S. Army. He serves as the deputy director and supervisor in training at the U.S. Army Family Life Chaplains' Training Program at Fort Benning, Georgia. His military experience includes 25 years in the reserve, National Guard, and active-duty components. He has participated in two extended deployments in Operation Joint Endeavor and Operation Iraqi Freedom. He is a fellow in the American Association of Pastoral Counselors, a clinical member of the American Association for Marriage and Family Therapists, and is licensed in marriage and family therapy. He is ordained in the Lutheran Church Missouri Synod.

KATHERINE A. WILSON is a graduate research assistant at the University of Central Florida's Institute for Simulation & Training. She is the lead graduate student on a project funded by the Army Research Laboratory examining multicultural team adaptability within Stability and Support Operations (SASO) environments. Her research interests also include team training and team performance in military and commercial aviation.